W9-CHY-865

Integrating Reading and Writing Instruction in Grades K–8

Ruth M. Noyce
University of Kansas

James F. Christie
Arizona State University

Allyn and Bacon
Boston ■ London ■ Sydney ■ Toronto

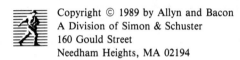 Copyright © 1989 by Allyn and Bacon
A Division of Simon & Schuster
160 Gould Street
Needham Heights, MA 02194

Series Editor: Sean W. Wakely
Production Administrator: Annette Joseph
Production Coordinator: Susan Freese
Editorial-Production Service: Oxnard Editorial and Production Services
Cover Administrator: Linda K. Dickinson
Cover Designer: Susan C. Hamant

Library of Congress Cataloging-in-Publication Data

Noyce, Ruth M., 1926-
        Integrating reading and writing instruction in grades K-8/Ruth M. Noyce, James F. Christie.
          p.   cm.
        Bibliography: p.
        Includes index.
        ISBN 0-205-11815-1
        1. English language—Composition and exercises—Study and teaching—United States. 2. Reading (Elementary)—United States. 3. Interdisciplinary approach in education—United States.
I. Christie, James F.   II. Title.
LB1576.N855 1988   88-22180
372.6—dc19   CIP

Printed in the United States of America
10 9 8 7 6 5 4 3 2 1   93 92 91 90 89 88

To John and Rosa, our loving spouses

Brief Contents

Contents

Preface

The need for a textbook reflecting current thinking on the reading/writing relationship and its implications for classroom practice inspired the writing of this book. Although the reading/writing relationship is currently a lively topic for researchers and practitioners, integration of instruction has yet to gain a foothold in most schools. But the movement is definitely under way. Our collaboration stems from our mutual interest, as reading and language arts educators, in this important new trend.

The purpose of this book is to help make the integration of reading and writing a reality in grades K–8 by suggesting teaching strategies that reflect the most recent classroom-based research. The book provides more than classroom methodology by focusing on theoretical aspects of the reading/writing relationship and presenting the basic rationale underlying each set of strategies. The instructional strategies are described in detail, and examples are given to demonstrate these strategies in action. Most strategies are generic and adaptable for use at various grade levels. In some instances, we have included adaptations for both younger and older students in our examples or indicated appropriate grade levels.

The strategies are organized into five groups: (a) early literacy; (b) writing for reading; (c) reading for writing; (d) content-area reading and writing; and (e) oral language. We have structured the integrated reading/writing strategies around the process approach to writing and the basal Directed Reading Activity, both of which are currently implemented on a wide basis. Two types of special features — Strategy Examples and Recommended Children's Books — are included throughout the book as a resource. In so doing, we hope to make it easier for teachers to incorporate the strategies into their regular teaching practices.

This book is intended as a basic text for undergraduate or graduate courses on integrating reading and writing instruction and for undergraduate communications methods courses which deal with both reading and writing. It is also appropriate as a supplementary text for basic reading and language arts methods courses at the graduate and undergraduate levels. In addition, the book is suitable as a reference for teachers, reading supervisors, and college instructors who are interested in integrating the language arts at the elementary- and middle-grade levels.

We are indebted to Victoria Chou Hare, The University of Illinois at Chicago; Verna Milz; John Pikulski, University of Delaware; Christine L. Roberts, The University of Connecticut; and Dixie Spiegel, The University of North Carolina at Chapel Hill, for their helpful comments and recommendations in reviewing preliminary versions of this manuscript. Special thanks to Victoria Chou Hare for her organizational suggestions.

1

Why Integrate Reading and Writing Instruction?

An Overview

> *Were I to make a prediction about the single most important change in language instruction that will take place in the next decade, it would be that we will no longer separate instruction in reading and writing. It is one of the most exciting prospects I can think of.*
> —Pearson, Changing the face of reading comprehension instruction

The integration of reading and writing instruction has been receiving increasing attention in recent years. The National Council of Teachers of English and the International Reading Association have led the way with journals such as *Language Arts, English Journal, The Reading Teacher,* and *Journal of Reading,* which regularly feature articles advocating the linking of reading and writing activities. Of particular importance were the May 1983 issue of *Language Arts* and an ensuing book, *Composing and Comprehending* (Jensen, 1984). Following these two landmark publications, the flow of research, edited books, and practical articles has been steadily increasing, supporting David Pearson's prediction that language arts integration is indeed the wave of the future.

What has given rise to this movement to teach reading and writing in an integrated manner? A key factor is the reaction against current instructional practices, typified by what Moffett and Wagner (1983) refer to as compartmentalization and fragmentation. *Compartmentalization* is the tendency to teach the language arts in isolation from one another. In a typical elementary school there is a one-and-one-half- to two-hour reading period, an English period, a spelling period, and an occasional handwriting period.

Rarely are the different aspects of written language linked together in any meaningful way. For example, the stories children read in their basal readers are not used as stimuli for writing assignments during English period, nor is writing used to help children better comprehend their basal reader selections. This lack of integration is not limited to reading and writing. There is no connection between the words taught in the reading texts and those taught in the spelling program, and little attempt is made to link spelling instruction with the words children actually use in their writing.

Fragmentation refers to the fact that most reading and writing instruction focuses on discrete subskills that are divorced from real texts or meaningful situations. In reading, the emphasis is on learning sight words, phonic generalizations, contextual analysis, and a myriad of comprehension skills such as recognizing main ideas, drawing conclusions, and separating fact from opinion. Similarly, English instruction consists primarily of drill and practice on parts of speech and mechanical skills such as capitalization, punctuation, and noun-verb agreement. Only a small percentage of the time in a typical reading or English period is spent reading or writing complete passages.

Birnbaum and Emig (1983) summarize current instructional practices in the language arts:

> Currently, in many American elementary schools, from 45 to 120 minutes a day are devoted exclusively to reading and . . . such concomitant skills as word attack and comprehension skills and vocabulary building. Of that time, Smith (1982) estimates that as few as four minutes may be allotted for whole reading experiences. If writing instruction appears at all in these schools, it is separated in time and place from reading instruction and in contexts where no parallels can be drawn between the processes. For example, children know that they write stories, but they do not know that the texts they read have authors. Moreover, much that passes for writing instruction is actually drill in usage, punctuation, and mechanics, divorced from production of whole texts. (pp. 87–88)

Many teachers are aware that this compartmentalization and fragmentation of the language arts curriculum results in a lack of transfer between reading, spelling, and English instruction. Another major problem is that, while children may have mastered isolated subskills, they often experience difficulty reading and writing whole texts. These concerns about the traditional language arts curriculum are the primary motivating force behind the integration of instruction movement.

Reports from major governmental commissions have provided another impetus to the integration of instruction movement. The Commission on Reading emphasized in its report *Becoming a Nation of Readers* (Anderson, Heibert, Scott, & Wilkinson, 1985) that writing experiences are valuable for reading. The report explained that writing develops phonics, spelling, and vocabulary skills and facilitates reading comprehension. It also encourages higher-level thinking by motivating students to read with the "eye of a writer." The commission alerts educators to the need for an integrated approach to literacy and language learning, pointing out that experiences with one language skill will foster development in others. Further confirmation of the need for integrating reading and writing has been found in the 1984 National Assessment of Educational Progress data (LaPointe, 1986). According to the results of testing in reading and writing, those students who read well are better writers; the two skills are systematically related.

Finally, a growing body of research has demonstrated that reading and writing are closely related and that both processes can be learned better in connection with each other rather than in isolation. This research casts doubt on the soundness of traditional, compartmentalized approaches to language arts instruction and has given rise to new theories of the reading/writing process. In the sections that follow we briefly review this research and these new theories. The chapter concludes with an overview of the instructional strategies covered in the remaining chapters of this book.

RESEARCH

■ ■ A number of studies have been conducted to determine the statistical relationship between students' reading and writing abilities. Stotsky (1983) summarizes the results of several dozen of these studies: "Correlational studies show almost consistently that better writers tend to be better readers, . . . that better writers tend to read more than poorer writers, and that better readers tend to produce more syntactically mature writing than poorer readers" (p. 636). Stotsky tempers this conclusion by pointing out that there are exceptions. For example, she cites Loban's (1976) thirteen-year longitudinal study of children's oral and written language development. Loban found that, while good reading and good writing were generally associated, there were a number of children for whom this pattern did not apply. At grade 4, one-quarter of the best readers were judged to be poor writers, and almost one-third of the poorest readers were ranked as good writers. Loban found that, as the students passed through the grades, these inconsistencies became less common and the relationship between reading and writing became stronger.

Tierney and Leys (1986), in another extensive review of reading/writing studies, came to the same conclusion: there is a positive correlation between reading and writing, but there are also a number of students who are good writers but not good readers and vice versa. They contend that these exceptions may be due, in part, to "the extent to which reading and writing opportunities are coordinated" (p. 17). Since reading and writing activities are usually isolated from one another, it is not surprising that some students show more growth in one area than in another. Thus, the good readers/poor writers and poor readers/good writers discovered in this research may be a by-product of the compartmentalized language arts curriculum.

Another important area of research has investigated the early language learning that takes place in home settings. Preschool children, of course, acquire nearly all of their oral language at home without formal instruction. Recent research, reviewed in depth in Chapter 2, has revealed that children also learn much about reading and writing before entering school. For example, most children learn to recognize words in their environment (e.g., on signs and cereal boxes), and many learn to write the letters of the alphabet and their names. A surprising number of children are "early" readers who are able to read and write a number of words, and in some cases entire stories, before entering school.

This early literacy learning takes place without any direct instruction. Instead, it occurs as a result of parent-child story-reading sessions, observation of adults using written language to accomplish real-life purposes, and independent play with books and writing materials. Reading and writing are merged together and often difficult to separate, and the texts children encounter are always whole and meaningful. Such activities differ markedly from the structured, isolated skill practice that typifies school reading readiness programs. The fact that children learn so much about written language through these kinds of informal activities has prompted many researchers and educators to propose that school reading and writing instruction should be made to more closely resemble the natural literacy events that children experience in home settings.

The final area of research consists of experimental studies of the effects of reading on writing and writing on reading. Stotsky (1983) reviewed the few experimental studies conducted to that date and concluded that there was little evidence that conventional, skill-oriented reading instruction had any effect on students' writing. Several experimental studies did indicate, on the other hand, that wide reading experience enhanced writing ability. Having students do additional reading appeared to have more effect on writing than traditional types of writing practice or grammar drills. Similarly, conventional writing instruction appeared to have little impact on reading. However, writing activities such as summarizing, paraphrasing, note taking, and outlining, when linked to texts that children were reading, significantly improved comprehension of those texts.

Since Stotsky's landmark review, additional research findings have been accumulating which support the contention that certain types of reading experiences enhance writing and that selected types of writing activities can promote reading comprehension. Studies by Eckhoff (1984) and others have shown that the books children read have a great impact on children's writing. Children who read large amounts of children's literature are exposed to models of elaborated structures and tend to write more maturely than children whose reading diets consist mainly of basal reader stories. A study we conducted (Noyce & Christie, 1983) showed that reading and writing experiences connected to children's books containing advanced syntactic structures enhanced third graders' reading comprehension and writing. Marino, Gould, and Haas (1985) reported that topic-related writing activities done prior to reading brought about significant gains in reading comprehension. These studies and others, which will be reviewed in detail in later chapters, are providing evidence that not only are reading and writing related, but selected types of reading activities promote growth in writing and vice versa.

THEORY

■ ■ Important differences do exist between reading and writing. The reader, for example, deals with a text that already exists and attempts to reconstruct the message embedded in the print. The writer, on the other hand, is engaged with an evolving text and attempts to compose a message in print. There is also an asymmetrical relationship between the processes in that "we can read indefinitely without writing; we cannot long write without reading — that is, rereading what we have written" (Birnbaum & Emig 1983). However, recent theories of the reading process indicate that the reading and writing processes are more similar than previously imagined, lending additional support for integrating instruction in the two skills.

Birnbaum and Emig (1983) refer to the traditional view of the reading/writing relationship as the "mirror" metaphor. In this theory reading is viewed as the inverse of writing: readers follow the same cognitive and linguistic steps as writers, but in the reverse order (Figure 1.1). Writers first decide on the meaning they wish to communicate then determine the language they will use to communicate that meaning, and finally arrange the language in linear sequences to produce a written text. Readers first decode the text sequences, identify the language underlying the text, and finally arrive at the meanings expressed by the author. In writing, meaning flows from the "top" (the author's mind) to the "bottom" (the words in the text). Reading is viewed as progressing in the opposite direction, from the "bottom" (the text) to the "top" (the reader's mind). Writing is considered to be an active process in which the writer composes meaning, whereas reading is seen as a passive process of decoding meaning constructed by someone else.

Recent research on reading comprehension, to be reviewed in Chapter 5, disputes this passive, bottom-up view of reading and has given rise to

FIGURE 1.1   The "Mirror" Metaphor

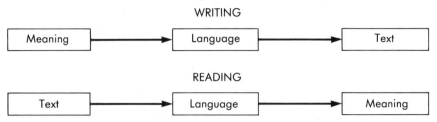

interactive theories of the reading process (e.g., Rumelhart, 1977). In interactive theories, reading comprehension is viewed as an active, constructive process that depends both on information in the text and on the reader's prior knowledge (Figure 1.2). Rather than being bottom-up, it is an interactive process in which both sources — text and mind — interact simultaneously as the reader reconstructs the meaning of the text. Pearson (1985) explains:

> The whole process of comprehension is much more *active, constructive,* and *reader-based* than older theories suggested. No longer can we think of comprehension as *passive, receptive,* and *text-based.* No longer can we think of meaning residing in the text. Instead, we must regard each and every text that students read as blueprints to guide them in building their own models of what the text means. The text sets some broad boundaries in the range of permissible meanings, but it does not specify particular meaning. Particular meanings are negotiations between an author and a reader.
>
> (p. 734)

Schema theory, whose roots trace back to the early twentieth-century Gestalt psychology, has been used recently to explain the mechanisms through which prior knowledge contributes to reading comprehension (Anderson & Pearson, 1984). According to this theory, knowledge is stored in schemata (plural of schema), which are networks of related concepts.

FIGURE 1.2   Interactive Model of the Reading Process

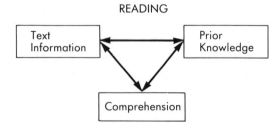

Comprehension occurs when text information is assimilated into an already existing schema or when the schema itself is changed so that it can accommodate new information from the text.

In order to illustrate how schemata work during the reading process, we will use the following example:

Joe blew out the candles and made a wish.

When reading this sentence, you undoubtedly assumed that it was about a birthday party, even though this fact is not explicitly stated in the text. As illustrated in Figure 1.3, most people's schema or knowledge of birthday parties involves at least seven subconcepts or slots:

1. Guests are invited to celebrate an honoree's date of birth.
2. Invited guests bring a gift.
3. There is a cake with candles—one for each year of the honoree's life.
4. The guests sing "Happy Birthday" while the candles are burning.
5. The honoree blows out the candles and makes a wish.
6. The honoree opens the gifts.
7. All participants celebrate with food, games, and party favors.

The words *blew out, candles,* and *wish* in the example sentence triggered your *birthday* schema, allowing you to infer that the sentence was about a birthday party. In addition, it is likely that other slots or concepts connected with the birthday schema were also called to mind: the cake was eaten, games were played, guests were present, gifts were brought, and so forth.

Schemata are also slots for learning new information while reading

FIGURE 1.3 Birthday Party Schema

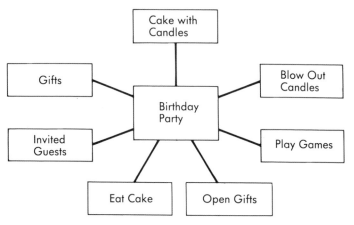

(McNeil, 1987). Due to the interactive nature of comprehension, schemata do not just help readers interpret and elaborate on information in a text; text information can also change their schemata. For example, if a young child does not know that birthday cakes typically have one candle for each year of the honoree's life (perhaps number-shaped candles have been used at the child's birthday parties), this fact may be added as another slot in the child's birthday party schema after being encountered in several books.

Schema theory highlights the active, constructive nature of reading comprehension. Readers do not simply identify words represented by text and passively absorb meaning. In order to achieve maximum comprehension, readers must constantly assimilate text information to their prior knowledge and make inferences by recognizing partial schemata and filling in the missing slots or concepts.

Schema theory also underscores the close connection between reading and writing. The same schemata that are used for reading comprehension are also utilized during the writing process. In order to write about a topic, authors must access their prior knowledge (schemata) of that topic. These schemata serve as the source of the content of the writing. Without schemata, writers would have nothing to write about.

The fact that reading and writing share the same schemata is an underlying rationale for many of the instructional strategies described in this book. As will be explained in later chapters, reading plays an important role in the writing process by supplying students with schemata (ideas) to write about. Reading also exposes students to models of skilled writing, the characteristics of which can be incorporated into their own compositions. Conversely, having students write about a topic prior to reading is an excellent way to facilitate reading comprehension. Such writing will activate the students' relevant schemata about the passage topic, making it easier to understand. Writing can also be a powerful stimulus for reading. If children want to write about a topic but do not possess adequate schemata, this can motivate them to read as much as they can about that topic.

The composition of meaning is obviously at the heart of writing. The fact that reading is an active process that utilizes the same schemata as writing has led some researchers to propose that reading is also a composing process. Tierney and Pearson (1983) explain:

> We believe that at the heart of understanding reading and writing connections one must view reading and writing as essentially similar processes of meaning construction. Both are acts of composing. From a reader's perspective, meaning is created as a reader uses his background of experience together with the author's cues to come to grips both with what the writer is getting him to do or think *and* what the reader decides and creates for himself. As a writer writes, she uses her own background of experience to generate ideas and, in order to produce a text which is considerate to her idealized reader, filters these drafts through her judgments about what her reader's background of experience will be, what she wants to say, and what she wants to get the reader to think or do.

In a sense both reader and writer must *adapt* to their perception about their partner in negotiating what a text means.

(p. 568)*

Tierney and Pearson (1983) have developed a "composing" model of reading that illustrates how reading and writing share some of the same basic processes. According to this model, reading and writing have the following characteristics in common: planning, aligning, drafting, monitoring, and revising. As illustrated in Figure 1.4, these aspects are not sequential steps; rather, they are continuous, recursive activities that occur during the reading and writing processes.

□ *Planning*

Both writers and readers set goals and mobilize existing knowledge. Writers make decisions about what they want to say and how they want to approach their topics. Both of these decisions are influenced by writers' prior knowledge. Readers decide how they want to approach a text and what they want to get out of it, based on their reading purposes and their prior experience with the text topic.

□ *Aligning*

Aligning refers to general ways of approaching a text. Both readers and writers make assumptions about their counterparts. A reader assumes that

FIGURE 1.4   The Composing Model of Reading and Writing
Source: Adapted from R. J. Tierney and P. D. Pearson.*

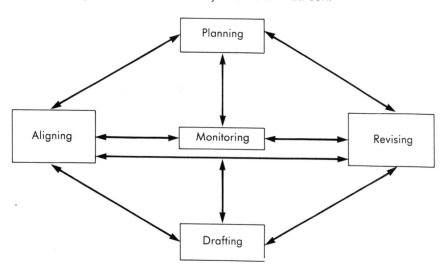

*From R. J. Tierney and P. D. Pearson, Toward a composing model of reading. *Language Arts.* Copyright © 1983 by the National Council of Teachers of English. Reprinted by permission of the publisher.

the author is either friendly, neutral, or antagonistic. These assumptions, in turn, influence how the reader interprets the text. Authors make similar assumptions about their audience, which influence their writing style and treatment of the topic. Readers and writers also adopt roles. Readers decide on the degree of their involvement in the story, ranging from detached observer to pretending to be an actual character in the story. Similarly, writers decide on the "voice" they wish to use in their writing.

☐ *Drafting*

Drafting is the "refinement of meaning which occurs as readers and writers deal directly with the print on the page" (1983, p. 571). Writers do this by making decisions about what information to include and exclude and about how that information should be arranged. Readers refine meaning by making inferences, adding information based on their prior knowledge. They in effect fill in the gaps left by the author.

☐ *Monitoring*

Proficient writers and readers constantly evaluate or monitor their efforts to see if they are achieving their goals. Writers have an alter ego or "inner reader" who is constantly reacting to what has been written. If the current text does not satisfy the writer's goals, then revising takes place. Readers also have an "inner reader" who is constantly making sure that what is being read makes sense and that the meanings being obtained match the goals set during the planning stage. If this is not the case, rereading ensues.

☐ *Revising*

Revising occurs when monitoring indicates that the writer's or reader's goals are not being achieved. Writers reread what they have written, adding or deleting information, rewording, and rearranging until they believe that their objectives will be realized. Early on in the composing process, most of the writer's revisions focus on content. Toward the end, attention shifts to issues of mechanics and style. It is also possible for readers to make revisions by reflecting on the ideas they are getting from the text and rereading portions to achieve better understanding, perhaps from a different perspective or alignment.

If reading and writing are both actually composing processes, this is yet another reason for integrating reading and writing instruction. Writing can help activate prior knowledge which will facilitate the construction of meaning during reading comprehension. Similarly, reading can supply the background knowledge—both about writing styles and mechanics and about topics for writing—that can help writers set and achieve their goals.

INSTRUCTIONAL STRATEGIES

■ ■   The research reviewed above, along with schema theory and the composing model of reading, provides strong support for integrating reading and writing activities. In the chapters that follow, we describe a number of strategies for accomplishing this goal.

Chapter 2 deals with early reading and writing instruction and presents three components necessary for effective kindergarten language arts programs. The first component involves creating a print-rich environment with a well-stocked classroom library, large supplies of writing materials, and ample displays of print of all types. The second component involves teacher-led demonstrations of literacy. Particular attention is given to the Shared Book Experience, which enables teachers to provide experiences similar to parent/child story-reading sessions, and the Language Experience Approach, which assures a perfect match between young readers and the texts they read. The final component concerns self-initiated engagement with written language. Strategies are described for encouraging children to engage in playful reading and writing activities and to use both forms of written language for functional purposes.

The next two chapters deal with how reading can be used to promote writing. We have organized these chapters around the process approach to writing instruction, the method of teaching writing which is currently favored by most experts in the field. In this approach, writing is viewed as a process involving prewriting, drafting, revising, editing, and publishing.

Chapter 3 describes how reading can be incorporated into the prewriting phase of the writing process, providing ideas and motivation for writing. We begin with several strategies for using basal reader stories as stimuli for writing activities and then move on to strategies involving children's literature. Included are strategies that use reading to help children generate original, creative ideas for writing. Other strategies encourage children to respond to basal stories and children's literature in personal ways and to channel their thoughts and feelings into writing. Annotated bibliographies of children's books that can be used to implement these strategies are included.

Chapter 4 details ways in which reading can enhance the composing and revising/editing phases of the writing process, ultimately leading to the acquisition of writing skills and conventions. First, through the use of strategies such as The Author's Chair, Getting Inside the Author's Head, and Book Characters Who Write, children can be encouraged to "read like a writer" (Smith, 1983) and focus their attention on technical and stylistic features of the texts they read. Second, reading also provides children with models of skilled writing, which can be used during the composing stage of the writing process. We describe how teachers can take advantage of this modeling process by encouraging the wide reading of children's literature, and through strategies such as the Integrated Sentence-Modeling Cycle and Rhetorical Imitation, which involve the purposeful imitation of specific writing skills and conventions. Third, reading is an essential part of the revising process. In order to polish and refine initial drafts into publishable works, writers must be able to read and evaluate their own writing. To this end, Group Paper Revision, Peer-Editing Groups, and the Press Conference are described as ways to help students become better reviewers and revisers of their own and other people's writing.

Chapters 5 and 6 examine the inverse perspective, describing how writing can be used to promote reading. We have organized the writing for reading strategies around the Directed Reading Activity, the lesson format used by most basal reading series. A typical basal Directed Reading Activity consists of three main parts: (a) prereading activities, which get students ready for the passage; (b) guided reading, in which the teacher sets purposes for reading, the students read silently, and then a discussion ensues about what has been read; and (c) skill-building activities, which provide instruction and practice on skills related to reading.

Chapter 5 describes how writing activities can be incorporated into prereading and guided reading phases of the basal lesson. We start by explaining how writing, done prior to reading, can facilitate reading comprehension by activating children's prior knowledge and by acquainting them with text structures used in stories. Several strategies, including Semantic Mapping, are presented as means for using writing to activate existing knowledge about passage topics. We then present several strategies which use writing to enhance the guided reading portion of the basal lesson. Strategies such as Question-Eliciting Questions, the Directed Reading and Thinking Activity, and Probable Passages are described as ways to use writing to help children set their own goals for reading by getting them to ask themselves questions and make predictions prior to reading. Another strategy, Save the Last Word for Me, uses writing to generate better postreading discussions.

Chapter 6 describes how writing can be used to supplement basal skill-building activities. First, strategies are presented which facilitate "basic" reading skills such as word recognition, vocabulary knowledge, and syntax. These activities include copying written passages, taking dictation (copying orally presented texts), and manipulating sentences. Strategies that directly facilitate reading comprehension by acquainting children with the structure of narrative stories are Story Templates, Macro-cloze Tasks, and Story Diagrams. Paraphrasing and text condensation activities that help readers reconstruct the meaning of text are also included. Next, we examine ways in which writing can facilitate "higher-order" reading skills such as inferencing, analyzing, and evaluating. Strategies such as Becoming Insiders and Self-Authoring are presented to help children to become critical readers, both of their own writing and the writing of other authors. Finally, several strategies are presented which use writing to build students' metacognitive or metacomprehesion skills. These strategies, including Quick Writes, Question-Answer Relationships (QAR's), and Think Alouds, can increase students' awareness of the cognitive processes used in reading and writing.

Chapter 7 focuses on strategies for teaching reading and writing in the various content areas of the curriculum such as science, mathematics, and social studies. In the first section, we explain how writing can improve students' comprehension of content area texts by familiarizing them with expository text structure and organization. Several strategies, including graphic organizers and pattern guides, are presented which accomplish this by helping students to write their own expository passages. In the second section, we examine writing as a mode of learning and present a number of "write to learn" activities including summary writing, Spin-Off Writing, I-Search, and Saturation Reporting. In the final section, we stress the need for students to practice reading and writing in each content area. Content-specific strategies are presented for teaching reading and writing in science, mathematics, and social studies. Sources of other teaching ideas for integrating reading and writing with each subject area are listed.

In Chapter 8 our interest centers on the oral and written language connection. Guidelines are given for unifying instruction in listening, speaking, reading, and writing, and patterns are described for integrating the language arts curriculum at the district, school, and classroom level. Then a number of specific strategies are presented for integrating oral and written language instruction. Two types of informal drama—role drama and story drama—are described as means to involve children in meaningful reading and writing activities. Next, several types of interviewing activities are recommended as unified communication processes. Finally, two types of oral reading activities—Quick Reads and Readers' Theatre—are presented which give children opportunities to read their own writing to interested audiences.

All of the strategies presented in this book involve whole, meaningful texts and are therefore quite different from the isolated skill activities found in many current reading and writing programs. We are not proposing that conventional basal reader series and English programs be discarded and replaced by the strategies described in this book. What we do advocate is for teachers to eliminate some of the more meaningless, fragmented activities in traditional programs and replace them with integrated experiences like the ones described in the chapters that follow. Ideally, time can be freed up in the reading period for interrelated writing activities, time made available during English periods for process-approach writing activities and reading to support this writing, and time devoted to both reading and writing activities during content area lessons. To this end we have organized strategies around the traditional basal reader lesson format, the process approach to writing, and content area instruction. We hope that this organization will help teachers find appropriate integrated activities to include in all three important aspects of the school curriculum.

The strategies described in Chapter 2 are primarily intended for kindergarteners and first-graders. Strategies in Chapter 3 through 8 are intended for use across the elementary grades, as supplements to traditional reading, English, and content area instruction. Many of the strategies described in these chapters can be easily adapted for use with both primary- and upper-grade students. In cases where strategies are only appropriate for a selected age group, we have labeled them as such. Otherwise, teachers are free to pick from strategies provided and to use them for all grade levels.

REFERENCES

Anderson, R. C., Heibert, E. H., Scott, J. A., & Wilkinson, I. (1985). *Becoming a nation of readers: The report of the Commission on Reading.* Newark, DE: International Reading Association.

Anderson, R. C., & Pearson, P. D. (1984). A schema-theoretic view of basic processes in reading comprehension. In P. D. Pearson (Ed.), *Handbook of reading research* (pp. 255–291). New York: Longman.

Birnbaum, J., & Emig, J. (1983). Creating minds, created texts: Writing and reading. In R. P. Parker & F. A. Davis (Eds.), *Developing literacy: Young children's uses of language* (pp. 87–104). Newark, DE: International Reading Association.

Eckhoff, B. (1984). How reading affects children's writing. In J. M. Jensen (Ed.), *Composing and comprehending* (pp. 105–114). Urbana, IL: ERIC/RCS.

Jensen, J. (Ed.). (1984). *Composing and comprehending.* Urbana, IL: ERIC/RCS.

LaPointe, A. (1986). The state of instruction in reading and writing in U.S. elementary schools. *Phi Delta Kappan, 68,* 135–138.

Loban, W. (1976). *Language development: Kindergarten through grade twelve.* Urbana, IL: National Council of Teachers of English.

Marino, J. L., Gould, S. M., & Haas, L. W. (1985). The effects of writing as a prereading activity on delayed recall of narrative text. *Elementary School Journal, 86,* 199–205.

McNeil, J. D. (1987). *Reading comprehension:* *New directions for classroom practice* (2nd ed.). Glenview, IL: Scott, Foresman.

Moffett, J., & Wagner, B. J. (1983). *Student-centered language arts and reading, K–13: A handbook for teachers* (3rd ed.). Boston: Houghton Mifflin.

Noyce, R. M., & Christie, J. F. (1983). Effects of an integrated approach to grammar instruction on third graders' reading and writing. *Elementary School Journal, 84,* 63–69.

Pearson, P. D. (1985). Changing the face of reading comprehension instruction. *The Reading Teacher, 38,* 724–738.

Rumelhart, D. E., (1977). Toward an interactive model of reading. In S. Dornic (Ed.), *Attention and performance, VI.* Hillsdale, NJ: Erlbaum.

Smith, F. (1982). *Writers and writing.* New York: Holt, Rinehart & Winston.

Smith, F. (1983). Reading like a writer. *Language Arts, 60,* 558–567.

Stotsky, S. (1983). Research on reading/writing relationships: A synthesis and suggested directions. *Language Arts, 60,* 627–642.

Tierney, R. J., & Leys, M. (1986). What is the value of connecting reading and writing? In B. T. Petersen (Ed.), *Convergences: Transactions in reading and writing* (pp. 15–29). Urbana, IL: National Council of Teachers of English.

Tierney, R. J., & Pearson, P. D. (1983). Toward a composing model of reading. *Language Arts, 60,* 568–580.

2

MAKING EARLY
CONNECTIONS
PROMOTING EMERGENT
LITERACY

Literacy learning begins in infancy. Reading and writing experiences at school should permit children to build upon their already existing knowledge of oral and written language. Learning should take place in a supportive environment where children can build a positive attitude toward themselves and toward language and literacy. For optimal learning, teachers should involve children actively in many meaningful, functional language experience, including speaking, listening, writing, *and* reading.
—Early Childhood and Literacy Development Committee of the International Reading Association, 1986

The past decade has witnessed a tremendous amount of research on the development of reading and writing in young children. This research has revealed that many children learn to read and write "naturally," without any direct instruction from parents or teachers. Even children who are not early readers have been found to learn a considerable amount about written language before they enter school. Especially pertinent to the focus of this book is the finding that writing plays an important role in learning to read.

These findings have led many researchers and educators to question traditional views of reading readiness and traditional methods of early reading instruction. There is a growing awareness that kindergarten and preschool reading/writing activities should closely resemble the types of natural literacy events that children experience in home settings.

This chapter begins with a review of research on children's early literacy development and a discussion of implications of this research for school reading programs. Then a number of strategies are presented which teachers can use to promote young children's emerging literacy skills.

FROM READING READINESS TO EMERGENT LITERACY

The traditional concept of reading readiness, which can be traced back to the mid-1920s, has had a great impact on how reading and writing have been taught to young children. Reading was viewed as being closely tied to physical and mental maturation. It was believed that children had to reach a certain level of intelligence — a mental age of 6.6 years — and develop non-reading skills such as visual memory, auditory discrimination, and motor coordination before they could learn to read (Durkin, 1987). According to this view, children were not ready to be taught to read until they had been instructed in the prerequisite nonreading abilities, also referred to as readiness skills. This concept of reading readiness was accompanied by the related belief that reading and writing should only be taught in formal school settings. Parents were cautioned not to try to teach young children to read or even to encourage early reading for fear the children might develop bad habits which would later have to be "untaught" by teachers. It was also believed that writing instruction should occur only after children had been formally taught to read.

These beliefs resulted in the concept that early childhood was a time during which only readiness skills should be taught as a prelude to "real" reading and writing (Teale & Sulzby, 1986). Accordingly, reading readiness tests were soon developed to assess children's readiness abilities, and reading readiness programs with workbooks full of perceptual-motor and other nonreading activities became popular. Although occasionally challenged, this traditional view of reading readiness predominated from the 1920s until the late 1950s. During this period, the beginning of first grade was devoted to readiness activities, and actual reading instruction was usually delayed until the middle part of first grade. Writing instruction was postponed until even later, often until second or third grade.

Sparked by the launching of *Sputnik* in 1957 and the resulting furor that American education "catch up with the Russians," attitudes about reading readiness finally started to change (Durkin, 1987). This event, combined with research pointing to the importance of early learning (e.g., Bloom, 1964) and a growing concern about the education of economically disadvantaged children, led to a movement to begin instruction in all academic areas, including reading, at a younger age. The result of this earlier-the-better attitude was to shift the timing of traditional practices downward, with readiness activities now being used in kindergartens and even some preschools (Durkin, 1987). Children were receiving the same reading readiness instruction, with its emphasis on motor development and perceptual skills, but at an earlier age. Actual reading experiences continued to be delayed, or, if they did occur, they were of a highly structured nature. For example, basal preprimers began to appear in some kindergartens.

Whether this new development in reading readiness instruction was an improvement over the old is debatable. Both approaches had serious shortcomings. The traditional approach withheld reading and writing activities from many children who were ready and eager to begin mastering written language, undoubtedly delaying the reading development of many, but not all, such children. As will be described below, some young children learned to read and write on their own, despite the benign neglect of the traditional approach. The earlier-the-better movement, on the other hand, forced other children to engage in structured instructional activities for which they were not ready, resulting in negative initial experiences with literacy learning. This was potentially more harmful than delays caused by the traditional approach, because initial failure can foster negative attitudes about the learning-to-read process that can be difficult to reverse.

Fortunately, at the same time that the downward shift of traditional readiness programs was underway, a new area of research emerged that would eventually lead to radically different conceptions of reading readiness and early literacy development. This research focused on early readers, children who learned to read without any formal instruction from their parents or teachers—that is, those who learned to read outside the confines of the traditional approach to readiness. Durkin (1966) and other researchers found that there were a number of such children, and that, contrary to popular belief, many early readers did not have exceptionally high IQs. Parental interviews revealed that these early readers had several characteristics in common:

1. They were curious about written language, asking many questions about letters, words, and print.
2. They showed an early interest in writing, and liked to scribble, write their names, send notes, and so forth.
3. They loved to have stories read to them over and over again.
4. They had a parent, older sibling, or other adult who answered their questions about written language and who read to them on a regular basis.

This discovery that some children of normal intelligence learned to read without formal reading instruction sparked interest in what children were learning about written language during the preschool years, giving rise to the field of emergent literacy research. Emergent literacy, a term that can be traced back to Clay's (1972) pioneering research in New Zealand, refers to reading/writing knowledge that is acquired naturally outside of school situations. Researchers began to use the same procedures used in oral language acquisition research to study the natural development of written language.

This growing body of research has revealed that children's literacy development begins long before they enter school and receive formal reading and writing instruction. Mason (1984) divides the early knowledge that children gain about written language into three categories: functions, form and structure, and conventions. We use these categories to briefly review some of the major findings about children's early literacy development:

1. *Functions of Print.*   Children learn that print represents spoken words and has meaning (Ferreiro & Teberosky, 1982). They can distinguish between pictures and print by age three (Harste, Woodward, & Burke, 1984). They also learn that print has many uses such as labels, signs, messages, shopping lists, entertaining stories. In addition, many children begin to identify written words. Goodman (1986) found that 60 percent of the three-year-olds in her study could recognize environmental print embedded in a context (e.g., the word *Pepsi* on a soft drink can). The percentage rose to 80 percent at ages four and five.

2. *Form and Structure of Print.*   Many children begin learning the names of letters and start writing letterlike symbols when they are three years old (Goodman, 1986; Heibert, 1981). They soon invent their own systems of spelling, initially based on their knowledge of letter names (Read, 1971). By the time children enter kindergarten, some have begun to learn the sounds that are associated with letters (Mason, 1984).

3. *Conventions of Reading.*   Preschool-age children learn how to handle books properly (Goodman, 1986). By kindergarten, many are familiar with terms associated with reading and writing, such as *letter, word, page,* and *cover,* although their understanding of the conventional, adult meanings of metalinguistic terms such as *letter* and *word* is usually not fully developed (Goodman, 1986).

Kontos (1986) gives a concise summary of children's normal progress in these three areas during the early childhood years:

Literacy acquisition has begun by age 3 when children learn to distinguish writing from other forms of print and begin to understand how and why print is used. Around age 4, children become environmental print readers and become interested in the graphic cues of print such as letters and letter names. Five-year-olds frequently can read some words out of context and are learning how to discuss and accomplish reading tasks. All of these abilities contribute to their later success in learning to read.

(p. 65)

It should be noted that these are general trends and that there are large individual differences in literacy development. As Teale and Sulzby (1986) point out, "Although children's learning about literacy can be described in generalized stages, children can pass through these stages in a variety of ways and at different ages" (p. xviii). As is explained below, part of this diversity is due to differences in home environment and parental behavior.

Research has also revealed much about the processes that bring about early literacy development. In general, it appears that the acquisition of written language shares much in common with the development of oral language. For example, both occur with very little *direct* adult instruction. Instead, much of language learning (both oral and written) is inductive and constructive in nature. Children build their own rules of oral grammar based on the speech they hear around them. These child-generated grammar systems are at first very different from adult grammar; however, with the passage of time, the child's rules gradually come to approximate the conventional rules of word ordering. In much the same manner, children construct their own rule systems for written language, based on their observations and explorations of print. For example, they invent their own rules for spelling, reflecting their growing understanding of written language. Gentry (1981, 1985) gives an illustration of how a child's spelling of the word *closed* goes through a sequence from random letters (*pls*); to a prephonetic stage, which shows some awareness that letters represent sound (*klz*); to a phonetic stage, during which words are spelled like they sound (*klosd*); to a transitional stage when children begin to attend to words' visual appearance (*clossed*); and finally to the correct spelling (see Table 2.1 for a more detailed description of these stages).

Teale (1982) explains that three ingredients are necessary for this type of inductive literacy learning to take place:

1. There must be print in the environment.
2. The child must be interested in print and have the desire to make sense out of it.
3. The child must engage in active exploration of print to extract its regularities and to invent his or her own system of rules to get meaning from written language.

Another characteristic that written language acquisition shares with the development of speech is that both rely heavily on social interaction. Teale (1982) argues that "the whole process of natural literacy development hinges upon the experience the child has in reading or writing activities which are mediated by literate adults, older siblings, or events in the child's everyday life" (p. 559).

One particular type of literacy interaction appears to be of utmost importance in children's early reading/writing development: storybook reading. Research by Snow and Ninio (1986) has shown that parent-child picture book reading often begins before a child's first birthday. These early book-reading sessions tend to be routinized, with the parent first focusing

TABLE 2.1   Richard Gentry's Invented Spelling Stages

Stage	Characteristics	Examples	Implicit Understandings Shown
Pre-Communicative	Random ordering of letters and other symbols known by child, sometimes interspersed with "letter-like" marks.	b + B p A = monster ≠ PAHIε = giant	• Speech can be recorded by means of graphic symbols
Semi-Phonetic	One, two and three-letter representations of discreet words. Letters used represent some speech sounds heard in word.	M S R = monster P = pie D G = dog	• Speech is comprised of discreet words. Recorded speech consists of written words. • Specific letters stand for specific speech sounds.
Phonetic	Spellings include all sound features of words, as child hears and articulates them.	P P L = people ChroBL = trouble	• Every sound feature of a word is represented by a letter or combination of letters. • The written form of a word contains every speech sound, recorded in the same sequence in which sounds are articulated when the word is spoken.
Transitional	Vowels are included in every recorded syllable; familiar spelling patterns are used, standard spelling is interspersed with "incorrect" phonetic spelling.	Highcked = hiked tode = toad come = come	• It is necessary to spell words in such a way that they may be read easily by oneself and others. • There are various ways to spell many of the same speech sounds. • Every word has a conventional spelling that is used in printed materials. • Many words are not spelled entirely phonetically.

Source: From Margo Wood. Invented spelling. *Language Arts.* Copyright © 1982 by the National Council of Teachers of English. Reprinted with permission of the publisher.

the child's attention on a picture and then asking the child to label the picture. If the child does so, the parent gives positive or negative feedback about the accuracy of the label. If the child does not volunteer a label, the parent provides the correct label. The help parents give children during these interchanges is called scaffolding (Cazden, 1983). This assistance enables children to accomplish tasks which they could not do on their own. As children mature, the nature of the scaffolding changes to accommodate their growing abilities. By age two or three, the emphasis shifts from labeling pictures to identifying printed words (Snow & Ninio, 1986). Since the same books are used over and over, repeated exposure to a small number of words can lead to the beginning of word recognition. These storybook-reading sessions also provide a context for children to ask questions about written language and to begin learning about books and how they should be handled.

Teale (1982) explains that interactive literacy events, such as storybook reading, serve two important functions. They are *substantive,* putting "the child in touch with the functions, uses, processes, and conventions of literacy in our society in general and in the child's family in particular" (p. 563). They are also *motivational,* serving to strengthen the child's desire to learn and write independently.

Children also learn about literacy by observing others, particularly their parents, using reading and writing in their everyday lives. As with literacy events, adult modeling of literacy activity serves both substantive and motivational functions. When children see their family members use print for various purposes, such as writing shopping lists, paying bills, looking up programs in the *TV Guide,* and writing notes to each other, they begin to learn about the uses of written language. Children who observe their parents reading books, magazines, and newspapers for pleasure are more likely to want to learn to read themselves and to be more interested in children's literature as a source of entertainment (Kontos, 1986).

One further major finding of emergent literacy research is that writing plays a crucial role in children's learning to read. Rather than developing after reading, as the traditional approach to reading readiness assumed, writing accompanies young children's growing interest in naming letters and reading print. Mason (1980), for example, found that preschool-age children began to write letters and words at approximately the same time they started to recognize printed words. Tierney and Leys (1986) explain that early attempts at writing "provide children with the opportunity to develop, test, reinforce, and extend their understanding about text" (p. 18). Writing also focuses children's attention on the visual features of print, aiding letter and word recognition. In addition, children's early invented spellings provide valuable practice with phonic skills such as segmentation (breaking words into parts), blending (putting sounds together to make words), and letter-sound correspondences (Chomsky, 1979).

Unfortunately, all children do not have equal opportunities to engage in early writing. Research on children's home environments indicates that there are wide discrepancies in the availability of writing materials. Durkin's (1966) home interviews revealed that the vast majority of parents of early readers regularly provided pencils, pens, paper, and other writing materials, whereas less than one-fourth of the parents of non-early readers reported doing so. Teale (1986), in his study of the home environments of twenty-four low-income two and three year olds, found that only four of the children had easy access to writing materials. He noted that these four children appeared to write more than the other children in the study. Lack of early writing experiences may be one of the reasons that low-income children in general have been reported to enter school with less knowledge of letters, letter-sounds, and words than middle-class children (e.g., McCormick & Mason, 1986).

The research on emergent literacy has several important implications for early childhood programs. It calls for the rejection of both the traditional and earlier-the-better conceptions of reading readiness instruction. Traditional readiness activities focus on perceptual-motor skills and do not involve actual reading/writing experiences, whereas the basal reader materials used in the "early" approach concentrate on isolated, abstract features of print and emphasize tedious drill-and-practice activities. Both approaches fail to take advantage of what children already know about written language, neglect early writing, and place little importance on reading as a pleasurable activity.

As an alternative, emergent literacy research suggests that preschool and kindergarten language arts programs should closely resemble the natural reading and writing instruction which takes place in home settings. In such a program, the teacher's role would involve: (a) providing ample reading and writing materials for children to play with and explore; (b) reading lots of picture books and stories to children; (c) engaging in literacy-centered conversations with children and answering their questions about print; (d) modeling both functional and pleasurable uses of written language; and (e) supplying children with opportunities to use reading and writing for a variety of meaningful, real-life purposes.

During these types of classroom literacy activities, teachers should provide scaffolding appropriate to the child's level of literacy acquisition. Mason (1984) has found that children are initially concerned with learning the functions of print and that print represents words. Later their attention shifts to naming letters and learning letter-sound correspondences. When working with children at the first level, teachers should focus their scaffolding on print awareness and on helping children to learn to match written words with the objects and actions they represent. When children understand that print has meaning and begin to read environmental print, then the focus of informal instruction can shift to letters and their sounds. Children's comments and questions about print can indicate when this shift in emphasis should occur. Kontos (1986) explains: "A focus on letters and print is only appropriate when children begin to get interested in and ask questions about graphic cues in print. It is at this point in the literacy acquisition process that some directed adult assistance in understanding letters and their sounds is appropriate and probably necessary" (p. 65).

Teachers should do everything possible to promote early writing. This can be accomplished by: (a) making writing materials readily available; (b) encouraging children to use these materials in their play; and (c) providing many opportunities for them to write stories and to use writing for real-life purposes (e.g., labeling pictures, writing notes to friends, making lists of things to be done). During these early writing activities, children's invented spellings should be encouraged and looked upon as an indicator of their growing knowledge of letter-sound relationships.

Finally, schools need to adopt a new concept of reading readiness. Reading readiness should not be viewed as a set of nonreading subskills; rather, it should be conceptualized as the relationship between the child's capacities and the demands of specific reading and writing tasks (Durkin, 1987). Viewed in this manner, all young children are ready for some types of literacy activities. In a typical kindergarten classroom, it would be likely that there will be some children who are ready for activities involving the identification of environmental print; others will be ready for activities dealing with letter-sound correspondences; and still others ready for the independent reading of children's books and stories. Similarly, there will be differences in readiness for different types of writing activities, with some children ready to experiment with writing their names and making letters; others will be ready for functional writing activities (e.g., writing lists of things to do); while some of the more advanced students may be ready to write their own creative stories.

STRATEGIES

■ ■   N. Hall (1987) has described three characteristics that can make preschool and kindergarten language arts programs similar to home language-learning environments and, in so doing, help the emergence of literacy to be a continuous process: "There must be an environment where literacy has a high profile and status; there must be access to valid demonstrations of literacy, and opportunity to engage in purposeful literacy acts which are acknowledged as valid literacy behaviour. All these must allow space and provision for discussion and reflection" (p. 82).*

While N. Hall's categories are not mutually exclusive (i.e., some activities can fit into more than one category), they provide a useful system for classifying strategies which teachers can use to promote young children's emerging literacy skills. The sections that follow describe strategies for

*Excerpts from *The Emergence of Literacy,* by N. Hall. Published by Hodder & Stoughton, Ltd., 1987.

creating a literacy-prominent classroom environment, demonstrating the uses of reading and writing, and engaging children in literacy activities.

■ Classroom Environment

Children's home and school environments can have a considerable effect on their literacy development. It is easier for children to learn about written language if many examples of written language are available and prominently displayed and if instruments for producing written language are easily accessible. Not only does such a setting provide models for children to observe and opportunities for children to interact with written language, but it also communicates to children that written language is important and worth mastering.

Several lines of research support the notion that print environment plays an important role in children's acquisition of written language. Studies of children's home environments have revealed that there is great diversity in the availability of literacy materials and the support that parents give to literacy activities (McCormick & Mason, 1986; Teale, 1986). It has also been found that the number of books in the home is positively related to children's reading achievement and attitudes toward reading (Sheldon & Carrillo, 1952; Hansen, 1969). Research on early readers reveals a similar pattern. Durkin's (1966) parental interviews revealed that these children grew up in a print-rich environment and had many opportunities to experiment with early writing.

It has been our experience that the print environment of school classrooms also varies greatly. Some preschool and kindergarten classes are neat, almost Spartan, with several beautiful, teacher-made bulletin boards, a few pieces of student artwork displayed on the walls, and a small collection of children's books tucked away on a shelf with other play equipment. In contrast, other classrooms have an abundance of print. These rooms feature large, well-stocked book corners; displays of children's books or book jackets; walls covered with student writing; written labels on equipment and storage areas; charts with written directions for children; and easily accessible writing materials distributed around the room. Such classrooms tend to be a bit cluttered and less pleasing to the adult eye than the neat classroom, but they are much more conducive to the emergence of literacy.

The following list, whose categories are adapted from a "survey of displayed literacy indicators" cited in N. Hall (1987), contains suggestions for making classrooms into literacy-rich environments:

1. *Book Area.* An inviting, well-stocked book area is a key element in creating an environment that encourages literacy development. At a minimum, the book area should contain shelves to store and display books, a table

and chairs, and an ample supply of books. Other desirable additions include rugs and throw pillows, which invite children to sit on the floor and browse through books, and parent-donated furniture, such as an old sofa or upholstered chair, which makes the reading area more homelike and comfortable.

Having books tightly bunched on a shelf with only their spines showing is an efficient use of space but not a very effective way to store books for young children. As many books as possible should be displayed so that their covers or pages are visible. This helps draw children's attention to the books and invites exploration. It also helps young children who cannot yet read decontextualized print to remember and locate specific books, using cover illustrations, size, color and other nonprint features as cues.

The books themselves are, of course, of utmost importance. The classroom collection should include children's favorites as well as high-quality books selected for the purpose of upgrading their literary tastes and opening new vistas for them. Teachers can keep up to date on the most popular titles through the "Children's Choices" book list published yearly in the October issue of *The Reading Teacher* and "The Web: Wonderfully Exciting Books," published quarterly by the Reading Center, The Ohio State University. The reference sources listed below will provide teachers with additional assistance in the selection of top-notch picture books:

Burke, Eileen. *Early Childhood Literature.* Allyn & Bacon, 1986.
Children's Book Council. *Children's Books: Awards and Prizes.* The Children's Book Council, 1987. (Published every two years.)
Cianciolo, Patricia. *Picture Books for Children.* American Library Association, 1981.
Coody, Betty. *Using Literature with Young Children.* William C. Brown, 1983.
Huck, Charlotte; Hepler, Susan; and Hickman, Janet. *Children's Literature in the Elementary School,* 4th ed. Holt, Rinehart & Winston, 1987.
Larrick, Nancy. *A Parent's Guide to Children's Reading.* Westminster, 1983.
Sutherland, Zena, and Arbuthnot, May Hill. *Children and Books,* 7th ed. Scott, Foresman, 1987.
Trelease, Jim. *The Read-Aloud Handbook.* Penguin, 1985.

2. *Writing Materials.* Things to write with—pencils, pens, chalk, felt-tip markers, and crayons—and to write upon—lined and unlined paper, note pads, and envelopes—should be in abundant supply and easily accessible to children. One particularly effective, but often overlooked, writing accessory is the individual chalkboard. These can be inexpensively constructed out of twelve-by-twenty-four-inch pieces of heavy cardboard. The edges should be covered with masking tape and both sides of the board painted with several coats of chalkboard paint. Small rags can serve as economical substitutes for erasers. Young children especially like to write on such chalkboards because of the ease with which they can erase and change what has been written.

A writing center, in which all of the above types of writing materials are concentrated, will encourage children to experiment with different writing media and can serve as the site for many of the adult-guided writing activities described below in the Engagement section. It is also important to have writing materials distributed around the room so that writing can be incorporated into other activities. For example, paper and pencils can be available in the dramatic-play area so that children will be encouraged to incorporate reading and writing into their make-believe episodes; in the book corner so that children can draw pictures and write about the books they are reading; in the science center so that notes can be written about the outcome of important "experiments"; and even by the door to the playground so that children will be encouraged to write down scores of the games they play.

3. *"World-Related Print."* Research has shown that much of the print which children encounter in their homes is of the utilitarian variety: reading and writing done to accomplish daily living routines such as shopping, paying bills, and finding out about television and movie entertainment (Teale, 1986). It is important that school classrooms also contain ample amounts of what N. Hall (1987) terms "world-related print" so that children can continue to learn about the important functions that literacy plays in our society. He recommends that teachers involve children in activities with items such as magazines, newspapers, *TV Guides,* cookbooks, phonebooks, products with labels (e.g., toothpaste tubes, cereal boxes, milk cartons, soft drink cans), calendars, logbooks, tickets, posters, and theater programs. He also recommends that teachers encourage children to bring these types of materials to class to share and to use in self-initiated activities.

4. *Display Spaces.* Samples of children's writing and dictated stories should be displayed everywhere possible: on walls, on bulletin boards, on mobiles hanging from ceilings, on cupboards. Such displays provide motivation for writing, as well as opportunities for children to read texts their peers have produced. These exhibits also communicate to children that writing is an important, high-status activity.

Displayed work does not have to be technically perfect. Invented spellings and nontraditional punctuation are to be expected during the kindergarten and primary-grade years. As children gain experience with printed language and engage in peer-editing sessions, described in later chapters, their technical writing skills will improve. With beginning writers, the most important goal is learning to put one's ideas down on paper. At this stage, content is much more important than mechanics.

5. *Labels.* Printed labels should be placed around the room in order to help children make associations between written words and their referents. Several different types of labels are useful: (a) environmental labels, which are placed on objects in the classroom (e.g., windows, doors, tables); (b) functional labels, which help children perform classroom routines (e.g., signs telling where to store different play material and where art materials can be found); and (c) explanatory labels, which explain or amplify exhibits or displays (e.g., captions on an incubator in the science center). Teachers should continually draw children's attention to these labels and the objects and meanings they represent.

The three types of labels described above will be particularly beneficial to children in Mason's (1984) first stage of literacy acquisition: ones who are primarily concerned with learning the functions of print. However, labels will also be useful to more advanced children, because repeated exposure and interaction with labels will lead to the eventual recognition of the words on the labels.

6. *Functional Print.*   In addition to the labels described above, there are several other types of functional print that can be used to assist in classroom routines and, at the same time, provide children with valuable experiences with written language. The following are some of the categories on N. Hall's (1987) list:

a. Messages about the current day—daily schedules, announcements, and notices about upcoming school events.

b. Directions for activities—charts, signs, or cards which help children to work independently. For example, there can be printed directions for games, instructions as to the maximum number of children allowed in the dramatic-play center, and so forth.

c. Recording sheets—charts or sheets which require children to record information. As an example, children can be asked to "sign in" when they first arrive at school. This can be done in several ways, depending on individual children's levels of literacy development. Less mature children can be taught to recognize their own name cards and then place these cards in a pocket chart. More advanced students can write their names on a sheet of paper next to the pocket chart. Pocket charts and record sheets can also be used by children to sign up for various classroom activities (e.g., painting, the dramatic-play center).

d. References—charts, books, lists, and catalogues should be available to support ongoing class activities. For example, there can be lists of common words, picture dictionaries, and alphabet charts to help children with their independent writing. Teachers should model using these resources and refer children to them when relevant questions arise. If a child asks the teacher how a word is spelled and that word is on a wall chart, the teacher can direct the child's attention to the chart rather than simply spelling the word for the child.

7. *Dramatic-Play Corner.*   As will be explained in the Engagement section, dramatic or make-believe play can be an important facilitator of literacy development. In order for this to occur, teachers need to provide an environment that is conducive to high-quality, literacy-oriented play.

A spacious housekeeping area equipped with replicas of kitchen appliances, table and chairs, dishes, utensils, dolls, and dress-up clothes will encourage children to engage in elaborate domestic dramatizations. The addition of literacy materials such as paper, pencils, note pads, cookbooks, and telephone directories will prompt children to incorporate reading and writing into their play episodes. N. Hall (1987) recounts the results of an experiment in which he transformed a traditional, nonliterate home center into a literate one by adding such materials: "The effects of these changes to the home center were dramatic. Children filled hundreds of sheets of paper with writing. They took messages, created restaurants and took orders. They also engaged in a lot of reading behaviours" (p. 44).

Dramatic play in the classroom can be further enriched by the addition of theme centers: settings that suggest specific themes such as a restaurant, doctor's office, or grocery store. Woodard (1984) gives examples of how to construct a variety of these centers, including an ice cream shop in which yarn pom-pom balls are used as scoops of ice cream, and a veterinarian's office with an office, examination room, and kennel composed of cardboard cages. Theme areas can, of course, be stocked with literacy materials. For example, the ice cream parlor can have a wall menu for customers to read and the employees can use pencils and note pads to take orders.

If there is ample space in the classroom, it is ideal to locate theme areas near the housekeeping center so that children will be encouraged to integrate play between the two settings (e.g., a family in the housekeeping center can take a trip to the ice cream parlor). This will result in richer, more complex dramatizations. However, if there is only room for one dramatic-play area, periodically transforming the housekeeping center into different theme areas is a viable alternative. Besides encouraging more diverse play episodes, theme centers tend to attract children, particularly boys, who are not interested in participating in domestically oriented play in housekeeping areas.

■ Teacher Demonstrations

Emergent literacy depends on more than just a print-rich environment. There must also be an adult or older siblings to demonstrate the uses of reading and writing, to show the conventions of written language (e.g., how books are handled), and to answer children's questions about print (Smith, 1982). Research on home environments has revealed that children from all social classes are exposed to numerous examples of how reading and writing can be used to do chores associated with daily living, such as paying bills, making shopping lists, leaving notes as reminders to other family members, and using a TV guide or newspaper to locate entertainment (Teale, 1986). Many parents, particularly those whose children are early readers, provide an additional type of demonstration: storybook-reading sessions (Durkin, 1966). These story-reading sessions allow parents to model the conventions of reading and also encourage rich adult-child dialogue and children's active participation in the reading process.

N. Hall (1987) contends that, if school language arts programs are to foster the continuance of emergent literacy, teachers need to provide demonstrations of reading and writing similar to those which children experience in home settings. Unfortunately, this is not always the case. Hall points out that, while teachers do engage in a large amount of literacy activity, most of the activity is instructional in nature. This communicates to children that reading and writing are activities to be taught and learned, but gives little cue as to what they are to be used for or why they are skills worth mastering. The impression is given that school reading and writing have little to do with everyday life.

Teachers can help broaden children's perceptions of literacy by allowing students to see them using reading and writing for a variety of purposes, both recreational and utilitarian. N. Hall (1987) suggests that teachers occasionally read for pleasure in the presence of their students and that they write with children and read some of what they write to their classes. Teachers can also make children aware of the reading and writing that they do for practical purposes: ordering films and supplies, keping records, answering letters, writing notes and reminders. Rather than hiding these activities from children, these practical uses of written language should be brought to children's attention.

Two other types of literacy demonstrations are particularly well suited to school settings: the Shared Book Experience and the Language Experience Approach. These activities allow children to observe teachers modeling conventions of reading and writing and provide a context in which teachers can give informal literacy instruction. In addition, these types of demonstrations can lead to rich dialogues between students and teachers, allowing children to get answers to their questions about written language.

☐ *Shared Book Experience*

There is almost unanimous agreement that reading to children plays an important role in literacy development. Teale (1981) cites a number of studies which report positive relationships between being read to at home and oral language development, vocabulary knowledge, eagerness to read, and success in early reading instruction. When children sit in their parent's lap and watch as favorite stories are repeatedly read to them, they not only develop positive attitudes toward reading, but also learn much about the purposes, structure, and conventions of written language (Snow & Ninio, 1986). The verbal interaction between parent and child appears to be a key factor, allowing children to ask questions and become actively involved in the story-reading process and providing parents with an opportunity to engage in informal teaching about written language and the world in general (see Taylor, 1986).

Reading to children is also common practice among the teachers of young children, though its frequency varies considerably from teacher to teacher. N. Hall (1987), for example, reported that observations in a large number of British schools revealed that some teachers read several stories a day to their students, whereas others only read one story a week. Needless to say, the more often stories are read in school, the better. Not only does frequent story reading provide children with models of book usage and valuable lessons about the conventions of reading, but it also shows that "reading has considerable value and status" (Hall, 1987, p. 88).

Teachers traditionally read picture books to their classes by holding the book so that the children can see the illustrations, pausing occasionally to solicit students' reactions to the story or to ask story-related questions. Holdaway (1979) contends that this traditional teaching method differs from parent-child storybook-reading interactions in several important ways: (a) the children can only see the pictures, not the print; (b) the teacher and children rarely engage in informal, story-related dialogue; and (c) the children do not actively participate by "reading along" on parts of the story they remember. As a result, reading to children loses much of its instructional value. In order to remedy this situation, Holdaway devised the Shared Book Experience, a strategy that uses enlarged print, teacher demonstrations, and increased pupil participation to make school storybook-reading sessions similar to those which occur at home.

To prepare for a Shared Book Experience, the teacher needs to select several stories to enlarge. Butler and Turbill (1984) recommend that these stories have: (a) an absorbing, predictable story line; (b) a predictable structure, containing "elements of rhyme, rhythm and repetition"; and (c) illustrations which enhance and support the text. These features make it easy for children to predict what is upcoming in the story and to read along with the teacher. Picture books containing versions of familiar folktales such as "Goldilocks and the Three Bears," "The Three Pigs," "The Three Billy Goats Gruff," "The Gingerbread Man," and "Henny Penny" are ideal stories to start with. We have found that Bill Martin's *Instant Readers* series, published by Holt, Rinehart & Winston, also fits the above characteristics. These books are excellent to adapt for Shared Book Experiences. A list of other predictable books that are suitable for use with this strategy can be found at the end of this chapter.

Once the books are selected, they are enlarged so the print can be seen clearly by children sitting twelve to fifteen feet away. This can be done by making transparencies of the pages of the storybook and showing them on an overhead projector, or by rewriting the story on chart paper, using one-to-two-inch-tall letters. If the latter is done, teachers need to make their own illustrations. However, as Holdaway (1979) points out, this is not too demanding a task: "We don't need to illustrate all of them [the pages] because the children will enjoy contributing their own illustrations to some of the books. Nor do the illustrations need to be polished pieces of art — the children will return to the normal-sized book in their independent reading and be able to savor the original illustrations at that time" (p. 66).*

Commercially produced Big Books are becoming increasingly available. Scholastic, for example, publishes enlarged versions of a number of high-quality picture books. These ready-made Big Books have the advantage of saving teachers time by eliminating the need to make enlarged texts. In addition, children can enjoy large versions of the original illustrations during shared reading experiences.

A typical Shared Book Experience involves the following steps, though the exact sequencing may vary:

*From D. Holdaway (1979). *The foundations of literacy.* Sydney, Australia: Ashton Scholastic.

1. *Warm-Up.* Familiar nursery rhymes, chants, and songs are read and sung, using enlarged print as a guide.

2. *New Story.* A new story is introduced to the children and then read by the teacher. Prior to reading, the illustrations are examined, the author and title discussed, and children encouraged to make guesses as to what the story might be about (Butler & Turbill, 1984). A pointer is used during reading, to help children follow along and to see the one-to-one relationship between print and oral language. The teacher pauses periodically to encourage children to predict what is coming next in the story. When finished, the children are encouraged to give their reactions to the story. The main focus of attention is on the story itself.

3. *Rereading of Favorite Stories.* Children choose a favorite story that was introduced in earlier lessons. During rereadings, more attention is given to student participation and informal instruction about written language. The teacher uses a pointer to make it easier for the children to follow the words being read and encourages them to read along on parts they remember. The teacher pauses periodically to discuss conventions of print, such as left-to-right sequence and punctuation.

Masking devices (see Figure 2.1) are used to isolate individual words and focus children's attention on the details of print. For example, the teacher might mask off several words, starting with the letter *d,* and help the children discover that they all start with the same sound. Oral cloze activities, in which the teacher deliberately omits words in a story and pauses for the children to supply the missing words, are used to promote prediction and contextual analysis. While reading an enlarged adaptation of Bill Martin's *Brown Bear, Brown Bear, What Do You See* (Holt, Rinehart & Winston, 1970), the teacher might omit the names of the animals:

Brown Bear, brown bear, what do you see?
I see a _____ _____ looking at me. (red bird)
Red bird, red bird, what do you see?
I see a _____ _____ looking at me. (yellow duck)

The repetitious structure of the text, plus the strong picture clues, make it easy for children to predict the missing words.

4. *Expressive Activities.* The children engage in related art, dramatic-play, and writing activities in which they are encouraged to recreate or innovate on the stories that have been read to them. For example, children might be asked to: (a) retell a story in their own words, using the illustrations in the enlarged text as a guide; (b) paint an illustration of their favorite part of the story, and perhaps write or dictate an accompanying caption; (c) adopt roles and dramatically reenact the story; or (d) make up a new story based on the pattern of that story (Butler & Turbill, 1984).

The last type of activity, called innovated stories, provides an excellent opportunity to link reading with writing. For example, after reading an enlarged version of *Brown Bear, Brown Bear, What Do You See?* several times, a teacher might encourage children to use invented spellings to write

FIGURE 2.1 Masking Device Used with an Enlarged Version of Bill Martin's *Brown Bear, Brown Bear, What Do You See?*

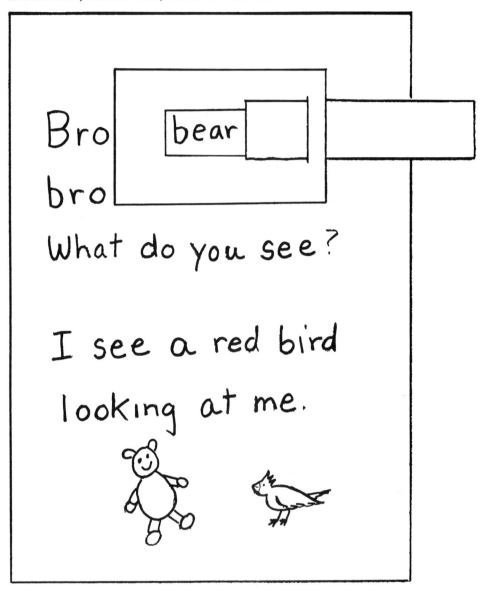

their own innovated story based on the *Brown Bear, Brown Bear, What Do You See?* pattern. Figure 2.2 is an example of one such story written by a kindergartener.

5. *Independent Reading.* Regular-sized versions of the enlarged books are available for the children to explore, pretend to read, or actually read (depending on individual children's level of literacy development).

FIGURE 2.2 Invented Story Based on *Brown Bear, Brown Bear, What Do You See?*

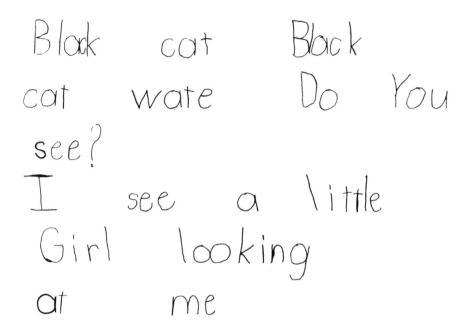

Black cat Black cat wate Do You see? I see a little Girl looking at me

The Shared Book Experience is an excellent strategy for promoting young children's emerging concepts about written language. Writing skills are developed through observation of teacher modeling and the composition of innovated stories. In addition, it provides opportunities for them to begin to develop basic reading skills such as sight vocabulary (words such as *brown* and *bear* will be recognized instantly after many repeated exposures), phonics, and contextual analysis. These skills are not formally taught to children in isolation as is the case of traditional reading readiness programs; rather, they are learned by children during enjoyable, meaningful experiences.

□ ***Language Experience Approach***
The Language Experience Approach involves using children's own oral language as reading material. Children first dictate stories about their experiences, either in groups of individually, and the stories are written down by their teacher. The dictated stories are then read by the teacher and by the children. The Language Experience Approach facilitates reading by assuring a perfect match between children and the material they read. Because the language patterns are determined by children's speech and the content is determined by their experiences, it is easy for children to predict and remember the text of experience stories.

This approach, which stems back to the story and sentence methods of reading instruction popular around the turn of this century, is an ideal way for teachers to demonstrate the interrelatedness of the language arts. Children watch while the teacher *writes* down their story as they *speak*. They then *listen* as the teacher reads the story, and finally they *read* the story themselves. This helps children realize that: (a) what they experience can be talked about; (b) what they talk about can be written down; and (c) what is written can be read. It also helps them grasp that written language has the same purpose as oral language: the communication of meaning (Allen, 1976; M. Hall, 1981). As teachers take dictation, they also have an excellent opportunity to demonstrate to children the conventions of written language: that it proceeds from left to right and from top to bottom, that words have spaces between them, that the first word in a sentence is capitalized, that sentences end with a period or other terminal punctuation, and so forth.

Experience stories can be composed by groups of children or by individuals. The same basic procedures are used in both cases:

1. *Stimulus.* There needs to be a meaningful experience for the children to write about. This might be a holiday (Halloween), recent school activity (field trip to the fire station), an interesting object brought to class (Jenny's butterfly collection), or a memorable out-of-school experience (exploits of the family pet). If a *group* story is to be composed, the experience must have been shared by all members of the group. In the case of *individual* stories, the stimulus can be any experience that is important to a specific child.

2. *Oral Discussion.* The teacher leads a discussion of the experience prior to the dictation of the story. This stimulates oral language development and will usually lead to better stories. Asking open-ended questions is a good way to get the discussion flowing.

3. *Dictation.* The teacher writes down the story as the children tell it. If a *group* story is being dictated, the story should be printed in large letters on the chalkboard or on a piece of chart paper (overhead transparencies can also be used). Children take turns adding sentences to the story. It is recommended that the teacher read each sentence back to the group after it is written down. This will promote continuity in the story by refreshing the next contributor's memory of the story line. *Individual* stories can be written on regular writing paper or in "blank books," pieces of blank paper sandwiched between covers made of construction paper.

With both group and individual stories, it is recommended that teachers try to preserve the children's oral language as much as possible. Grammatical editing should be kept to a minimum. However, if the meanings of sentences are not clear children should be asked (and helped, if necessary) to rephrase their ideas. Teachers can pause occasionally during dictation to comment on the conventions of print. Figure 2.3 presents an

FIGURE 2.3   Individual Experience Stories

A kindergarten class went on a field trip to a nearby Native American Museum. Upon returning to school, each child dictated an individual experience story about the trip. The teacher wrote their stories on sheets of writing paper, and then the children drew pictures to accompany their stories. The following are examples of the stories they dictated:

It was a great field trip. I liked it. I saw the buffalo and the Indians. I saw the ponies. I saw the teepee. I like Indians.

Indians have teepees. The Indians catched the buffalo. Indians have bows and arrows and canoes. I like them.

Indians liked buffaloes. They had poisonous snakes. They killed those snakes and wore their skin. They were friends of turtles and owls.

example of an individual experience story composed by a kindergarten child.

4. *Reading.* After a story has been dictated, the teacher reads it out loud to the individual child or to the group. This allows the teacher to model reading orally with expression and proper intonation. While reading, the teacher can use a pointer (as in the Shared Book Experience) to help children follow along. Teachers can also encourage children to make revisions to their stories at this point, helping them begin to realize that what has been written is not "set in stone" but can be easily modified. This concept is an important prerequisite for the peer group editing activities to be described in later chapters.

The story is then read orally by the individual child or group. With individual stories, the child can first read the story with the teacher and then alone. With group stories, the teacher can have the children read the story in unison with and then without her accompaniment. This can be followed by having children volunteer to read the story by themselves. Group stories can also be rewritten on ditto masters and duplicated so that each child has a copy to read. As the children read, teachers should prompt children on unknown words in order to insure success and to promote fluent oral reading.

5. *Follow-up Activities.* Once experience stories have been recorded and read, there are a number of things which can be done with them in order to extend children's literacy learning:

   a. *Illustrations.* Children can make pictures to go with their stories. As M. Hall (1981) points out, this is a very popular activity with children and provides motivation for composing experience stories. Illustrations can also serve as stimuli for stories. Telling a story about a picture that one has drawn or painted is an easy way for young children to begin the Language Experience Approach.

   b. *Class Books.* Collections of children's individual experience stories or duplicated copies of different group stories can be made into books by stapling them between covers made of construction paper. These books can then be placed in the classroom library for children to read independently. In addition to providing valuable reading practice, class books give children an additional reason for composing experience stories: they know that their friends will be able to read their stories.

   c. *Key Words and Word Banks.* The key word strategy, developed by Sylvia Ashton-Warner (1963), is an excellent adjunct to the Language Experience Approach. In this strategy, children choose words that are personally meaningful and that they would like to learn to read. Language experience stories and favorite children's books are primary sources for these "key" words. After taking dictation or conducting a Shared Book Experience, teachers can ask individual children to pick a favorite word from the story. This word is written down on a large card while the child watches. The child then engages in various activities with the word in order to become familiar with it. The Strategy Example below presents a number of key word activities recommended by Jeanette Veatch and her associates.

Each child's word cards are kept in a box or on a ring file known as a "word bank." Periodically, the teacher can have children review the words in their banks. If a word is not recognized instantly, it is removed from the word bank. With very young children it is probably best to discard such words, since they lack sufficient personal significance. Veatch et al. (1979) recommends giving an explanation such as "Oh, that just wasn't a good enough word to remember" (p. 29). With older children, these words can be placed in a second file, a "Words I Need to Learn" bank. These words are also periodically reviewed with the teacher. After the child recognizes a problem word a specified number of times, it is returned to the regular word bank.

Besides providing opportunities for children to practice recognizing key words, word banks serve other valuable functions. They provide children with a concrete record of their reading vocabulary growth. It is very motivating for children to see their collections of words grow larger and larger. In addition, the words can be used to assist and personalize reading instruction. For example, when working on the *d* letter-sound correspondence, the teacher can have children assemble and review all the cards in their word banks that begin with that letter.

——————— STRATEGY EXAMPLE 2.1 ———————

Key Word Activities

Group Activities

1. Retrieving Words from the Floor. The children's words (usually the words of a group or half the class are best) are placed on the floor face down. On the signal, each child is to find her own word, hold it up, and tell it to whoever is watching.
2. Claiming the Cards. The teacher selects many words from the class, holds them up, and the child who "owns" each word claims it.
3. Classifying Words. Certain kinds of topics—for example, desserts, television characters, funny words, places, scary words—are chosen. Topics are selected according to the classification. All the children who have a "dessert" word, for example, would stand in one spot. The teacher might want to label the spot with a sheet of

paper that says "dessert." Children who have words of other classifications also stand in their designated areas.

4. Acting Out Words. If the key word is conducive to "acting out," the child can sometimes dramatize her word for others to guess.

Individual Activities

1. Making Alphabet Books. After children are sure they know their words and can claim them for their own, the words are recorded in the correct section of an alphabet book that is divided by initial letters.
2. Illustrating. The child can draw a picture about the key word, then dictate a caption for the teacher to write on it.
3. Making Sentences. The children write their words on a piece of paper or on the chalkboard and then proceed to add other words, such as service words, to make sentences of varying length. The following are some examples of sentences written for key words: Get the *lion.* Casper, the *ghost,* can fly.
4. Finding Words. The child can find a word in a book, magazine, or newspaper.

Source: From J. Veatch, F. Sawicki, G. Elliot, E. Flake and J. Blakey. *Key words to reading: The language experience approach begins.* Copyright © 1979 by Merrill Publishing Co. and reprinted by permission.

Microcomputers are an excellent medium on which to record children's experience stories. A number of word processors are available, such as Bank Street Writer and Apple Writer, which are easy for teachers (and children) to learn to use. Children enjoy watching while the words of their story appear on the computer monitor. Once completed, the story can be read from the screen and revisions can easily be made (much more quickly and neatly than when written experience stories are changed). The final version of the story can then be printed out and stored in the child's story folder or attached to pages of a blank book.

The Language Experience Approach and the Shared Book Experience complement each other. The Shared Book Experience makes beginning reading easier through its illustrations, predictable story structure, and repeated language patterns. The Language Experience Approach assists early reading by providing a precise match between children and the language patterns and content of the material they read.

The two strategies acquaint children with different aspects and uses of written language. The Shared Book Experience, with its enjoyable stories, introduces them to the entertainment function of print. It is a powerful motivator for learning to read for pleasure. The Language Experience Approach, on the other hand, personalizes reading and writing and links these skills with children's real-life experiences. Holdaway (1979) explains: "Where shared-book experience is strong in providing emotional and aesthetic satisfaction, language experience has its strength in learning about the real world and channeling intellectual motivations into reading and writing. It integrates well with science and social studies and helps to turn these interests to literate use" (p. 144).

When used simultaneously, the two approaches tend to stimulate and build on each other. Holdaway gives the example of how, after being read an enlarged version of *The Very Hungry Caterpillar* in a Shared Book Experience, children's interest in insects was heightened. Children began to bring insects to class, and field trips were taken to observe them in natural settings. This, in turn, prompted many children in class to compose experience stories about insects and undoubtedly heightened their interest in storybooks with insects as main characters. In addition, Holdaway found that children began to use language structures (idioms, phrasing, sentence patterns) from the enlarged books in their own dictated stories. For example, after being read Maurice Sendak's *Where the Wild Things Are,* children began to use phrases like "In and out of weeks and through a day" when they referred to the passage of time in their experience stories.

■ Child Engagement

In addition to a literacy-prominent environment and adult demonstrations of reading and writing, children also need ample opportunities to engage in these activities (Smith, 1982). They need to be able to explore the functions, structure, and conventions of print in the context of *self-initiated, purposeful* activities which are similar to literacy events experienced in the home. Such activities are far superior to isolated practice of letter and word recognition, phonics, and handwriting found in traditional readiness programs. Readiness drill activities sever reading and writing from their real-life functions and have the potential for creating negative attitudes toward literacy instruction.

Rudolph and Cohen (1984) point out that repetition is necessary in order for children to learn skills such as handwriting. Having children sit alone and copy letters on ditto sheets provides this repetition, but it is also boring and devoid of meaning. If, on the other hand, the repeated writing of letters of the alphabet occurs in the process of a self-initiated activity such as dramatic play or some type of functional writing activity (e.g., writing a note to a friend or to the teacher), the "repetition presents exciting experimentation, surprising effect and a sense of accomplishment" (p. 296).

The children not only learn how to write letters; they also discover what the skill can be used to accomplish and why it is worth mastering.

In the sections that follow, we present strategies for engaging children in three categories of purposeful literacy activities: self-initiated reading, self-initiated writing, and dramatic play. All three types of engagement are needed for an effective school literacy program. In discussing the reading and writing strategies a distinction is made between play and functional activities. Play refers to activities pursued for their own sake; the activity is of primary importance and any outcome or product is secondary. Functional activities, on the other hand, are performed to achieve some real-life goal or purpose. The outcome of such activities is more important than it is in play. Both types of literacy activity are meaningful, enjoyable ways for children to explore and practice aspects of reading and writing.

☐ *Reading*

Demonstrations of reading are more effective when accompanied by opportunities for the children to have active engagement with similar reading material. After a Shared Book Experience with an enlarged text, copies of the actual children's book can be made available for children to explore and play with. Similarly, after language experience stories have been dictated they can be made into books and placed in the reading corner. Large numbers of predictable books and other high-quality picture books should also be available in the reading area, arranged in a manner so as to catch children's attention (see Classroom Environment section above).

Young children at all levels of literacy development can profit from engagement with books. Infants' and toddlers' independent activity with books is sensory-motor in nature. They carry books around the room, thumb through the pages, and point to favorite pictures. Preschoolers begin to imitate the reading behaviors that they have observed during adult demonstrations of reading, i.e., they pretend to read. Those who are not yet able to remember stories that have been read to them make up their own stories to go along with the illustrations in a book. More mature children use picture cues and their memory to recite favorite lines and paraphrase the rest of the story. Children with some word recognition skills will actually read part or all of the book. Crowell, Kawakami, and Wong (1986) describe the range of playlike reading activities which occurred as their kindergartners engaged with easy picture books during independent reading time:

> Edwin turned pages of *Cowboy Andy* (Chandler, 1959). He told a story of going to "Sam's Daddy's friend's house" and taking his gun, lasso, and pony. Although no one was paying attention to him, he worked his way through the whole book. Rayleen chose *Thump, Thump, Thump!* by Anne Rockwell. She read "Thump, Thump, Thump" on every page that it appeared, filling in the gist of the story for the words that she couldn't read. She beamed when she

reached the last page. Esther proudly read and showed pictures of *Snow* (McKie and Eastman, 1962) to several interested children.

(pp. 148–149)

Play-like reading enables children to experience some of the importance and status associated with reading, providing important motivation for learning to read. N. Hall (1987) explains:

> When collecting children's accounts of learning to read I found two children who remembered a time before they could "read." They told me: "When I couldn't read I pretended I could read and so everybody thought I was grown up" and: "I used to pick up my Dad's thick books and sit down and would flick through the book slowly, pretending to read just looking at the pictures. I used to love doing this. It made me feel big and proud of myself." Those two children had . . . identified being able to read as an achievement to be proud of. For them, being literate had social status and was a desirable goal.
>
> (p. 20)

Besides serving as a motivational force, make-believe reading directly contributes to reading development by gradually leading children to recognize printed words. Play reading is initially imitative, heavily dependent on memorization and picture cues. Children simply recite the parts of stories they remember, prompted by pictures and their memory of the story structure. In time, pretend reading becomes increasingly print focused, with printed words rather than pictures prompting memory of the story. Eventually many children begin to recognize and remember some of the words in their favorite books, and "real" reading begins.

Pretend reading also sets the stage for later reading by encouraging active comprehension. The following Strategy Example presents Holdaway's (1979) transcript of four-year-old Leslie's play reading of Sendak's *Where the Wild Things Are*. Notice how Leslie is not merely repeating the story from memory, but is filling in parts she did not remember with words from her own vocabulary, based on her understanding of the story. She is actively constructing meaning as she "reads." As explained in Chapter 1, this type of composing is a crucial component of reading comprehension.

--------------------- **STRATEGY EXAMPLE 2.2** ---------------------

Leslie's Playlike Reading of *Where the Wild Things Are*

Test	Reenactment
and an ocean tumbled by with a private boat for Max and he sailed off through night and day	Max stepped into his private boat and sailed off one day and one night

and in and out of weeks and almost over a year to where the wild things are.

And when he came to the place where the wild things are they roared their terrible roars and gnashed their terrible teeth and rolled their terrible eyes and showed their terrible claws.

till Max said "BE STILL!" and tamed them with a magic trick of staring into all their yellow eyes without blinking once and they were frightened and called him the most wild thing of all

and made him king of all the wild things. "And now," cried Max, "let the wild rumpus start!"

No text. [Picture of wild dance]

then when he came to where the wi—oh oh look at that thing—he's blowing smoke out of his nose

and where the wild things are they lashed their terrible claws—*oh no!* they lashed their terrible teeth— Hrmmm! [Interviewer: "What did they gnash?"] They *lashed* their terrible claws!—showed their terrible claws and showed their terrible yellow eyes (but we've got blue eyes)

til Max said, "BE STILL!" that's what he said. One of these ones have toes [turns the page to find the toed monster] Toes! [Laughs] until Max said "BE STILL" into all the yellow eyes without blinking once. And all the wild things said, "You wild thing!"

And then Max said, "Let the wild rumpus start!"

That's got no words, has it? He'd better pull his tail out of the way.

Source: Holdaway, D. (1979). *The foundations of literacy.* p. 41. Sydney, Australia: Ashton Scholastic.

The teacher's main role in promoting child engagement with books is to provide an abundant supply of good children's literature in the classroom and ample opportunities for children to engage with these books. (See the Shared Book Experience section of this chapter for help in selecting high-quality picture books.) Teachers may also occasionally become involved in their students' book play, serving as an audience for children's play reading and encouraging their efforts. Children find this type of role reversal very motivating.

As we explained earlier in this chapter, many of children's home-reading experiences are functional in nature. They watch their parents and older siblings use reading and writing to accomplish real-life purposes. They often get to join in these activities (e.g., reading food labels and signs in the environment). It is important that teachers provide opportunities for children to continue to learn about functional qualities of reading and writing in the classroom.

Mason and Au (1986) have suggested a number of functional reading activities for use in kindergarten classrooms. These include:

1. *Name Cards.*   Children's names can be printed on cards and then used for a variety of purposes. They can be placed on children's desks and storage spaces. Teachers can also use the cards to call roll and to excuse children to go for snacks or recess. At first, the teacher needs to say each pupil's name as his or her card is held up. Eventually, only the cards will be needed for these activities. Name cards can also be used in pocket charts to designate children who will serve as monitors or perform other special services during the day. Mason and Au point out that such activities not only teach children to recognize their own names but also the names of their fellow students.

2. *Signs and Labels.*   Labels can be placed on many objects and places in the classroom. For example, shelves can be labeled to indicate the location of art supplies. Toy shelves can have labels showing where different play materials should be stored, greatly facilitating cleanup after free play periods. Lists of rules and directions can be placed in different learning centers. For example, a sign might be placed outside the housekeeping corner indicating the maximum number of children allowed in the center, or instructions might be given about how to feed the goldfish in the science center.

3. *Daily Schedule.*   A pocket chart can be used to inform children of the activities scheduled for the day. Mason and Au recommend using a combination of clock pictures (to represent the times) and words. The teacher can go over this chart at the beginning of each day and refer children to it when they inquire about upcoming events.

4. *Song Lyrics.*   Lyrics for songs to be sung during opening ceremonies or music time can be written on large pieces of chart paper, overhead transparencies, or the chalkboard. The teacher points to the words as they are sung. Children will soon find that these written lyrics are useful in remembering the words of different songs.

5. *Special Events.*   Information about special activities can be written on the chalkboard or on chart paper. For example, the teacher might write, "On Tuesday we will take a field trip to the fire station." The message can then be read to the children. If they have prior knowledge of the event, the teacher might encourage them to try to figure out the message on their own.

□ ***Writing***

Opportunities for children to engage with writing are every bit as important as early reading activities. One of the most commonly reported characteristics of children who learn to read prior to entering school is that they show an early interest in writing, initially producing scribblelike forms to represent letters and words (see Figure 2.4). Holdaway (1979) explains how these

FIGURE 2.4   Kelli's Scribble Writing: Early Kindergarten

early attempts at writing are closely connected with young children's interest in environmental print:

> During the leisurely period of three to four years of active literacy-learning before school entry most . . . children become fascinated in print as a mystery that is well worth solving. They begin to play with writing in the same way as they play with reading, producing writing-like scribble, the central feature of which, for them, is that it *carries a message.* They learn to write their names, and explore creating letters and letter-like symbols with a variety of writing devices. They show intense interest in the print around them of signs, labels, advertisements, and TV, and often imitate these forms in inventive ways.
>
> (p. 47)

This playlike writing provides opportunities for children to learn about the form and functions of print, and ultimately leads to the ability to write and recognize the letters of the alphabet.

As soon as children learn to write letters, they begin to use invented spelling to make words. These spellings are initially random but soon come to reflect children's growing knowledge of letter names and letter-sound relationships, progressing through prephonetic, phonetic, and transitional stages (see Table 2.1).

Figures 2.5 and 2.6 show examples of five-year-old Matthew's spelling during phonetic and transitional stages. Notice how in the phonetic-stage sample, in which he is explaining how to make a peanut butter and jelly sandwich, several syllables do not contain vowels (*frst, tk, pnut, butr*). In the transitional-stage sample, every syllable has a vowel, showing that Matthew has acquired this important spelling principle.

Invented spelling does more than simply reflect children's understandings about print; it directly contributes to their knowledge of letter-sound correspondences and to later word recognition. Carol Chomsky (1972) detailed how children's invented spellings of words can lead to the ability to read those words:

> The composing of words according to their sounds . . . is the first step toward reading. Once the child has composed a word, he looks at it and tries to recognize it. The recognition is slow, for reading the word seems much harder than writing it. Often the child works it out sound by sound, the reverse of the process by which he wrote it, and then recognition dawns all at once.
>
> (p. 120)

FIGURE 2.5 Matthew's Phonetic-Stage Spelling

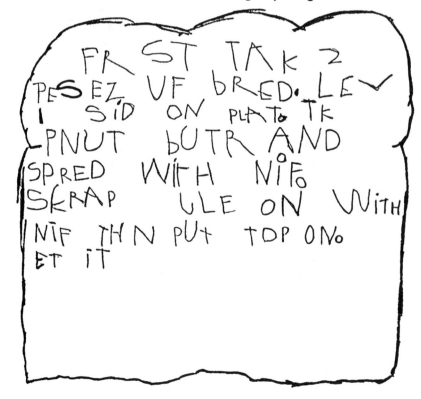

FIGURE 2.6   Matthew's Transitional-Stage Spelling

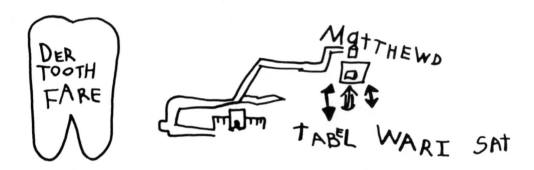

I LOST MY FERST TOOTH

TODA AT LUNCH I THenk.

LOOK FOR IT PLEZ.

DER TOOTH FARE

MatTHEWD

TABEL WARI SAT

The fact that young children find it much easier to write words with their own spellings than to read words written by others has prompted Chomsky to advocate a "write now, read later" sequence for early literacy instruction.

Traditionally, educators have worried that permitting children to use invented spellings would interfere later with their ability to learn the conventional spelling words. Recent research has refuted this belief, with a number of studies showing that, if children are simply allowed to engage in large amounts of writing, invented spellings gradually give way to the conventions of mature writing (Henderson & Beers, 1980). Invented spelling errors are not permanent; children abandon them as soon as they learn more about letter-sound relationships and the irregular spellings of certain words. Judith Newman's (1984) case study of six-year-old Shawn's journal entries is a superb example of this natural development of invented to conventional spelling.

This research on invented spelling has several important instructional implications. The first is that invented spellings should be accepted by teachers and looked upon as signs of young children's literacy development rather than as errors in need of correction. Second, it is useful for teachers to become familiar with the features that appear in the different stages of invented spelling so that they can monitor and understand individual children's spelling development (see Table 2.1). The third implication is that school literacy programs should provide opportunities for children to engage in large amounts of both playful and functional writing activities. The more that children are allowed to write, the faster they can progress through the stages of invented spelling.

The following are strategies teachers can use to promote young children's writing development:

1. *Playlike Writing.* Distribute a variety of writing instruments (pencils, felt tip pens, crayons) and materials (lined paper, unlined paper, blank books, note pads) about the room in dramatic-play areas, at learning centers, on tables, and so forth. Plastic letters and letter blocks should also be available, since these materials encourage young children, who do not have the small motor control needed to write letters, to experiment with spelling words (Chomsky, 1971). During free-play period, children can be encouraged to try writing the alphabet, their names, and captions for their artwork, and to incorporate writing into their dramatizations (see Group Dramatic Play section below). After dictating language experience stories, children can be encouraged to experiment at writing their own stories. Some children, who tire of waiting for the teacher to get around to them to take individual dictation, will do this spontaneously. In all these early writing efforts, scribble writing and invented spellings should be accepted, praised, and treated as meaningful written language.

2. *Functional Writing.* Provide opportunities for children to use writing for a variety of real-life purposes. N. Hall (1987) suggests that children "sign in" when they arrive at school and "sign up" for various activities during the day. For example, they can be asked to write their name on a sign-up sheet in order to paint at an easel or play in the housekeeping center. Other functional writing activities include: making notices about upcoming classroom events (e.g., a field trip to the fire station); invitations to parties; holiday greeting cards; notes to fellow classmates, teachers and custodians ("Plez do not muv my pitjur"); signs with rules; lists of supplies needed for special projects; and recipes for food to be prepared in class. Figure 2.7 shows two signs Jami, a preschooler, made for a cage in her classroom in which chicken eggs were hatching. Children tend to pay more attention to such regulatory signs when they have a hand in making them.

3. *Interactive Writing.* Engage children in written dialogue. This approach, known as "written conversations" (Watson, 1983) or dialogue journals (Hall & Duffy, 1987), can help link writing with oral language and make children's writing more spontaneous and natural by helping them to find their writing "voice." The teacher and child use shared writing paper or blank books (journals) to take turns writing to each other and reading each

FIGURE 2.7 Signs Made by a Preschooler for an Animal Cage in the Classroom Science Corner

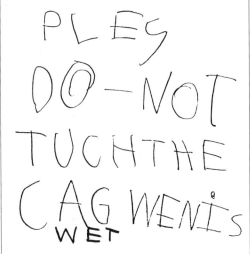

other's comments. The teacher initiates the conversation by writing brief messages to individual students, who in turn read what the teacher has written and write a response back to the teacher. The teacher then reads these responses and writes additional comments, and this continues in a chainlike fashion. Figure 2.8 presents a segment of a written conversation between a teacher and a first-grader.

Hall and Duffy (1987) recommend that teachers begin by making declarative statements about personal experiences rather than asking children questions. Duffy found that when she asked questions the children gave brief, stilted replies (similar to their oral responses to verbal interrogation by a teacher). For example:

> T: Did you do anything nice on Sunday?
> C: No. (p. 526)

On the other hand, when she wrote personal statements to the children, they responded more spontaneously:

> T: I am upset today.
> C: What is the matr with you?
> T: My dog is sick. I took her to the vet and he gave her some medicine.
> C: I hope she get betr sun did the medsn wok. (p. 527)

FIGURE 2.8   A Written Conversation between a Teacher and a First-Grader   Source: From Dorothy J. Watson. Bringing together reading and writing. In *Teaching Reading with the Other Language Arts*, edited by U. H. Hardt. Reprinted with permission of Dorothy J. Watson and the International Reading Association.

Your baby rabbits are so cute! Thank you for bringing them. How are they today?

They are fin How are your KIDS   One girl is not feeling very well but the other one is fine. She is singing in a play tomorrow night

That Is hrs

What are you doing today? Weeken
What are you working on? weeK
What work?

(worKing oN deT TadeTs

Where did you get dot to dots?

FROM YOU

Me! No! I don't remember that. What else are you doing?   a POTea
What is the poster about?   me
What does it tell about you? I'm a semr
What else? a diver
How did you learn to dive?
all You GaT To do Is Jeeaq

It would scare me to jump. Do you jump off a high board? Yes

In this strategy, the teacher serves both as model of spontaneous writing and as a real audience for children's writing. Having an interested audience is a powerful motivator for writing, as will be explained further in the section on sharing writing.

Once children get used to engaging in written conversations with their teachers, they will naturally want to engage in written exchanges with their peers. Martinez & Teale (1987) describe how a "postal system/pen pal" program was successfully implemented in several Texas kindergartens. The students in morning half-day classes wrote weekly letters to pen pals in afternoon classes, and students in full-day programs were assigned pen pals in other classrooms. They report that student response was "overwhelmingly positive."

In addition to facilitating fluent, natural writing and motivating the writing process, written conversations have the additional advantage of providing children with valuable reading practice. We will return to the dialogue journals in Chapter 3, in which we explain how they can be used to elicit personal responses to literature from older children.

4. *Sharing.* Provide opportunities for children to share their early attempts at writing with a supportive audience. Written conversations are one means of doing this. Children should also be encouraged to share their independent writing with small groups of students or with the whole class. Young children at all levels of literacy development can do this because, as Mavrogenes (1986) explains, "Even at the scribbling stage, children can read what they have written because it has meaning to them" (p. 177).

The sharing of writing is important for several reasons. It provides motivation for writing and gives children pride in their creations. An interested audience is one of the best reasons for wanting to write. Sharing also gives children valuable experiences in reading and listening comprehension. The sharer gets to read his or her own writing, and the audience learns to listen attentively and to ask questions about unclear points. Finally, sharing encourages children to view themselves as authors. The strategy, "The Author's Chair," described in Chapter 4, is ideal for this purpose.

Another way to share children's writing is to keep a folder with samples of each child's writing collected over the course of the school year. This folder can be shared with parents so they can proudly view the progress their children are making in writing. If papers are collected in this fashion and shown to parents during teacher conferences, teachers can explain about the development of written language and allay any parents' concerns about invented spellings (Mavrogenes, 1986).

□ ***Group Dramatic Play***

Group dramatic play is an advanced form of play in which two or more children adopt roles and work together to enact a story. For example, several children might take on roles of family members and pretend to eat an imaginary meal, or they might become witches and ghosts and act out a fantasy tale. This type of play, which first appears at about age two and reaches its peak during the preschool and kindergarten years, is believed to make many important contributions to children's intellectual and social development. For example, group dramatic play has been linked with growth in children's ability to think abstractly, to see things from other people's perspectives, and to cooperate with others (Johnson, Christie, & Yawkey, 1987). It also has been found to promote the development of skills more directly related to literacy such as vocabulary growth, story comprehension, and knowledge of story structure (Christie, 1987; Christie & Noyce, 1986).

In addition to building underlying skills needed for reading and writing, dramatic play also provides a context for children to engage in meaningful engagements with literacy. N. Hall (1987) recounts that some of the best literacy activities he has observed in British preschools have occurred in connection with dramatic play. He recounts one instance in which he watched children playing at running a puppet theater and a clinic for babies:

> In both cases, print became an integral part of the play. The children made use of the freedom they had, the materials available, and the support of adults. Some of the children working on the puppet theatre had been to theatres. They brought in programmes and other print deriving from their visits. The children were soon making tickets, programmes and posters. Finally, and with some adult support, they created a seating plan and numbered the chairs in front of the puppet theatre . . . The baby clinic had to have, like the one they had visited, a receptionist who spent much time on the phone taking appointments and "writing" cards.
>
> (p. 89)

While engaging in dramatic play, it is not uncommon for children to make lists for imaginary shopping trips, to jot down orders while playing the role of waiters, and to write tickets when pretending to be Highway Patrol officers. Because literacy plays an important role in so many aspects of everyday life, it is hardly surprising that children will eagerly incorporate literacy behaviors into their dramatizations, provided suitable reading and writing materials are available in their play settings.

A number of recent research studies have investigated factors which affect the amount and quality of dramatic play in school settings. These studies have revealed that there are several things teachers can do to promote frequent, high-quality dramatic play in their classrooms (see Figure 2.9). The most important of these provisions for play are:

1. *Time.* Dramatic play takes time for children to plan, organize, and execute. Prior to the start of such play, children must: (a) recruit other players; (b) assign roles; (c) designate the make-believe identities of objects; and (d) agree on the story line to be dramatized. In addition, the dramatiza-

FIGURE 2.9 Prerequisites for High-Quality Dramatic Play

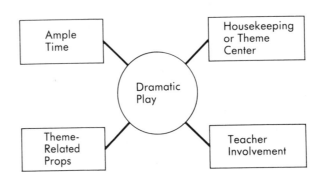

tions themselves often take considerable time to enact. Many of the benefits of the group dramatic play arise from the planning and problem solving necessary to sustain lengthy, multiepisode dramatizations (e.g., planning dinner, going shopping, serving dinner, and then cleaning up). If play periods are too short, children will either engage in very simple, one-episode dramatizations or forgo dramatic play altogether and engage in simpler forms of play (e.g., sensory-motor play) which can be accomplished in short periods of time.

Research has shown that preschoolers engage in a significantly higher proportion of group dramatic play during thirty-minute periods than during shorter, fifteen-minute periods (Christie, 1987b). We therefore recommend that classroom play periods last a minimum of thirty minutes. Half an hour a day is not too much time to devote to such an important activity as dramatic play.

2. Space and Materials. Theme-related props and settings are key ingredients in encouraging group dramatic play. We have unfortunately observed many instances of kindergarten classrooms which contain very few dramatic play materials. Inevitably, the children in such classrooms rarely engage in group dramatic play during free-play periods. In one instance, the amount of dramatic play was so low that permission was asked to introduce theme-related props into the classroom (Johnsen, Christie, Peckover, & Tracy, 1987). The result was a dramatic increase in the amount of group dramatic play.

At a minimum, kindergarten classrooms should have a spacious, well-equipped housekeeping center (see Classroom Environment section above). The scope of children's dramatizations can be broadened by providing groups of props related to a variety of themes. This can be accomplished by setting up theme centers (See Classroom Environment section) or by providing collections of objects known as prop boxes. Prop boxes contain real-life objects related to a theme or occupation. The Strategy Example below presents examples of four prop boxes. Notice that all four contain literacy materials: (1) automobile mechanic — auto supply catalogues; (2) forest ranger — nature books, logs; (3) beautician — paper and pencil; and (4) plumber — hardware supply catalogues. Additional literacy materials could easily be added to each box. For example, the auto mechanic box could have paper and pencils for writing work orders and ordering parts. For further suggestions for prop boxes, see Johnson, Christie, and Yawkey (1987).

─────── STRATEGY EXAMPLE 2.3 ───────

Prop Boxes

Automobile Mechanic
Used (and washed) motor parts: spark plugs, filters, carburetors, cable sets, gears
Tools: hammers, pliers, screw drivers
Oil funnel
Empty oil cans
Flashlight
Wiring
Air pump
Windshield wipers
Key carrier and keys
Rags, old shirts, gloves
Automobile supply catalogues
Repair manuals

Beautician
Mirror
Curlers
Hairpins
Hairnets
Dryer
Aprons or large bibs
Combs
Towels
Magazines
Empty shampoo bottles (plastic)
Plastic basin
Emery boards
Pencil, paper
Money

Forest Ranger
Canteen
Flashlight
Rope
Mosquito netting
Canvas for tent
Knapsack
Food supplies
Nature books
Small logs

Plumber
Piping: all lengths, widths, and shapes for fitting together
Spigots
Plungers
Tools
Hose and nozzles
Spade
Old shirt, cap
Hardware supply catalogues

Grill   Measuring devices
Binoculars   Plumbing manual
Maps

Source: From J. Bender, "Have you ever thought of a propbox?" from *Young Children, 26,* 1971. Copyright by the National Association for the Education of Young Children.

3. *Teacher Involvement.*   Until recently, it was commonly believed that teachers should not intervene in children's play. The teacher's role was simply to set the stage for play and then observe. In the late 1960s, however, Smilansky (1968) conducted a study in Israel that undermined the "hands-off" position regarding adults participating in play. Smilansky had pre-school and kindergarten teachers intervene in their students' play in order to encourage and model group dramatic play. Results showed that teacher involvement in play increased the frequency and quality of the children's group dramatic play and also resulted in gains on cognitive measures. Researchers in the United States, Canada, and England have replicated Smilansky's study with similar results: adult intervention in play improved not only the play itself but also brought about gains in cognitive development and social competence (see Johnson et al., 1987).

Three major types of teacher involvement in play have been found to be beneficial:

   a. *Thematic Fantasy Training.*   The teacher helps children enact familiar folktales (e.g., "Three Billy Goats Gruff," "Little Red Riding Hood"). The teacher first reads the tale to the children and then helps them act it out. The story is usually enacted several times with children switching roles.

   b. *Outside Intervention.*   The teacher makes suggestions and comments which encourage children to engage in group dramatic play. For example, the teacher might suggest that a child take on a role, such as a fire fighter, and use an object in a make-believe manner— for example, use a rope as if it were a fire hose. This type of intervention is called "outside" because the teacher does not actually join in the play episode.

   c. *Inside Intervention.*   The teacher actually takes a role, joins in the play, and demonstrates how to engage in dramatic-play behaviors. For example, the teacher might take on the role of fire fighter and demonstrate how to use a rope as a make-believe hose, encouraging other children to join in the episode and engage in similar pretend behaviors.

Research has shown that all three types of teacher involvement in play can increase the amount and quality of dramatic play in the classroom and can also result in gains in cognitive and social development. For detailed descriptions of these procedures, see Johnson et al. (1987).

One note of caution is necessary. These strategies should not be overused because, if teachers take over too much control of children's play activities, the activities cease to be play. It is recommended that teachers only intervene when children appear to be unable to engage in group dramatic play on their own or if a play episode has grown stale and is in need of enrichment. Once children begin engaging in rich, imaginative play on their own, teacher involvement should be phased out.

By providing time, theme-related props (including literacy materials), and guidance, teachers can enhance the quality of the dramatic play that occurs in their classrooms. The resulting play will make important contributions to children's cognitive and social development. At the same time, the play will be providing situations which will enable children to have meaningful engagements with reading and writing.

SUMMARY

■　■　The research reviewed at the beginning of this chapter indicates that children's literacy development begins long before they enter school and begin receiving formal instruction. Through story-reading sessions, watching their parents and older siblings use reading and writing for practical purposes, and playful exploration of print, most children learn much about the functions, form, and conventions of written language. This finding has led many educators to question traditional methods of early reading instruction and the concept of reading readiness upon which such practices are based.

There is a growing awareness that kindergarten reading programs should provide reading and writing activities which closely resemble the types of natural literacy that occur in the home. By supplying such experiences, school reading programs can build on the knowledge of written language young children already possess and can help make the acquisition of literacy a continuous process.

In the strategy section we reviewed three major components necessary for effective emergent literacy programs. The first component involves creating a print-rich environment, with a well-stocked classroom library; large supplies of writing materials; "world-related" print, such as phonebooks and TV guides; displays of children's writing and dictated stories; signs and labels; and functional print, such as daily schedules and sign-up sheets for class activities. In addition, it is important to have a well-equipped dramatic-play area complete with theme-related literacy materials. Such a classroom environment provides many opportunities for children to learn about literacy through both observation and active exploration.

The second component involves teacher demonstrations of literacy. Teachers can help broaden children's perceptions of literacy by allowing children to observe them using reading and writing for a variety of recreational and practical purposes in the classroom. Two other types of teacher-led demonstrations are particularly effective: the Shared Book Experience and the Language Experience Approach. Shared experiences with enlarged texts enable teachers to provide story-reading experiences similar to those children receive at home, and the Language Experience Approach assures a perfect match between young readers and the texts they read.

The final component concerns self-initiated child engagement with written language. We suggested a number of ways to encourage children to engage in playful activities with books and to use reading in functional ways. We also described how to engage children in playful, functional, and interactive writing activities. Particular stress was placed on the need for teachers to accept young children's scribble writing and invented spellings. If children are allowed to engage in large amounts of meaningful reading and writing activities, their invented spellings will naturally give way to the conventions of adult language. Finally, we described the important role dramatic play can have in literacy development and described how teachers can promote frequent, high-quality dramatic play by providing adequate time, theme-related materials, and appropriate intervention.

Through the provision of print-rich environments, teacher demonstrations, and self-initiated child engagement, schools can provide children with reading and writing experiences that are far superior to those found in traditional reading readiness programs. Instead of forcing children to forget what they already know and enjoy about written language, emergent literacy programs can build on children's existing competence and insure initial success in learning to read and write.

RECOMMENDED CHILDREN'S BOOKS

Predictable Books

Aardema, Verna. *Why Mosquitoes Buzz in People's Ears*. Dial, 1978.
Aliki. *Go Tell Aunt Rhody*. Macmillan, 1974.
Allen, Pamela. *Bertle and the Bear*. Putnam, 1984.
Barton, Byron. *Buzz, Buzz, Buzz*. Penguin, 1979.
Baum, Arline and Joseph. *One Bright Monday Morning*. Random House, 1962.
Brown, Ruth. *A Dark Dark Tale*. Dial, 1981.
Burningham, John. *The Shopping Basket*. Crowell, 1980.
Carle, Eric. *The Very Hungry Caterpillar*. Collins World, 1969.
_____. *The Grouchy Ladybug*. Crowell, 1977.

_____. *The Very Busy Spider.* Philomel, 1984.

Chess, Victoria. *Poor Esmé.* Holiday House, 1982.

Domanska, Janina. *Busy Monday Morning.* Greenwillow, 1985.

Emberley, Barbara. *Drummer Hoff.* Prentice-Hall, 1967.

Emberley, Ed. *Klippity Klop.* Little, Brown, 1974.

Farber, Norma, and Lobel, Arnold. *As I Was Crossing Boston Common.* Creative Arts Books, 1982.

Hayes, Sarah. *This Is the Bear.* Lippincott, 1986.

Hoberman, Mary Ann. *A House is a House for Me.* Viking, 1978.

Hoquet, Susan. *I Unpacked My Grandmother's Trunk.* E. P. Dutton, 1983.

Hutchins, Pat. *Good-night Owl!* Macmillan, 1972.

_____. *Don't Forget the Bacon!* Penguin, 1978.

_____. *You'll Soon Grow into Them, Titch.* Greenwillow, 1983.

Jonas, Ann. *When You Were a Baby.* Greenwillow, 1982.

Kraus, Robert. *Whose Mouse Are You?* Collier, 1970.

_____. *Where Are You Going, Little Mouse?* Greenwillow, 1986.

Lobel, Anita. *King Rooster, Queen Hen.* Greenwillow, 1975.

Lobel, Arnold. *A Treeful of Pigs.* Greenwillow, 1979.

_____. *The Rose in My Garden.* Greenwillow, 1984.

Martin, Bill. *Brown Bear, Brown Bear, What Do You See?* Holt, Rinehart & Winston, 1970.

_____. *Fire! Fire! Said Mrs. McGuire.* Holt, Rinehart & Winston, 1970.

Noble, Trinka. *Jimmy's Boa Ate the Wash.* Dial, 1984.

_____. *Jimmy's Boa Bounces Back.* Dial, 1984.

Numeroff, Laura. *If You Give a Mouse a Cookie.* Harper & Row, 1985.

Pearson, Tracey C. *Old MacDonald Had a Farm.* Dial, 1984.

Peek, Merle. *Mary Wore Her Red Dress and Henry Wore His Green Sneakers.* Clarion, 1985.

Quackenbush, Robert. *She'll Be Comin 'Round the Mountain.* Lippincott, 1973.

Rice, Eve. *Goodnight, Goodnight.* Greenwillow, 1980.

Silverstein, Shel. *A Giraffe and a Half.* Harper & Row, 1964.

Stevens, Janet. *The House That Jack Built.* Holiday House, 1985.

Tafuri, Nancy. *Have You Seen My Duckling?* Greenwillow, 1984.

Westcott, Nadine B. *I Know an Old Lady Who Swallowed a Fly.* Little, Brown, 1980.

Wood, Audrey. *The Napping House.* Harcourt Brace Jovanovich, 1984.

REFERENCES

Allen, R. V. (1976). *Language experiences in communication.* Boston: Houghton Mifflin.

Ashton-Warner, S. (1963). *Teacher.* New York: Simon & Schuster.

Bender, J. (1971). Have you ever thought of a prop box? *Young Children, 26*(3), 164–169.

Bloom, B. S. (1964). *Stability and change in human characteristics.* New York: Wiley.

Butler, A., & Turnbill, J. (1984). *Towards a reading-writing classroom.* Portsmouth, NH: Heinemann.

Cazden, C. B. (1983). Adult assistance to language development: Scaffolds, models, and direct instruction. In R. P. Parker & F. A. Davis (Eds.), *Developing literacy: Young children's uses of language* (pp. 3-18). Newark, DE: International Reading Association.

Chomsky, C. (1972). Write first, read later. In C. B. Cazden (Ed.), *Language and learning in early childhood education* (pp. 119-126). Washington, DC: National Association for the Education of Young Children.

Chomsky, C. (1979). Approaching early reading through invented spelling. In L. B. Resnick & P. A. Weaver (Eds.), *Theory and practice of early reading* (Vol. 2, pp. 43-65). Hillsdale, NJ: Erlbaum.

Christie, J. F. (1987). Play and story comprehension: A critique of recent training research. *Journal of Research and Development in Education, 21*, 36-43.

Christie, J. F., Johnsen, E. P., & Peckover, R. (In press). The effects of play period duration on children's play patterns. *Journal of Research in Childhood Education*.

Christie, J. F., & Noyce, R. M. (1986). Play and writing: Possible connections. In B. Mergen (Ed.), *Cultural dimensions of play, games, and sport* (pp. 129-136). Champaign, IL: Human Kinetics Publishers.

Clay, M. M. (1972). *Reading: The patterning of complex behaviour*. London: Heinemann.

Crowell, D. C., Kawakami, A. J., & Wong, J. L. (1986). Emerging literacy: Reading-writing experiences in a kindergarten classroom. *The Reading Teacher, 40*, 144-149.

Durkin, D. (1966). *Children who read early*. New York: Teachers College Press.

Durkin, D. (1987). *Teaching young children to read* (4th ed.). Boston: Allyn & Bacon.

Early Childhood and Literacy Development Committee (1986). Literacy development and pre-first grade: A joint statement of concerns about present practices in pre-first grade reading instruction and recommendations for improvement. *Young Children, 41(4)*, 10-13.

Ferreiro, E., & Teberosky, A. (1982). *Literacy before schooling*. Exeter, NH: Heinemann.

Gentry, J. R. (1981). Learning to spell developmentally. *The Reading Teacher, 34*, 378-381.

Gentry, J. R. (1985). You can analyze developmental spelling—And here's how to do it. *Early Years, 15(9)*, 44-45.

Goodman, Y. M. (1986). Children coming to know literacy. In W. H. Teale & E. Sulzby (Eds.), *Emergent literacy: Writing and reading* (pp. 1-14). Norwood, NJ: Ablex.

Hall, M. (1981). *Teaching reading as a language experience* (3rd ed.). Columbus, OH: Merrill.

Hall, N. (1987). *The emergence of literacy*. Hodder & Staughton Ltd. Portsmouth, NH: Heinemann

Hall, N., & Duffy, R. (1987). Every child has a story to tell. *Language Arts, 64*, 523-529.

Hansen, H. S. (1969). The impact of home literacy environment on reading attitude. *Elementary English, 46*, 17-24.

Harste, J., Woodward, V., & Burke, C. (1984). *Language stories and literacy lessons*. Portsmouth, NH: Heinemann.

Heibert, E. H. (1981). Developmental patterns and interrelationships of preschool children's print awareness. *Reading Research Quarterly, 16*, 236-260.

Henderson, E. H., & Beers, J. W. (1980). *Developmental and cognitive aspects of learning to spell*. Newark, DE: International Reading Association.

Holdaway, D. (1979). *The foundations of literacy*. Sydney, Australia: Ashton Scholastic.

Johnsen, E. P., Christie, J. F., Peckover, R., & Tracy, D. B. (1987, March). *Enriched environments and pretense in kindergarten*. Paper presented at the meeting of the Association for the Anthropological Study of Play, Montreal.

Johnson, J. E., Christie, J. F., & Yawkey, T. D. (1987). *Play and early childhood development*. Glenview, IL: Scott, Foresman.

Kontos, S. (1986). What preschool children know about reading and how they learn it. *Young Children, 42*, 58-66.

Martinez, M., & Teale, W. H. (1987). The ins and outs of a kindergarten writing program. *The Reading Teacher, 40*, 444-451.

Mason, J. M. (1980). When do children begin to read: An exploration of four-year-old children's letter and word reading competencies. *Reading Research Quarterly, 15*, 203-227.

Mason, J. M. (1984). Early reading from a developmental perspective. In P. D. Pearson (Ed.), *Handbook of reading research* (pp. 505–543). New York: Longman.

Mason, J. M., & Au, K. H. (1986). *Reading instruction for today*. Glenview, IL: Scott, Foresman.

Mavrogenes, M. A. (1986). What every teacher should know about emergent literacy. *The Reading Teacher, 40,* 174–178.

McCormick, C. E., & Mason, J. M. (1986). Intervention procedures for increasing preschool children's interest in and knowledge about reading. In W. H. Teale & E. Sulzby (Eds.), *Emergent literacy: Writing and reading* (pp. 90–115). Norwood, NJ: Ablex.

Newman, J. (1984). *The craft of children's writing*. Portsmouth, NH: Heinemann.

Read, C. (1971). Pre-school children's knowledge of English phonology. *Harvard Educational Review, 41,* 1–34.

Rudolph, M., & Cohen, D. H. (1984). *Kindergarten and early schooling* (2nd ed.). Englewood Cliffs, NJ: Prentice-Hall.

Sheldon, W. D., & Carrillo, R. (1952). Relation of parent, home and certain developmental characteristics to children's reading abilities. *Elementary School Journal, 52,* 262–270.

Smilansky, S. (1969). *The effects of sociodramatic play on disadvantaged preschool children.* New York: Wiley.

Smith, F. (1982). *Understanding reading* (3rd ed.). New York: Holt.

Snow, C. E., & Ninio, A. (1986). The contracts of literacy: What children learn from learning to read books. In W. H. Teale & E. Sulzby (Eds.), *Emergent literacy: Writing and reading* (pp. 116–138). Norwood, NJ: Ablex.

Taylor, D. (1986). Creating family story: "Matthew! We're going to have a ride." In W. H. Teale & E. Sulzby (Eds.), *Emergent literacy: Writing and reading* (pp. 139–155). Norwood, NJ: Ablex.

Teale, W. H. (1981). Parents reading to their children: What we know and need to know. *Language Arts, 59,* 902–912.

Teale, W. H. (1982). Toward a theory of how children learn to read and write naturally. *Language Arts, 59,* 555–570.

Teale, W. H. (1986). Home background and young children's literacy development. In W. H. Teale & E. Sulzby (Eds.), *Emergent literacy: Writing and reading* (pp. 173–206). Norwood, NJ: Ablex.

Teale, W. H., & Sulzby, E. (1986). Emergent literacy as a perspective for examining how young children become writers and readers. In W. H. Teale & E. Sulzby (Eds.), *Emergent literacy: Writing and reading* (pp. vii–xxv). Norwood, NJ: Ablex.

Tierney, R. J., & Leys, M. (1986). What is the value of connecting reading and writing? In B. T. Petersen (Ed.), *Convergences: Transactions in reading and writing* (pp. 15–29). Urbana, IL: National Council of Teachers of English.

Veatch, J., Sawicki, F., Elliot, G., Flake, E., & Blakey, J. (1979). *Key words to reading: The language experience approach begins.* Columbus, OH: Merrill.

Watson, D. J. (1983). Bringing together reading and writing. In U. H. Hardt (Ed.), *Teaching reading with the other language arts* (pp. 63–82). Newark, DE: International Reading Association.

Wood, M. (1982). Invented Spelling. *Language Arts, 59,* 707–717.

Woodward, C. Y. (1984). Guidelines for facilitating sociodramatic play. *Childhood Education, 60,* 172–177.

3

Using Reading in the Writing Process I
Prewriting

It begins with the paraphrasing of reference sources (called "reports") and the plot summaries (called "book reports"), which are really just checks on the directed reading. It continues through the "critical papers," "research papers," "term papers," and "essay questions" of college. . . . What all this writing has in common is that it monitors assigned reading and tests coverage of given content.
—Moffett, Hidden impediments to improving English teaching

Schools have traditionally linked reading with writing by requiring students either to write brief summaries of a book just read or to write answers to factual questions about their reading. The major purpose of these activities is not to promote writing ability but rather to confirm that the students really did read the books and understand what they read. Moffett is emphatic about the negative effects of such activities on students' attitudes toward both reading and writing: "Reading and writing are brought into a stupefyingly negative relationship to each other that makes students want to avoid both. Every time you read, you have to write something about it to show that you got the point. That is, the punishment for reading is having to write" (1985, p. 53). As a result, the traditional means of using reading as a stimulus for writing may actually inhibit growth in both skills. Current research on the writing process and on reading/writing relationships has revealed that there are much better ways to use reading to promote growth in writing.

Some recent trends in writing instruction emphasize the writing process more than the written product (Emig, 1971; Hillocks, 1986). A basic assumption of this instructional movement, commonly referred to as the process approach to writing instruction, is that students learn to write by writing extensively and by discussing their writing with others. The writing process is most often described as a series of interactive, recursive steps involving prewriting, drafting, revising, editing, and publishing. Process-oriented classrooms have a workshop atmosphere that promotes the learning of skills while writing is in progress rather than after a paper has been "corrected" by the teacher.

Reading skills are used throughout the writing process. During the prewriting stage, students find topics to write about and prepare to write through such activities as brainstorming, recollecting, talking, planning, and *reading*. After generating ideas in prewriting experiences, they compose a first-draft paper. The revising process begins when they reread and evaluate their own writing, making desired changes in content and organization. The second step in revision includes *reading* their papers to a response-group audience and receiving feedback from peers. A common procedure followed by response groups is to comment, first, on the strengths and positive aspects of the writing, and then to make constructive suggestions for improvement. At this point attention is given only to the content of the piece that has been read. After the response-group session, students revise their first drafts, incorporating any suggestions from peers they wish to follow, and prepare a final version of the paper. In this phase of the process they are instructed to give careful attention to conventions such as spelling, punctuation, and noun-verb agreement. Editing of the revised paper is often done in a second peer-group meeting during which students *proofread* each others' papers and discuss grammatical issues. The last stage of the process allows students to share their edited papers with audiences other than their peer groups, in publishing activities ranging from *reading* them aloud to the entire class or posting them around the classroom to including them in a book or newspaper.

In this chapter we will examine how reading can function during the prewriting phase of the writing process, acting as a stimulus to writing in three ways: (a) by motivating children to want to write; (b) by generating ideas for writing; and (c) by evoking personal responses to literature, which in turn stimulate writing. The focus of the strategies described in this chapter will be on using reading to promote writing fluency, the ability to put one's ideas down in writing. These activities can be used with basal reader stories and with trade books to get the writing process flowing. In Chapter 4 we will explore how reading can contribute to the style and mechanics of students' writing during the composing and revising/editing stages of the writing process.

THE IMPORTANCE OF
PREWRITING EXPERIENCES

■ ■ With the change of focus in writing instruction from product to process, both researchers and practitioners are stressing the importance of involving children in prewriting experiences before expecting them to write. During the prewriting stage, ideas for writing are generated by exploring new information or prior knowledge through activities which encourage a free flow of thought. Through such experiences, children discover they have something to say when they write. Activities such as brainstorming, mapping, and fantasizing stimulate experimentation with ideas, helping students to decide what to write about and how to go about it.

Opinions differ as to the importance of various kinds of prewriting experiences. Hillocks (1975) prefers that students' prewriting experiences involve personal observation, explaining that writers tend to avoid empty generalizations and pay more attention to details when they are writing about what they have actually observed. In his view, writing from vicarious experience tends to be trite and uninteresting. Dixon (1967) adds that writing about observations is likely to be more effective when students have been given the opportunity to discuss them before writing. Moffett (1986) also recognizes the need for students to have the stimulation of discussion before trying to "talk" on paper.

Others recommend that prewriting experiences take advantage of children's natural motivation for expressive writing by having them start with what they know. Frank (1979) suggests that prewriting activities focus on the self, a subject the writer knows about and probably enjoys sharing with others. Kirby and Liner (1981) remind teachers that children have the knowledge, feelings, and words to write about their likes and dislikes, memories, and personal experiences. Students are given techniques for "inventorying" their experiences by Tchudi and Tchudi (1984) in *The Young Writer's Handbook*. Memory-jogging questions are used to help students list what they have seen, what they have done, and what they think is important. These personal data are then used in later writing.

Some researchers describe the prewriting process as going beyond the idea-generating stage to include a rehearsal period during which students experiment with ideas in different ways (Graves, 1979; Murray, 1982; Hennings, 1986). They believe that children should engage in talking, pictorializing, and planning before beginning to write. Boiarsky (1981) has identified four stages through which a writer passes during prewriting:

1. Participating in an event.
2. Giving meaning to that event through activities such as discussion and brainstorming.

3. Selecting an angle for communicating meaning, style, tone, point of view, and voice.
4. Developing an organizational structure, based on the angle, to create an effective piece of written discourse.

Prewriting experiences are as important for beginning writers as they are for older students. Graves's (1979) study of the prewriting rehearsal process in first-grade writers produced a number of implications for primary-grade teachers, including:

1. Teachers must ask children to choose their own topics for writing from the wealth of their daily experiences. Assigned topics are unnecessary and cheat the child of an important writing task.
2. Children need to rehearse before they write. They may need to draw, play, or talk before they write.
3. Children need permission to explore, experiment, and make errors. Rigid standards of correctness and neatness restrict children to writing about what they can spell correctly and express without a struggle.
4. Children need a writing classroom where active rehearsal is encouraged. Writers need breaks from writing to achieve distance. They will need to move in the room, draw, and talk.

(p. 835)*

After studying writing instruction in American classrooms, Applebee (1981) concluded that most students are given approximately three minutes to think of a topic during a typical writing lesson. Other students are more fortunate in that they are warned a day ahead of time to have a writing topic. Given these conditions, it is hardly surprising that many students are not highly motivated to write. In the classrooms where students are given limited time to come up with a topic, a spontaneous groan often accompanies the announcement that it is time to write. It is essential that students be given prewriting experiences to prepare and motivate them to write.

The value of reading as a prewriting experience cannot be overemphasized. Researchers have called our attention to the fact that reading is a search for meaning, causing readers to generate ideas in response to literature. Students confirm predictions and compose meaning as they read stories. These ideas and feelings that stem from reading can be used to stimulate writing in several ways. First, the reading of literature can serve as a source of motivation for writing, encouraging students to want to write their own stories, essays, or poems. Second, reading can be used alone or in conjunction with other strategies (e.g., clustering) to generate ideas for writing. Finally, reading literature can produce personal responses and feelings which can be channeled into expressive writing.

*Condensed from D. Graves. A six-year old's writing process: The first half of first grade. *Language Arts.* Copyright © 1979 by the National Council of Teachers of English. Reprinted by permission of the publisher.

There is evidence that children borrow words, content, and structure from their reading to use in writing. Jaggar, Carrara, and Weiss (1986) interviewed avid child readers about the effects of reading upon their writing and discovered that these children claim to utilize reading for both content and technique. When asked if reading made her a better writer, one child replied, "Yeah, 'cause reading gives you an idea of how you write. It gives you ideas and ways to form the piece. If you never read a book, you wouldn't know how to write a book" (1986, p. 297). Burris (1985) reported that when third-graders in her study wrote their own folktales they combined characters, themes, and plots from folktales they had heard or read. For example, one child's story, "Big Bear, Little Bear," included characters from Minarik's *Little Bear,* Zolotow's *Mr. Rabbit and the Lively Present,* and Flack's *Ask Mr. Bear.* Burris concluded that a good story may be the best story "starter." Dionisio (1983) also has reported that reading helped stimulate her sixth graders' writing by exposing them to new topics.

Several researchers have explored the effects of prewriting experiences involving the reading and discussion of literature upon the quality of children's writing. Mills (1968) found that the writing of fourth-graders who read or listened to and then discussed children's books as a prewriting activity rated higher on a quality assessment than the writing of children who did not have a prewriting experience with literature. McConaghy (1985) observed that her first-grade students' writing was often a direct outcome of their trade book reading. Whether the reading was done at home or at school, it had a strong influence on their writing throughout the school year. Her students responded in three ways to the literature they read: (a) "literal" responses, in which children simply transferred characters and events directly into their own stories; (b) "role-playing" responses, where they included themselves as they used elements from literature ("Once Upon a Time and Me"); and (c) "meaning-making" responses, in which the students transferred underlying themes and messages to their own stories and illustrated the ability to use literature to better understand themselves. McConaghy concluded that prewriting experiences with children's literature are effective in creating good writers because children use literary experiences as a resource for their own writing.

We have grouped reading-related prewriting strategies into two categories: (1) writing with basal reader stories; and (2) writing with children's literature. The distinction we make between the two kinds of material is that in the basal reader children are exposed briefly to excerpts from books, short stories, and poetry, while in the trade books they experience a deeper involvement with characters, plot, and theme that is more likely to trigger personal responses. We have included these strategies in this chapter because the main outcome of the activities appears to be writing fluency and practice. The reader should keep in mind that, due to the reciprocal nature of the reading and writing processes, most of the strategies also will promote students' reading abilities.

BASAL READER STORIES

■ ■ Buckley (1986) has described a number of strategies used by teachers in Berkeley, California, to get children to respond to basal reader stories through writing. Some of the activities include:

1. Write a preface to the story, describing what might have happened *before* the story began. Where are the characters? What are they doing? What events led up to the story beginning as it did?

2. Write a sequel to the story, continuing the plot while bringing in new complications, events, and, perhaps, characters.

3. Write a different ending for the story, exploring the range of possibilities and selecting one that logically relates to the development of the story.

4. Write the story from another point of view, noting what changes are made when perspective is altered.

5. Write the story in another setting, observing how changes in time and setting affect the story, and making whatever adjustments are needed to make the changes plausible.

6. Identify the main event in the story that determines the outcome and then change the event, discussing and writing the results of the change.

7. Rewrite the story in dialogue, producing a script. If needed, include a narrator.

8. Write a comparison/contrast between two characters in the story or between a character in one story and a character in another story.

(pp. 374–375)*

Many basal teacher manuals contain activities which involve writing in response to stories or which can be adapted for such purposes. These suggestions are usually contained in the "enrichment" portion of the basal lesson. For example, a story entitled "Bears Aren't Everywhere" is found in the third-grade reader, *How It is Nowadays*, in the Ginn Reading 720 series (Silver, Burdett & Ginn, 1976). It is about a boy named Danny who, while walking through the woods, hears a noise he thinks is caused by a bear. He gets scared and runs home. Later, he and his father discover that the noise was actually made by a squirrel. The Ginn teacher's manual suggests several follow-up activities in the "Interrelated Activities" portion of the lesson, including:

1. *Creating Stories Containing Imaginary Fears.* Remind pupils of Danny's imaginary fears in "Bears Aren't Everywhere." Encourage the children to create oral stories containing imaginary fears.

On the chalkboard write *Once I heard a strange noise.*

*Condensed from M. H. Buckley. When teachers decide to integrate the language arts. *Language Arts.* Copyright © 1986 by the National Council of Teachers of English. Reprinted by permission of the publisher.

. . . Read the following paragraph as a story sample:

Once I heard a strange noise from the attic of my house. I was afraid. I called the police. I did not dare to go to the attic alone. I thought thieves were there. When the police arrived, we walked up the stairs to the attic. We discovered that our cat had knocked over a pile of boxes.

Allow volunteers to tell their own *"Once I heard a strange noise"* story.

2. *Suggesting Multiple Hypotheses.* Encourage the children to use their imaginations to think of a number of improbabilities or "just suppose's" in connection with "Bears Aren't Everywhere." Read or write on the chalkboard these hypotheses and let the children discuss them in groups.

a. Just suppose Danny had really seen a bear in the woods. What might have happened then?

b. Just suppose Danny and his Dad learned that the noise they heard was caused by a bear. What might they have done?

c. Just suppose Danny and his father caught a bear. Would Danny still be afraid of bears? What else might have happened?

(p. 158)*

The above are intended to be oral activities, but could just as easily involve writing. Children could write their own "Once I heard a strange noise" stories and "just suppose" hypotheses.

It has been our experience that the "enrichment" portion of basal reader lessons tends to get overlooked in many classrooms, undoubtedly due to pressure to cover all of the skill activities in the teacher's manual and student workbooks. This is unfortunate, because many worthwhile language activities are included in that section of the lesson. One way to provide more time for reading literature, writing, and enrichment activities is to follow the example of the Berkeley teachers (Buckley, 1986) and carefully evaluate the usefulness of each story, skill activity, and workbook assignment in the basal system. Activities which are not obligatory for the children's reading development can then be eliminated. As a result of this type of careful scrutiny, the Berkeley teachers were able to free up ample time for integrated language activities.

Another approach we recommend for deriving prewriting experiences from basal reader stories is to use these stories in conjunction with two creative-thinking strategies: (a) Rico's (1983) Clustering strategy, a brainstorming approach that combines the recalling of prior knowledge with the production of new images, and (b) Eberle's (1984) SCAMPER model, which facilitates imaginative thinking by suggesting various thought processes to use for problem solving and divergent thinking. Both are promising vehicles for extending basal reader stories into writing activities. The two strategies, explained below, can also be used in conjunction with children's literature.

*Condensed from Teacher's Edition of *How It Is Nowadays* of the READING 720 series by Theodore Clymer and others. Copyright © 1976, 1969 by Silver Burdett & Ginn Inc. Used with permission.

■ Clustering

Clustering is a brainstorming process in which students generate ideas and images around a stimulus word until they see connections or patterns to write about. By enabling them to map out their thoughts on a subject, it helps them to select the ideas they want to use, making it easier and more enjoyable to write.

The stories and poetry children read in the basal program can provide both the central focus and the storehouse of information and images for Clustering. For example, if "Picture Puzzle Piece" from Shel Silverstein's *A Light in the Attic* (Harper & Row, 1981) were included in a primary-grade basal reader, teachers might involve their students in the following group Clustering experience:

> 1. "Picture Puzzle Piece" by Shel Silverstein is read to the class. In this poem the poet imagines where a puzzle piece lying on the sidewalk might be from.
> 2. Teacher and students discuss past experiences with puzzles, including these questions: Have you ever worked a puzzle down to the last piece and found that the piece was lost? Can you remember the pictures of some of those puzzles and describe them? Would you like to try being in the opposite situation, having only one piece of a puzzle, as the poem describes?
> 3. The teacher displays a large green puzzle piece made of poster board and asks the class to imagine the picture puzzle from which it came. Ideas brainstormed by the children are arranged in a Clustering model on the chalkboard.
> 4. Partners are instructed to select a puzzle piece from an assortment provided by the teacher and to think of as many ideas as they can about the picture from which it came, following the Clustering model. After this brainstorming experience together, they are each asked to put an asterisk by the idea they like best in their cluster and then write a vignette (mini-story) about it.

A sample from this Clustering experience in a second-grade classroom appears in Figure 3.1.

■ SCAMPERing

SCAMPERing is a technique for promoting original thinking by manipulating images and generating new ideas to link with existing ones (Eberle, 1984). It is an enrichment tool teachers can use to increase the flexibility of students' responses to basal reader stories and to improve their divergent thinking skills. SCAMPER is an acronym describing the searching around for ideas and images. Each letter in the word is the first letter of the name of a creative thinking technique included in the process: Substitute, Combine, Adapt, Modify/Magnify, Put to use, Eliminate, Rearrange/Reverse.

FIGURE 3.1   Cluster Sample: Students' Ideas about the Picture on the Puzzle from Which the Piece Came

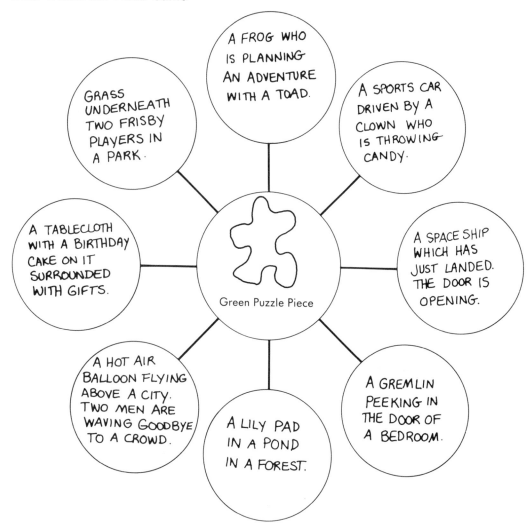

Martin, Cramond, and Safter (1982) have modified the SCAMPERing process so that it can be used as a prewriting strategy in conjunction with any story. Here is an example of how the SCAMPERing prewriting strategy would work with "Cinderella":

S	Substitute	What might have happened if Cinderella had dropped her handkerchief instead of her glass slipper as she left the ball?
C	Combine	In what ways were Cinderella and Snow White alike?

A	Adapt	If the music at the ball had been so loud that Cinderella could not hear the clock striking twelve, what could she have done to make sure she got to the coach on time?
M	Modify	What do you think the Prince would have done if the glass slipper had not fit any lady in his kingdom?
	Magnify	Describe a day in Cinderella's life after her marriage to the Prince.
P	Put to use	How many ways could Cinderella have put one glass slipper to use?
E	Eliminate	How might Cinderella have met the Prince without the help of her fairy godmother?
R	Rearrange	Imagine that Cinderella had not been home to try the glass slipper on when the Prince's pages came. Rewrite the ending of the story.
	Reverse	Rewrite the story as it might have been if Cinderella's sisters had been loving and kind.

The designers of this application of the SCAMPERing strategy suggest that teachers integrate reading, discussion, and writing by encouraging children to share their writing and to talk about their reasons for answering the questions as they did.

CHILDREN'S LITERATURE

■ ■   When children are encouraged to respond to literature in personal and creative ways, the reading of literature takes on new dimensions for them and both reading and writing improve. Huck (1979) maintains that "as children relate what they are reading to their background of experience, they internalize the meaning of the story" (p. 705). Research has documented the importance of children's responses to literature. Church and Bereiter (1984) found that high school students who responded personally and affectively to literature were more likely to notice characteristics of the writing style of passages they read than other students. They termed such students "aesthetic readers," and speculated that aesthetic response is "the necessary foundation on which 'reading like a writer' is built":

> It seemed that when aesthetic readers switched over to analysis of style, they had a sense of what they were looking for, because they already had an aesthetic response that told them what the text was doing. Style analysis then becomes a search for what it is about the text that affected you in a certain way. Style analysis not based on prior aesthetic response would seem sterile . . . especially for young readers.
>
> (p. 90)

Writing assignments which help children learn to respond personally to literature not only provide valuable writing practice; such activities promote reading like a writer, which, as will be explained in Chapter 4, can improve children's knowledge of writing skills and conventions.

As we mentioned in the introduction to this chapter, postreading writing activities traditionally have been restricted to formal book reports. Such assignments do not encourage personal responses from students. Moffett (1986) explains that activities requiring reportage involve students in the least personal forms of writing by requiring them to place themselves in an objective role, at some distance from the literature, and by encouraging them to write literally rather than figuratively and implicitly. In his classification of the various thinking processes used by writers, he calls this factual kind of thinking/writing *looking into*. He contrasts *looking into* with other kinds of writing which require critical and creative thinking, such as *thinking up* (producing stories and poems) and *thinking over* (producing personal essays). If children are to grow as writers, they must have experiences which allow them to write in their own voices, reacting honestly to what they read through the thinking/writing processes of *thinking up* and *thinking over,* as well as *looking into.*

Many teachers were first introduced to the concept of having children write in response to the reading of literature through the Project English units, *A Curriculum for English*, developed by groups of elementary teachers (Nebraska Curriculum Development Center, 1966). Each of the seventy literature units was developed around one children's classic, representing one of the nine literary genres included at each grade level— folktale, fanciful, animal, adventure, myth, fable, other lands and peoples, historical fiction, and biography. After two decades, these units remain in print and are counted among the richest sources of discussion questions, composition activities, and language explorations related to children's literature. Background information for teachers, suggested procedures, and listings of related books are included in each unit. By composing their own stories, following patterns to which they were exposed, children who participate in the unit activities grow beyond expressing at second hand someone else's ideas to demonstrating their own mastery of literary conventions. By interacting with literature through personal writing, they develop a broader range of composing and comprehension skills than traditional book reports and "lit crit" activities promote. If teachers are fortunate enough to have access to these units, we heartily recommend their use.

In this section we describe other strategies that can be used to encourage children to write personal responses to the books they read. Our first three examples—Similar Experiences, Topics from Classical Poetry, and Book Contracts—were developed by teachers for use with classical literature. Other strategies that follow—Reading Journals, Dialogue Journals, Response Heuristic, Creativity Training, and Type One Interest Centers— are illustrated with activities using children's popular fiction and folk literature as a springboard to writing. With the exception of Topics from Classical Poetry, the strategies described below can be used with all forms of literature. For example, Book Contracts can be used with popular fiction and folktales as well as with classical literature.

■ **Similar Experiences**

The writing assignments in Jo Etta Alwood's classroom often ask students to write about an experience similar to the one they have just read about (Alwood, 1984). After a discussion of rebellion related to the story of Prometheus in a mythology unit, she asked her high school students to write about a time when they either felt like rebelling or actually rebelled against something. Her rationale for this approach is that following in the footsteps of great writers by telling stories of their own will not only increase students' appreciation of literature but also help them to appreciate their own writing.

Elementary- and middle-grade children might enjoy writing about experiences of their own which are similar to those of either classical or popular book characters in the following examples:

1. Marcy Lewis, the overweight heroine of Paula Danziger's *The Cat Ate My Gym Suit* (Delacorte, 1974), was too embarrassed about her body to change into a gym suit in the locker room before gym class. She always had an excuse like "The cat ate my gym suit" or "My little brother misplaced his security blanket and is using my gym suit instead." Have you ever made up excuses for not doing something you should have done?

2. In Betsy Byars's *The Glory Girl* (Viking, 1983), Anna saves her family from injury and possible disaster in a bus accident. Have you ever helped someone avoid danger or trouble?

3. The greatest honor in Charley Cornell's school is to carry the flag in the daily parade to the bus (*Did You Carry the Flag Today, Charley?* by Rebecca Caudill; Holt, Rinehart & Winston, 1966). Not being the helpful type, Charley thought he would never win the award, but he did in his own way. Can you think of a time when you wanted to do something very badly and were not able to do it?

4. There are several instances in Lloyd Alexander's *The Book of Three* (Holt, 1964) where Taran prejudges people. When Eilonwy and Taran came to a dead end in the tunnel she wanted to explore (in "The Barrow" chapter), Taran told her that he knew all along that she didn't know where she was going. He said he was sure from the beginning that they would get lost, because she didn't know anything about tunnels. Write about a time when you prejudged someone or someone prejudged you.

5. In *Sarah, Plain and Tall*, by Patricia MacLachlan (Harper & Row, 1985), the children write letters to the stepmother they have not met, describing themselves. If you were getting a new stepmother, what would you write about yourself in a letter to her?

■ **Topics from Classical Poetry**

Hearing the poetry of such great authors as Shakespeare, John Donne, and William Blake has inspired students in Kenneth Koch's (1973) third-through sixth-grade classes to write poetry of their own. Koch's objective in introducing his students to literary models was to provide motivation for writing and topics for students to write about rather than structures for them to imitate.

His technique was to read classical poetry to his classes — for example, William Blake's "The Tyger," which begins:

> Tyger! Tyger! burning bright
> In the forests of the night,
> What immortal hand or eye
> Could frame thy fearful symmetry?

After reading the poem Koch initiated a discussion, developing one idea or issue stemming from the work. With "The Tyger" he focused on the point that Blake is asking the animal how it got to be the way it is. The discussion brought forth imaginative thinking from the students based on their experiences with other creatures, leading them to write their own poetry in which they asked the same question. Below are examples of their poems, taken from Koch's (1973) book, *Rose, Where Did You Get That Red?**

> Dog, where did you get that bark?
> Dragon, where did you get that flame?
> Kitten, where did you get that meow?
> Rose, where did you get that red?
> Bird, where did you get those wings?
> *—Desiree Lynne Collier* (p. 39)

> Oh Rose, where did you get your color?
> Dog so beautiful, how do you learn how to bark? Will you teach me?
> Ant, the most precious, where did you get your body?
> Beautiful butterfly, where did you get your wings?
> Rose: there once was a red sea and I fell in.
> Dog: my mother gave me lessons.
> Ant: three rocks were stuck together, then lightning hit me.
> Butterfly: one day a kid in Mrs. Fay's class drew a butterfly, then it got
>   loose and it was raining, then it was alive the next day.
> *—Arlene Wong* (p. 39)

Koch's students experienced great enjoyment when he read good literature to them. His strategy channeled this pleasure so that it could be used as motivation for writing. The strategy is, of course, not limited to use just with poetry. It can be adapted easily for use with other types of literature, as illustrated in the Book Contracts that follow.

■ Book Contracts

The Book Contract is a strategy teachers in the Bay Area–National Writing Project have used successfully for stimulating personal reactions to reading. Hailey (1978) describes the Book Contract as a packet of activities related to a book, prepared by the teacher for individual, small group, or whole class use. Under an illustrated cover, the Book Contract contains all or most of these materials: (a) a set of instructions for completing the requirements of the contract; (b) a page for daily assignments and record keeping; (c) a vocabulary page; (d) a page for summarizing factual information about plot and characters; (e) a series of questions and activities to motivate thinking/ writing; and (f) suggestions for creative writing.

"Contracts are excellent vehicles for integrating writing into reading," Hailey comments. "Interpretive and applicative questions used in writing situations such as Book Contracts encourage writing as one process of thought. All too often writing is merely the poor sister of reading. Asking only factual questions does not utilize the potential writing has to help us think clearer and discover what we think" (1978, p. 97).

Teachers who have designed Book Contracts have found the *Taxonomy of Educational Objectives: Cognitive Domain* (Bloom, 1956) to be a valuable resource for use in developing critical and creative reading questions. Definitions of the Bloom Taxonomy categories, with illustrative questions for use with *The Book of Three* by Lloyd Alexander (Holt, 1964), are presented below:

1. *Knowledge.* Recalling previously learned information.
   What did Taran do for a living?
2. *Comprehension.* Translating, interpreting, and/or inferencing from what is read.
   Why did the author call it *The Book of Three*?
3. *Application.* Using knowledge in new situations.
   What kinds of magic do people, even in this Space Age, believe in today?
4. *Analysis.* Relating elements of what is read.
   What was the author's purpose in having Taran and Eilonwy give each other constant "put downs"?
5. *Synthesis.* Putting parts together to create a new pattern or whole.
   Pretend that you are Princess Eilonwy and write to your kinsmen explaining why you won't be home for awhile.

6. *Evaluation.*   Making judgments based on definite criteria.
   Would you recommend this book to a friend? Why or why not?

Book Contracts, if prepared and introduced properly, are as appropriate for use with primary-grade children as they are with older children. Bay Area–National Writing Project participants recommend that teachers demonstrate the first contract in a group or whole-class situation, modeling the reading and writing skills students will be expected to use. After this experience they should be given the opportunities to complete contracts individually or in groups. A Sample Book Contract for *The Ugly Duckling* (Hans Christian Andersen, Scribner's, 1965) appears in Appendix 3.1. This was designed by a group of primary-grade teachers.

Teachers who have constructed and used Book Contracts in their classrooms have found the following resources especially useful:

1. *The Web (Wonderfully Exciting Books)*, ed. Charlotte Huck and Janet Hickman. Columbus, OH: The Center for Language, Literature and Reading, College of Education, Ohio State University.

Published quarterly, *The Web* presents reviews of the best in current children's books with a wide range of suggestions for involving students with the books in creative and personal ways. Teachers share their experiences with these books, and many of the ideas offered are classroom tested. In each issue one particular book or theme is developed in web form, moving out in a variety of directions with activities and ideas for motivating children to respond to literature.

2. *Response Guides for Teaching Children's Books*, by Albert Somers and Janet Worthington. Urbana, IL: National Council of Teachers of English, 1979.

Experiences with high-quality books focus on creative interactions with and enthusiasm for these stories. Discussion questions ranging from interpretation through evaluation are, in many instances, applicable to other books as well. There are stimulating ideas for composing throughout the book.

3. *A Two-Way Street: Read to Write/Write to Read*, ed. Maryellen Hains. Urbana, IL: National Council of Teachers of English, 1982.

Teachers in the Michigan Writing Project based this collection of follow-up writing activities for selected books on the format of the writing process, describing ideas for prewriting, composing, revising, and publishing. There are abundant opportunities for children to participate actively with good literature.

4. *Read to Write: Using Children's Literature as a Springboard to Writing*, 2nd ed., by John Stewig. New York: Holt, Rinehart & Winston, 1980.

In a three-step process, this book promotes the understanding and appreciation of good literature. After exposure to a story children discuss it critically and then use the story as a springboard for writing their own stories and poems. Samples of children's writing inspired by a broad range of literature are included.

5. *Writing is Reading: 26 Ways to Connect*, by Eileen Tway. Urbana, IL: National Council of Teachers of English, 1985.

Many activities to help children live literature through their own writings are offered in this resource book. Literature is used as a model for writing as well as a springboard for ideas to write about. Children's literature is the main resource for making reading/writing connections.

■ Reading Journals

Response-based teaching starts with children, rather than with traditional analysis of literature, because it is based on the premise that readers become interested in literature according to how it affects them. Kirby and Liner (1981) recommend that teachers begin to solicit personal responses to reading by asking students to write a first reaction to something they have read, saying whatever they like, without penalty (with the exception of "I like it" or "I don't like it"). They suggest alternatives to book reports, such as responding to a quotation, writing to an author, continuing a story, writing letters as a character, and writing a brief version of a story from another point of view.

The Reading Journal is an ideal vehicle for this kind of expressive writing. Children can write fluently without fear of criticism because they are not burdened with the task of polishing their writing for another reader. Journal writers are free to answer the question, "What do I honestly think of that?" as they read, think, and write.

Teachers who require journal writing on a regular basis in their classrooms frequently structure the experience to help students make connections between what they read and their own prior knowledge. Ed Youngblood (1985) selects lead-in sentences from a list of generic questions about literature in order to generate written responses to literature from his older students. The questions that follow, chosen from the list he developed, are appropriate for use with elementary-school children:

1. This character reminds me of somebody I know because . . .
2. This character reminds me of myself because . . .
3. This section makes me think about _____ because . . .
4. I like/dislike (name of character) because . . .
5. This situation reminds me of a similar situation in my own life. It happened when . . .
6. The character I admire most is _____ because . . .
7. If I were _____ at this point, I would . . .

(pp. 47–48)

A primary advantage of Reading Journals is that they combine the first-person focus of the diary with an academic focus on facts and ideas from literature. Students who write regularly in Reading Journals are equipped not only with a record of the content of their reading but also with first-draft thought pieces that can be developed into final papers when desired. A daily ten-minute period of uninterrupted journal writing provides enough time for most students to record and react to what they read. This daily writing practice will also promote students' writing fluency.

The journal-writing process generates additional paperwork for teachers to read. However, teachers who are journal advocates have solved that problem in several ways: (a) circulating through their classes during the journal-writing period, reading excerpts and making comments to individual students; (b) asking students to put an asterisk by the entries they particularly want the teacher to read and responding to those entries in writing; or (c) giving credit based on the total number of entries a student turns in, reading and responding to selected entries.

■ Dialogue Journals

The basic idea behind the "learning log" type of Dialogue Journal is that teacher and student can carry on a written dialogue at a different level than the regular dialogue that takes place in the classroom. Craig (1983) maintains: "By making written comments in student journals, asking questions and encouraging written response on the part of the student, the teacher can make the journal experience a two-way street and enter into conversation with the student in a manner which may help the student think more deeply and respond more honestly" (p. 377). The frequent writing which occurs in Dialogue Journals helps promote students' writing fluency, and the reading of teachers' comments provides valuable reading experience as well.

Unfortunately, in actual practice this type of Dialogue Journal has had limited success in the nation's classrooms due to the excessive time demands it places on the teacher. Linda Gambrell (1985) suggests that teachers who are interested in experimenting with learning logs try working with one reading group or randomly selected group for a period of at least three weeks. Every child in the class could, in turn, be in a group that works on these journals with the teacher. This arrangement enables the teacher to respond to a manageable number of journals daily, while insuring that all children will have an opportunity to participate in the Dialogue Journal experience.

A variation of this strategy, the student-directed Dialogue Journal, is proving to be practical and effective for developing critical reading and reflective thinking skills. In this journal format, students take notes from their reading and add their own reflections in two columns that are in dialogue with each other. Students draw a line down the middle of the journal page and use the left-hand column for note-taking, quotations, and summaries, while using the right-hand column for recording their own comments and raising questions. The "note-making" column of the Dialogue Journal becomes a rich source of ideas for elaboration in future writing. It is recommended that students first read the story noncritically for enjoyment before engaging in this process. A model student-directed Dialogue Journal page for Tomie de Paola's *Strega Nona* (Prentice-Hall, 1975) appears in the Strategy Example.

----------- **STRATEGY EXAMPLE 3.1** -----------

Student-Directed Dialogue Journal Page for *Strega Nona* by Tomie de Paola

Note-Taking

This folktale takes place in a town called Calabria.

Strega Nona asked Big Anthony to watch (and not touch) her magic pasta pot while she was away. He said the magic words he had heard her repeat over the pot and it started working.

The pasta kept pouring from the pot and it seemed as though it would bury the town. Everyone, including the mayor, was worried. Big Anthony didn't know the magic words to shut it off.

Strega Nona came home just in time to save the town.

Note-Making

My friend Corinne calls her grandmother "Nona" and it means grandmother in Italian. This town must be in Italy.

It's really important to follow the directions given by people who are holding you responsible. You can get into serious trouble if you don't.

This story reminds me of Rumpelstiltskin. Nobody knew his magic power either.

I wonder what would happen if Strega Nona hadn't come back in time to stop the pasta from running all over the town.

Who would save us if that happened in our town? The firefighter? police? national guard?

Strega Nona saved Big Anthony from hanging by suggesting that the punishment fit the crime and he was sentenced to eating all of the pasta covering her bed.

Witches aren't always bad, I guess. She was fair to Big Anthony.

I remember one time I ate too much spaghetti and got sick. Looking at Big Anthony when he is eating all that pasta brings back memories of that awful time.

■ Response Heuristic

Some students will have problems with strategies described above because they do not get personally involved in their reading. Such students' Reading Journal entries and responses to Book Contract questions tend to be a literal parroting of the story. This lack of personal involvement, of course, not only affects the quality of these students' written responses to literature, but also limits understanding of what is being read (see Chapter 5).

The Response Heuristic, developed by Bleich (1978), is ideally suited for these "uninvolved" readers. The Response Heuristic is a structured strategy "designed to promote students' response to literature by helping them independently analyze and interpret literary texts" (Tierney, Readence, & Dishner, 1985). It provides a means for students to examine their thoughts and reactions and attempts to get them into the habit of responding to the texts they read. In so doing, the Response Heuristic can lead to better reading comprehension and improved written responses to literature.

The strategy involves three steps: perceptions, reactions, and associations. The following are second-grader Jenny's written responses to *The Beast in Ms. Rooney's Room*, by Patricia Reilly Giff (Dell, 1984), a story about a second-grade boy with a problem many young readers can identify with:

1. *Perceptions.* What is important in the book?
   "Richard and his reading class. Richard's friend Mattew [sic]."
2. *Reactions.* Write about how the story makes you feel.
   "Sad for Mattew [sic]. He wets his pants. Happy and sad for Richard. Happy for Emily."
3. *Associations.* Have you had any experiences the book reminds you of?
   "I'm in 2nd grade too. I know a boy with the same problem."

We recommend that this strategy be used selectively with intermediate- or upper-grade students who have difficulty responding to literature.

Students who already respond personally to reading do not require the structure inherent in this method. In fact, the structure might inhibit the creativity of such students' responses.

It is recommended that the teacher introduce the strategy by modeling it in connection with a story that students have just read. The students are then encouraged to give their own oral responses for each step of the process. Next, after another shared reading experience, the students write their responses for each step, possibly using a handout partitioned into three sections, each containing directions for one step of the strategy. The students should then share their written responses, exposing them to differing interpretations of the same text.

If students respond well to this structured approach, they can be encouraged to use it when writing in their reading journals. Once students get into the habit of reacting personally to what they read, the strategy can be phased out, permitting freer responses to reading.

■ **Creativity Training**

Jones (1972) defines creativity as "a combination of the flexibility, originality, and sensibility to ideas which enables the learner to break away from usual sequences of thought into different and productive sequences" (p. 7). Divergent thinking is a prerequisite for creative reading and writing. Unfortunately, students are seldom directly taught creative thinking techniques or given an operational definition of creativity to help them understand what thought processes to use in carrying out creative writing assignments.

Researchers confirm that creativity can be taught as well as nurtured (Torrance, 1974; Turner & Alexander, 1975). They remind teachers that creative readers and writers develop in classrooms where there is freedom in decision making, opportunity for open-ended thinking, and encouragement for intellectual risk taking. The questions teachers ask can elicit creative behavior if they invite invention and fantasy, divergent thought, and speculation. Through direct instruction, students can learn and practice specific creative thinking techniques such as problem solving and "hitch-hiking" (building upon the ideas of others in the class to come up with new ones). Although creativity training has not permeated the regular elementary school curriculum to any great extent, it is considered an important aspect of programs in gifted education, providing students with the process skills necessary to become self-directed, independent learners.

Swicord (1984) suggests that modeling creativity is an effective way to teach it. In order to facilitate thinking about creative behavior, teachers might try the approach used in the Torrance Tests of Creative Thinking (Torrance, 1966) to evaluate their own behavior in terms of fluency (ability to generate many ideas), flexibility (ability to generate varied ideas that fall into different categories), originality (ability to generate unique ideas not produced by others), and elaboration (ability to provide details to an idea). By learning and practicing these components of creativity teachers can encourage creative thinking in their students through example. According to Swicord, "creativity breeds creativity" (p. 29). As a result, teachers who teach creativity to children often become more creative thinkers themselves in the process.

Naumann (1980) has developed a method of linking Creativity Training with children's literature to serve as a prewriting activity for use with primary- and intermediate-grade students. She theorized that children who actually understand the nature of creativity should be able to think and write more imaginatively than others. In order to test her hunch she developed a strategy for teaching her third-graders about the characteristics of creativity. She introduced the concept by distributing her own version of the Torrance "Circle Test" (twenty unconnected circles on a single sheet of paper) and asking her students to draw things with the circles for ten minutes. After completing this task the children learned about Torrance's four elements of creativity—fluency, flexibility, originality, and elaboration—by discussing and evaluating their tests.

Naumann devised simplified definitions for the Torrance creativity categories, and the class adopted them as their creativity standards:

Fluency	the number of ideas expressed (circles used)
Flexibility	the number of different categories represented (animals, fruits, flowers)
Originality	the number of ideas different from anyone else's
Elaboration	the number of details used (eyes, fingers)

The children evaluated their own creativity as they judged their use of circles, noticing that there were differences in creative strengths among the class members. One child combined all the circles to form a letter game; another used very few circles but designed them intricately; one combined several circles at a time to make mechanical things; another sketched twenty bugs.

After discussing the nature of creativity in this context, the class agreed to apply their standards to poetry selections read by the teacher from Shel Silverstein's *Where the Sidewalk Ends* (Harper & Row, 1974), trying to identify these elements of creativity in the poems. In order to simplify this exercise, Naumann assigned one of the characteristics to each child so that several children were listening for fluency, several others for originality, and others for flexibility or elaboration.

The poem, "My Rules," was the unanimous favorite of the class. It is about a boy who presents his girlfriend with a list of exacting rules that she must follow if she is to marry him, such as raking leaves, shoveling snow, and keeping his shoes spotlessly shined. The girl responds by walking away, much to the boy's surprise. After reading this poem and discussing the elements of creativity contained in it, the students decided to follow up by writing their own sets of rules. During the next session they examined each others' lists of rules, identifying examples of fluency, flexibility, originality, and elaboration.

After this practice exercise was completed, Naumann distributed creative writing suggestions based on the poems in *Where the Sidewalk Ends*, and students selected one to complete. A few examples follow:

"Smart"	Once there was a kid (about nine years old) who thought he was really SMART . . . but he wasn't so smart after all. Write a story about this kid. Tell what happened.
"Who"	Write some wild exaggerations about things you like to do. The wilder, the better.
"Point of View"	In a story, describe yourself from your brother's or sister's point of view. Be honest.
"Recipe for a Hippopotamus Sandwich"	Create your own animal sandwich without leaving out a single ingredient. Please don't bring me a sample to try.
"Afraid of the Dark"	Write a dialogue between you and your mother for excuses to stay up.
"One Inch Tall"	Imagine what life would be like if you were only one-inch tall. Make a list of the advantages and disadvantages of this teeny-weeny life. Imagine what life would be like if you were twenty feet tall. Make a list of advantages and disadvantages. (p. 76)*

Naumann's strategy of helping students to identify the elements of creativity in a piece of literature and then using these elements as a springboard to writing can be used in conjunction with any book or poem that contains creative elements. Torrance (1974), an expert on creativity in children, particularly recommends those books which: (a) open new worlds for children; (b) capture their interest through words and language; (c) present original plot lines; and (d) feature unique titles, content, and imaginative formats. A list of such books, appropriate for children in grades K–6, is presented at the end of this chapter.

Naumann concluded that the study of creative thinking in conjunction with children's literature was worthwhile and enjoyable, both in its own right and as a stimulus for writing. The stories which the students wrote after the prewriting activities showed a marked increase in creativity. In

*Reprinted from N. Naumann, *Instructor,* February 1980. Copyright © 1980 by the Instructor Publications, Inc. Used by permission.

addition, Naumann noted that the students in her classroom showed increased interest in reading poetry as a result of their experience with the Silverstein poems, so their attitudes toward reading profited as well as their writing.

■ Type One Interest Center

In presenting the rationale for his Enrichment Triad model, a tool for differentiating instruction to meet individual needs, Renzulli (1977) stresses that Type One enrichment is good for all learners, regardless of ability. Type One activities are general exploratory activities which expand the horizons of students, motivating them to explore a topic by exposing them to a wide variety of potentially interesting areas related to the topic. They are ideal prewriting experiences due to the abundance of ideas they supply. (Type Two enrichment involves training in the higher-level thinking processes, and Type Three activities are individual and group investigations.)

Interest centers stocked with materials that arouse curiosity about a topic or area of study are recommended as a strategy for Type One enrichment. Various kinds of books related to a field of interest are the chief focus of most interest centers, although other media are useful for drawing attention to the center and illustrating concepts. Renzulli emphasizes that the teacher's role is to design a dynamic center with challenging materials that will attract students.

Renzulli recommends that teachers not impose too much structure on children in the center by requiring them to complete specific assigned tasks; rather, teachers should explain that the purpose of the interest center is to discover a topic worth pursuing in depth through an individual or group project. Because the reading that occurs in the center is a natural stimulus for writing, many projects involve some form of writing activity. These activities can be tailored for individual children. Some children, due to limited interest or ability, may participate only to the extent of browsing and selecting a book for independent reading. In these cases teachers might require a written review that will be published in a class book, "Junior Reviews." Students whose interest and curiosity is sparked by the materials in the center can embark on much more challenging writing projects culminating in peer publishing of books and plays.

In order to appeal to a variety of reading abilities and interests, Type One Interest Centers should include as wide an assortment of books and materials as teachers can gather. For example, an American folklore interest center might contain informational books with accumulated knowledge about folklore, favorite American folktales, tall tales, collections of stories about folk heroes and heroines, "how-to" books describing how a folklorist works, folksongs on cassette tape, primary materials such as the *Farmer's Almanac*, and student products such as peer-produced books. Specific books, appropriate for an intermediate- or upper-grade Type One Interest Center on American folklore, are listed at the end of this chapter.

Written publications stemming from an American folklore interest center might include:

1. *American Folklore "How-To" Books.* Students gather information about how folklorists and genealogists work and prepare guides for class-mates to use for folklore and family history projects.

2. *Family History Plays.* After interviewing relatives about interesting ancestors and past events, students choose a favorite episode and write a play for presentation to the class.

3. *Local Folklore Collections.* Students investigate origins of regional folksongs and folklore, documenting each entry and describing the circum-stances under which it was collected.

4. *Living History Albums.* Students assign a page of a loose-leaf note-book to each family member and prepare a book of photos, information, and anecdotes. A page can be added every year for each person.

5. *Family Legends.* Students contribute a story, for which there is some basis of truth from their family's past, to a class book.

6. *Guinness Tall Tales.* Children choose one of the incredible facts or characters in the *Guinness Book of Records* and exaggerate the details enough to create an original tall tale or ballad for a class book.

SUMMARY

■ ■   After describing the process approach to writing instruction and emphasiz-ing the importance of prewriting experiences, we explained in this chapter how reading can serve as a stimulus for writing. We described two catego-ries of strategies which use reading as a prewriting activity: (a) writing with basal reader stories; and (b) writing with children's literature or trade books.

We began with the basal story strategies since these are the types of stories with which children have the most contact. Buckley's ideas for using basal reader stories to inspire young writers were presented, followed by two creative thinking strategies that can be used to help children generate imaginative ideas for writing: Rico's Clustering strategy, in which students map out their images stemming from the reading of a story or poem; and Eberle's SCAMPERing technique (Substitute, Combine, Adapt, Modify/ Magnify, Put to Use, Eliminate, Rearrange/Reverse), which can increase the fluency and originality of students' responses to stories. Both are well suited for extending basal reader stories into writing activities.

We then described how children's literature can also serve as a source of ideas for young writers and presented a number of prewriting strategies based on trade books. The first three strategies—Similar Experiences,

Topics from Classical Poetry, and Book Contracts—use classical literature to provide motivation for writing. Reading Journals and Dialogue Journals use personal involvement in literature to stimulate first-draft, expressive writing. The Response Heuristic strategy helps children channel their thoughts and feelings into writing as they respond to literature. Creativity Training helps children identify the elements of creativity in the literature they read and to use these elements as a springboard for writing. The last strategy, the Type One Interest Center, uses collections of related books to stimulate ideas for writing.

All of the strategies described in this chapter use reading to promote writing fluency—the ability to put one's ideas effortlessly down on paper. These "reading for writing" strategies can also stimulate growth in reading skills. The reading of literature that occurs in each of the motivational prewriting strategies provides children with valuable reading "mileage" or practice. The prewriting techniques which use literature to stimulate creative thinking are likely to result both in more creative writing and in more creative reading, with children making more imaginative and original interpretations of what they read. Finally, when children are encouraged to respond personally to literature they are likely to exert more effort and concentration during reading and to relate what they read to their own experiences, all of which will lead to better reading comprehension.

RECOMMENDED CHILDREN'S BOOKS

Part 1
Books for Promoting Creativity

The books listed below are especially recommended for stretching imaginations of children and for use as prewriting stimuli. They are appropriate for children in grades K–6.

Adoff, Arnold. *The Cabbages are Chasing Rabbits*. Harcourt Brace Jovanovich, 1985.
Allard, Harry. *Miss Nelson Has a Field Day*. Houghton Mifflin, 1985.
Barrett, Judy. *Cloudy with a Chance of Meatballs*. Atheneum, 1978.
Barrett, Ron. *Hi Yo, Fido*. Crown, 1984.
Cameron, John. *If Mice Could Fly*. Atheneum, 1979.
Chevalier, Christa. *Spence Isn't Spence Anymore*. Whitman, 1985.
Galdone, Paul. *The Teeny Tiny Woman: A Ghost Story*. Houghton Mifflin, 1984.
Gardner, Beau. *Guess What?* Lothrup, 1985.
Gerstein, Mordicai. *William, Where Are You?* Crown, 1985.
Graves, Robert. *The Big Green Book*. Macmillan, 1985.
Hasler, Eveline. *Winter Magic*. Morrow, 1985.
Herman, Emily. *Hubknuckles*. Crown, 1985.
Hughes, Shirley. *The Trouble with Jack*. Merrimack, 1986.
Hurwitz, Johanna. *The Adventures of Ali Baba Berstein*. Morrow, 1985.

Joyce, William. *George Shrinks*. Harper & Row, 1985.

Jukes, Mavis. *Like Jake and Me*. Knopf, 1984.

Lester, Allison. *Clive Eats Alligators*. Houghton Mifflin, 1986.

Lester, Helen. *It Wasn't My Fault*. Houghton Mifflin, 1985.

Lorenz, Lee. *A Weekend in the Country*. Prentice-Hall, 1985.

Mahy, Margaret. *The Boy Who Was Followed Home*. E. P. Dutton, 1986.

Martin, Bill, Jr. *The Ghost-Eye Tree*. Holt, Rinehart, & Winston, 1985.

Modell, Frank. *Look Out, It's April Fool's Day*. Greenwillow, 1985.

Most, Bernard. *What Ever Happened to Dinosaurs?* Harcourt Brace Jovanovich, 1984.

Nozaki, Akihiro. *Anna's Hat Trick*. Philomel, 1985.

Poppel, Hans, and Bodden, Iloan. *When the Moon Shines Brightly on the House*. Barron's Educational, 1985.

Schwartz, David. *How Much Is a Million?* Lothrup, 1985.

Sharmat, Marjorie. *What Are We Going to Do About Andrew?* Macmillan, 1980.

Spier, Peter. *Dreams*. Doubleday, 1986.

Stanley, Diane. *A Country Tale*. Macmillan, 1985.

Steig, William. *Solomon, the Rusty Nail*. Farrar, Straus, & Giroux, 1985.

Stevenson, James. *Are We Almost There?* Greenwillow, 1985.

Van Allsburg, Chris. *Jumanji*. Houghton Mifflin, 1981.

Wildsmith, Brian. *Daisy*. Pantheon, 1984.

Part 2
Books for a Type One Interest Center
on American Folklore

Collections of American Folklore by Alvin Schwartz, including notes, sources, and a bibliography:

1972 *A Twister of Twists, A Tangler of Tongues*. Lippincott.
1973 *Tomfoolery*. Lippincott.
1973 *Witcracks*. Lippincott.
1974 *Cross Your Fingers, Spit in Your Hat*. Lippincott.
1975 *Whoppers*. Lippincott.
1976 *Kickle Snifters and Other Fearsome Critters*. Lippincott.
1979 *Chin Music: Tall Talk and Other Talk*. Harper & Row.

Books of Folklore

Caney, Steven. *Kids America*. Workman, 1978.

Coffin, Tristram, and Cohen, Hennig. *Folklore in America*. Anchor/Doubleday, 1970.

_____. *Folklore from the Working Folk of America*. Anchor/Doubleday, 1974.

Thomas, Robert. *The Old Farmer's Almanac*. Yankee, 1974.

Trout, Lawana. *Tales, Talk, and Tomfoolery: A Collection of Folklore*. Scholastic, 1975.

Wiggington, Eliot. *The Foxfire Book*. Anchor/Doubleday, 1972.

Tall Tale Trade Books

Aylesworth, Jim. *Hush Up!* Holt, Rinehart & Winston, 1980.
_____. *Shenandoah Noah.* Holt, Rinehart & Winston, 1985.
Blassingame, Wyatt. *How Davy Crockett Got a Bearskin Coat.* Garrard, 1972.
Calhoun, Mary. *Big Sixteen.* Morrow, 1983.
Cohen, Caron Lee. *Sally Ann Thunder and Whirlwind Crockett.* Greenwillow, 1985.
DeLeeuw, Adele. *Old Stormalong.* Garrard, 1967.
_____. *Paul Bunyan Finds a Wife.* Garrard, 1969.
Dewey, Ariane. *Pecos Bill.* Greenwillow, 1983.
_____. *Febold Feboldson.* Greenwillow, 1984.
Domanska, Janina. *What Happens Next?* Greenwillow, 1983.
Felton, Harold W. *Mike Fink.* Dodd-Mead, 1960.
Fleischman, Sid. "The McBroom Series." *Atlantic Monthly,* 1976–1984.
Keats, Ezra Jack. *John Henry.* Pantheon, 1965.
Kellogg, Steven. *Paul Bunyan.* Morrow, 1984.
Rounds, Glen. *Casey Jones.* Golden Gate Books, 1968.
Shapiro, Irwin. *Heroes in American Folklore.* Messner, 1962.
Stoutenburg, Adrien. *American Tall Tales.* Viking, 1963.

REFERENCES

Alwood, J. E. (1984). Polly doesn't want just another cracker. *English Journal, 73(5),* 68–70.

Applebee, A. N. (1981). Looking at writing. *Educational Leadership, 38,* 458–462.

Bleich, D. (1978). *Subjective criticism.* Baltimore: Johns Hopkins University Press.

Bloom, B. S. (Ed.). (1956). *Taxonomy of educational objectives: The classification of educational goals. Handbook I: cognitive domain.* New York: David McKay.

Boiarsky, C. (1981). Prewriting is the essence of writing. *English Journal, 71(4),* 44–47.

Buckley, M. H. (1986). When teachers decide to integrate the language arts. *Language Arts, 63,* 369–377.

Burris, N. A. (1985). Third-graders write folktales. *Educational Horizons, 64(1),* 32–35.

Church, E., & Bereiter, C. (1984). Reading for style. In J. M. Jensen (Ed.), *Composing and comprehending* (pp. 85–91). Urbana, IL: ERIC/RCS.

Craig, S. T. (1983). Self-discovery through writing personal journals. *Language Arts, 60,* 373–379.

Dionisio, M. (1983). Write? Isn't this reading class? *The Reading Teacher, 36,* 746–750.

Dixon, J. (1967). *Growth through English.* Reading, England: National Association of Teachers of English.

Eberle, R. F. (1984). *Scamper on.* Buffalo, NY: D.O.K. Publishers.

Emig, J. (1971). *The composing processes of twelfth graders.* Urbana, IL: National Council of Teachers of English.

Frank, M. (1979). *If you're trying to teach kids how to write, you've gotta have this book.* Nashville, TN: Incentive.

Gambrell, L. B. (1985). Dialogue journals: Reading-writing interaction. *The Reading Teacher, 38,* 512–515.

Graves, D. (1979). A six-year-old's writing process: The first half of first grade. *Language Arts, 56,* 829–835.

Hailey, J. (1978). *Teaching writing K–8.* Berkeley, CA: University of California Press.

Hennings, D. G. (1986). *Communication in action: Teaching the language arts* (3rd ed.). Boston: Houghton Mifflin.

Hillocks, G., Jr. (1975). *Observing and writing.* Urbana, IL: National Council of Teachers of English.

Hillocks, G., Jr. (1986). *Research on written composition.* Urbana, IL: ERIC/RCS.

Huck, C. (1979). *Children's literature in the elementary school.* New York: Holt, Rinehart & Winston.

Jaggar, A. M., Carrara, D. H., & Weiss, S. E. (1986). The influence of reading on children's narrative writing (and vice versa). *Language Arts, 63,* 292–300.

Jones, T. P. (1972). *Creative learning in perspective.* New York: Wiley.

Kirby, D., & Liner, T. (1981). *Inside out: Developmental strategies for teaching writing.* Montclair, NJ: Boynton/Cook.

Koch, K. (1973). *Rose, where did you get that red?* New York: Random House.

Martin, C. E., Cramond, B., & Safter, T. (1982). Developing creativity through the reading program. *The Reading Teacher, 35,* 568–572.

McConaghy, J. (1985). Once upon a time and me. *Language Arts, 62,* 349–352.

Mills, E. B. (1968). An experimental study in the use of literary models in written composition. *Dissertation Abstracts International, 28,* 3900–A.

Moffett, J. (1985). Hidden impediments to improving English teaching. *Phi Delta Kappan, 67,* 50–55.

Moffett, J. (1986). *Active voices IV.* Montclair, NJ: Boynton/Cook.

Murray, D. (1982). *Learning by teaching.* Montclair, NJ: Boynton/Cook.

Naumann, N. (1980). Dancing pants and a hippopotamus sandwich. *Instructor, 90*(7), 74–76.

Nebraska Curriculum Development Center. (1966). *A curriculum for English.* Lincoln: University of Nebraska Press.

Renzulli, J. (1977). *The enrichment triad model: A guide for developing defensible programs for the gifted and talented.* Mansfield Center, CT: Creative Learning Press.

Rico, G. L. (1983). *Writing the natural way.* Los Angeles: Tarcher.

Swicord, B. (1984). Creativity — It's not just kid-stuff. *G / T / C,* March/April, 28–29.

Tchudi, S., & Tchudi, S. (1984). *The young writer's handbook.* New York: Scribner's.

Tierney, R. J., Readence, J. E., & Dishner, E. K. (1985). *Reading strategies and practices* (2nd ed.). Boston: Allyn & Bacon.

Torrance, E. P. (1966). *Torrance test of creative thinking.* Princeton, NJ: Personnel Press.

Torrance, E. P. (1974). Ten ways of helping young children gifted in creative writing and speech. In R. B. Ruddell (Ed.), *Resources in reading — Language instruction* (pp. 250–258). Englewood Cliffs, NJ: Prentice-Hall.

Turner, T. N., & Alexander, J. E. (1975). Fostering early creative reading. *Language Arts, 52,* 786–789.

Youngblood, E. (1985). Reading, thinking and writing using the reading journal. *English Journal, 74*(6), 46–48.

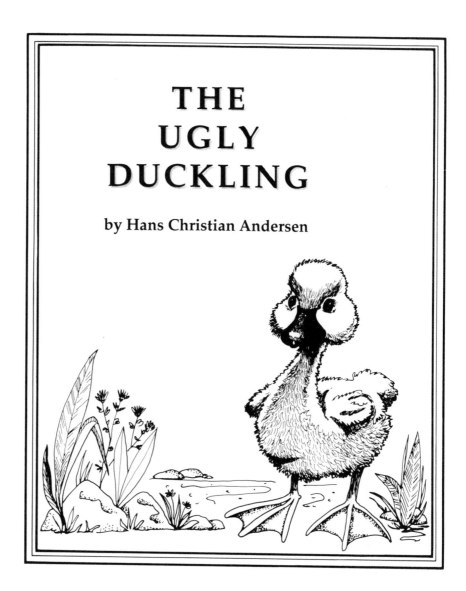

Appendix 3.1 Book Contract for *The Ugly Duckling* Source: Courtesy of Merrillee Cooper, Pat Newton, and Cathy Bates.

THE UGLY DUCKLING
GENERAL DIRECTIONS

1. You will have two weeks to complete the reading of *The Ugly Duckling* and the assignments on the following pages.

2. Your dates for beginning and ending are

   _____ to _____.

3. Each day, bring this packet of materials, paper, pencil, and your journal to class. Books will be kept in the classroom.

4. Each activity page will have instructions for you to follow. Mark your Reading Record (page 2) each time you work on this project.

5. All activities completed are to be kept together in your folder until completion date.

6. Sign this contract after you have completed the requirements listed and turn it in with your folder.

   1. Reading Record _____ (✔)

   2. Vocabulary _____

   3. Summary of Main Characters _____

   4. Journal Questions (3) _____

   5. Hans Christian Andersen question (1) _____

   6. Ducks and Swans question (1) _____

   7. Writing Activities (2) _____

   Signed _____
   Your Name

Page 2

READING RECORD

Directions: Every time you work on this project, record your progress. For example, if you read from page 11 to page 15 on one day, make your entry as shown in the example. If you complete two study questions on another day, indicate by entering the information in the last column.

EXAMPLE

DATE	STARTING PAGE	STOPPING PAGE	WORK ACCOMPLISHED
3–3	p. 11	p. 15	
3–7			answered 2 questions

Page 3

VOCABULARY

Directions: As you read the story *The Ugly Duckling* write down on this page any words that you do not know or that are interesting to you. When you have finished reading, find definitions for each word by using the dictionary.

Example: 1. rushes—grasslike plants that usually grow in wet places.

1. _____
   _____

2. _____
   _____

3. _____
   _____

4. _____
   _____

5. _____
   _____

6. _____
   _____

7. _____
   _____

8. _____
   _____

9. _____
   _____

10. _____
    _____

Page 4

SUMMARY OF MAIN CHARACTERS

Pick four characters, including the ugly duckling, to describe briefly below. You could choose the mother duck, the old duck, Sonnie the cat, Chucky Low Legs, the farmer, or the old woman. You've read quite a bit about how the ugly duckling acted and felt and only a little about the other characters. Look back at the dialogues and descriptions of the others and decide whether they were likeable characters or not. Write about why or why not.

NAME: The Ugly Duckling
PERSONALITY DESCRIPTION:

NAME:
PERSONALITY DESCRIPTION:

NAME:
PERSONALITY DESCRIPTION:

NAME:
PERSONALITY DESCRIPTION:

JOURNAL WRITING

Directions: Choose 3 questions to answer in your journal.

1. How do you think the ugly duckling felt about being different?

2. What would you have done in response to the other animals' cruelty?

3. What was the difference between the ugly duckling and his brothers and sisters?

4. Do you think it was a good idea for the ugly duckling to run away? Why?

5. How do you think the ugly duckling must have felt when he discovered that he was a swan?

6. Can you compare how the ugly duckling felt about being different to feelings you have had? How were they alike? How were they different?

7. Find another version of the same story in the room. After reading it, which do you prefer? Why?

8. Do you know why there might be several different versions of the same story?

QUICK WRITE QUESTIONS

Directions: Use the classroom library to help you answer these questions. Pick *one* of the questions about Hans Christian Andersen and *one* of the questions about ducks and swans to answer.

QUESTIONS ABOUT HANS CHRISTIAN ANDERSEN

1.   Read about the life of Hans Christian Andersen and tell about three parts of his life that you think are particularly sad.

2.   *The Ugly Duckling* is often considered to be much like Mr. Andersen's own life. Describe some of the likenesses you see.

3.   Hans Christian Andersen used his stories to show how ridiculous people could be. Read *The Emperor's New Clothes* and then describe the message you think Andersen was trying to tell.

QUESTIONS ABOUT DUCKS AND SWANS

1.   Tell about ducks being hatched. Be sure to tell where the nest might be located, how many eggs she usually lays, how long it takes for the eggs to hatch, how large the eggs are, what the baby ducks are like when they first hatch, and one more interesting fact that you find.

2.   Tell about swans. Be sure to tell where swans live, what they eat, what they do in the winter, how large they get when full grown, and two more interesting facts that you find.

3.   Describe the interesting features of ducks that make them able to swim, dive and fly so well.

MORE WRITING ACTIVITIES

Here are some activities to make you think about the story of *The Ugly Duckling* in a different way. Choose the two that you like best and write about them in your journal.

1.   If you could meet one of the characters in the story—the mother duck, one of the other ducklings, the old duck, the turkey, one of the wild ducks, Sonnie, the cat, Chucky Low Legs, the hen, the old woman, the boy who saved the duckling from the ice, one of the swans, or the duckling himself—which one would it be? Write a paragraph telling why you would choose that character and what you would say to or ask him or her.

2.   The duckling was treated badly by most of the characters he met in the story. What if they had liked him and had been nice to him? How would the story have turned out? Write a new ending for the story.

3.   The duckling grew up and became a beautiful swan. What do you think his life was like after that? Write another chapter for the story and tell about new adventures the beautiful swan might have. Give it a new title. (*The Ugly Duckling II, Revenge of the Swan, Adventures of the Swan*—you make one up!)

4.   Have you ever been away from your family and felt very lonely, just like the ugly duckling? Write about a time when you were very sad and/or lonely. What happened to change your situation?

5.   Pretend you are a newspaper reporter and that you are assigned to interview the new swan in the stream. What questions would you ask him? Write up your interview like a newspaper article. Tell who it is about, where and when the story took place, how you found out about the story, and why it is of interest.

6.   People sometimes treat each other unkindly, too, just like the other animals treated the ugly duckling in the story. Write your own story that is something like *The Ugly Duckling,* but use people for the characters. Give it a new title, illustrate it, and bind it as a book for the library corner.

4

Using Reading in the Writing Process II

Composing and Revising/Editing

Read, read, read. Read everything . . . and see how they do it. Just like a carpenter who works as an apprentice and studies the master—Read! You'll absorb it. Then write.
—William Faulkner, *The Writer's Quotation Book*

Reading can do more than serve as a stimulus for writing. It also plays an important role in acquainting students with the rules and characteristics of skilled writing. So, in addition to being an excellent means of getting the writing process started, reading helps children acquire the skills used during the composing and revising/editing stages of the writing process.

This chapter begins with a review of research which indicates that students' writing ability is affected both by the amount of reading they do and by the types of texts they read. Smith's "reading like a writer" theory, which attempts to explain how reading can improve writing competence, is also examined. Then a number of strategies are presented for using the reading of literature to promote students' writing skills and to increase their knowledge of writing styles and conventions.

RESEARCH

■ ■   An impressive body of research indicates that large amounts of reading can have positive effects on students' overall writing abilities. In his excellent literature review, Krashen (1984) cites six correlational studies which found that good writers tend to do more reading outside of class than poor writers. Krashen also cites a number of experimental studies which have reported that increased reading was more effective in promoting writing skills than additional grammar study or writing practice. Stotsky (1983) came to a similar conclusion in her comprehensive study of reading/writing research. This research indicated that additional reading may be as effective as additional writing practice in improving students' writing abilities. She concluded that reading is an essential aspect of a good writing program.

Other researchers have examined the effects of particular types of reading experiences on children's writing. Eckhoff (1984) analyzed the writing of second-graders who had been reading in two very different basal reader series. One series was written in a tightly controlled style, using simple sentence structures, whereas the other used a more natural, complex style similar to children's literature. She found that the children's writing mirrored certain characteristics of passages they had been reading. For example, students who read in the more tightly controlled basal wrote simpler sentences and tended to copy stylistic features peculiar to that series, such as putting each sentence on a separate line and starting sentences with "And" and ending them with "too." Students who read in the series that contained more complex sentence patterns used more complex syntax in their own writing.

A growing number of case studies of individual children have reported similar findings. Jaggar, Carrara, and Weiss (1986) illustrated how several fourth-graders incorporated elements from books they had read into their own writing. When asked why she included parts in her story which were not true, one girl replied: "Because some parts should be fiction to be funny. Like Judy Blume. She puts fiction parts. She knows a fat person named Blubber and made a book out of her and added funny parts that really didn't happen to Blubber. That's what I'm doing here" (p. 297).

Butler and Turbill (1984) related how an eight-year-old boy's first attempts at nonfiction writing resembled the narrative stories to which he had had wider exposure. For example, he would use phrases like, "Now I am going to tell you abuot [sic] turtles." However, after six weeks of reading nonfiction trade books, his style of writing began to reflect the established conventions of expository writing; now he was using phrases like, "Animals are in evry cuntry [sic] and in every sea." According to Butler and Turbill, the boy began to use the nonfiction "register" as a result of reading many nonfiction books.

The findings of Eckhoff's (1984) research and these case studies indicate that what children read influences how they write. The implication

new oral therapy

actigall™

u r s o d i o l

300-mg capsules

The "write" option for gallstone patients who can't or won't have surgery

Please consult full Prescribing Information on final pages.

C I B A

for teachers is that, if children are going to become skilled writers, they must be provided with models of elaborated written structures through the reading of good literature in addition to the skill-building material of the basal reader series.

A theory has recently been developed to help explain reading's positive effects on writing. Frank Smith (1983) has proposed that, given certain conditions, one will effortlessly and unconsciously learn the rules and conventions of writing while reading. These conditions include: (a) the absence of pressure or anxiety; (b) a clear understanding of what is being read; and (c) the perception of one's self as a writer who will have an opportunity to write the same type of text. When these factors exist, the reader subconsciously becomes sensitive to the style and mechanics of the text, and reads like a writer. Smith explains:

> To read like a writer we engage with the author in what the author is writing. We anticipate what the author will say, so that the author is in effect writing on our behalf, not showing how something is done but doing it with us. . . . Every nuance of expression, every relevant syntactic device, every turn of phrase, the author and learner write together. Bit by bit, one thing at a time, but enormous numbers of things over the passage of time, the learner learns through *reading* like a writer to *write* like a writer.
>
> (pp. 563–564)

Smith contends that only through such unconscious learning stemming from reading can we possibly learn the multitude of rules and conventions connected with different types of writing. He recommends that teachers surround students with a variety of good books, encourage ample recreational reading, and provide frequent opportunities for children to write texts similar to the ones they are reading.

Krashen (1984) has extended Smith's theory by adding the distinction between writing competence (the subconscious knowledge that one has about writing) and writing performance (the ability to use this knowledge in actual writing). He maintains that writing competence develops from large amounts of reading like a writer. This wide reading is a necessary but not sufficient condition for good writing; a good writer must also learn about the composing process through writing. Repeated practice is needed to discover effective planning and revision strategies that will enable students to use their writing competence. Krashen points out that instruction is also necessary in order for students to learn about certain performance aspects of writing which cannot be acquired through reading.

This chapter focuses on ways in which reading can be used to build children's writing competence by acquainting them with the styles and conventions of skilled writing. The first group of strategies — reading like a writer — can be used to help children think of themselves as members of the author "club," a prerequisite for learning about writing through reading. The second group — reading as a source of patterns and models — describes how teachers can use literature to acquaint children with different types and styles of writing to use during the composing stage of the writing process. The last group—reading for revising/editing—are strategies for helping children evaluate their own writing and the writing of others.

READING LIKE A WRITER

■ ■   Frank Smith (1983) contends that children must first perceive themselves as authors—members of the writing club—before they will be able to read like writers. They need to realize both that they are capable of writing something similar to what they are reading and that they will likely have an opportunity to do so. Belonging to the club supplies the motivation for reading like a writer. Smith explains: "We find ourselves pausing to reread a passage . . . because something in the passage was particularly well put, because we respond to the craftsman's touch. This is something we would like to be able to do ourselves, but also something that we think is not beyond our reach. We have been reading like a writer, like a member of the club" (p. 563). On the other hand, if children do not consider themselves authors and do not expect to ever write something similar to what they are reading, reading like a writer will not take place. They have no reason to pay attention to the style or other characteristics of the passages they read.

Smith (1983) offers some broad recommendations for helping children join the author's club. First, teachers need to provide opportunities to do purposeful writing in the classroom, since only through frequent writing will children come to view themselves as writers. This also creates the expectation for children that they will soon have an opportunity to write passages similar to those they are reading. Smith also recommends that teachers write with their students. By doing so, teachers demonstrate that writing is an interesting, worthwhile activity. In addition, they are acting as a model that many students will want to imitate.

The strategies that follow are other ways to help children perceive themselves as authors.

■ The Author's Chair

Graves and Hansen (1984) have developed a strategy that, when used in conjunction with a workshop approach to writing instruction, can help primary-grade children develop a sense of authorship. A chair is designated as the Author's Chair. The teacher reads trade books from this chair, giving biographical details about the adult author, and sometimes reads books that the students have written, treating them in the same manner as the trade books. Children also take turns reading from the Author's Chair. They read three types of books: (a) books that they have written themselves; (b) books that other children in class have written; and (c) adult-authored trade books. Regardless of who is doing the reading or what type of book is being read, the children in the audience always have an opportunity to receive the story that was read and then ask questions of the author or reader. Receiving involves making comments about the story—talking about one's favorite part or one's view of what the story was about. Then the students ask questions about the story. They may ask for additional information or ask why a particular event happened in the story. Hansen (1983) explains what happens when children read each others' books to the class:

> A child reads and the class applauds. Then all those hands wave and the child graciously receives the comments. Before long the questions begin. . . . The person who reads the book tries to answer the questions. These children learn that sometimes authors leave out too much information and may have to explain their texts. But the questioners learn much more than just the answers to their questions. They have gathered to respond to another author's work, and they continue to learn it's their responsibility as readers to ask questions.
> (p. 973)

When the book is a trade book written by a professional author, the teacher and children speculate on how the author might answer the questions.

The key to the Author's Chair strategy is that the chair serves as a link between child-authors and adult-authors. When children sit in the chair and read their published books, their books are treated just like those of professional writers. They are received and questioned in the same manner. This helps children perceive themselves as belonging to the same club as the adult authors. In addition, when children attempt to answer questions addressed to the authors of trade books, they have the experience of placing themselves in the adult writer's shoes. Furthermore, this strategy can make them more active readers by getting them into the habit of constantly questioning what they are reading.

■ Getting Inside the Author's Head

Marilyn Woolley and Keith Pigdon have developed a strategy for helping children identify more closely with adult writers by getting them to speculate on the processes the author might have gone through to produce the finished piece of writing (Butler & Turbill, 1984). Three steps are involved:

> 1. *Reading/Listening*. The students read the book silently or the teacher reads it to them on a daily basis. Once the book is completed, it is discussed in order to ascertain that the students understood the story.

2. *Preparation.* The teacher copies key passages from the book onto overhead transparencies. The teacher also prepares questions that will help the students "get inside the author's head." These questions focus on the author's possible intentions, the message the author is trying to convey, the information needed to write the story, and the style or register that the author employed. The following are examples of questions prepared for use with the story *Magpie Island* by Colin Thiele and Roger Haldane:

What did he [the author] need to know about magpies?
What did he need to know about Eyre Peninsula of
   South Africa and the local sea birds?
How would he get to know these things?
How did he choose to write the book?
How did he choose to present the information?
                                        (Butler & Turbill, 1984, pp. 75–76)

The questions are duplicated for the students to use during small group discussions.

3. *Reading as a Writer.* The students meet in small groups. First, the key passages (on transparencies) are reread orally and discussed in relation to the whole book. Then the children are asked to answer the prepared questions, using the key passages as references. In answering the questions, the students imagine that they are the author.

As in the Author's Chair, this strategy gives students experience in viewing writing from an adult writer's perspective. In so doing, children are confronted with the fact that they make similar choices and decisions in their own writing. This can lead to clearer conceptions of authorship, help students link their writing with adult literature, and encourage reading like a writer.

■ Professional Writers Tell Them How

A 160-page book, *A Gift From Maine,* resulted from a letter-writing strategy planned by James Plummer (1984) for his sixth-graders. The purpose of the project was to "start their creative juices going." The children wrote letters to well-known professional artists and writers in their state, Maine, asking them to tell about their sources of motivation for creating art or written works. Through the letters they received in answer to their requests, the students "learned firsthand how simple ideas evolve into stories and works of art; how feelings contribute to creative works; and why it's important to write from personal experience" (p. 37).

The book contains letters and original contributions from sixty-two Maine artists, writers, and organizations. Among the "gifts" were letters from writers John Gould, E. B. White, and Theodore Enslin. Gould's advice was to practice thinking about the impossible. He quoted the Queen of Hearts in Lewis Carroll's *Alice in Wonderland,* who boasted, "Why, sometimes I've believed as many as six impossible things before breakfast!"

and then encouraged the students to try a prewriting experience in which they: (a) think about things they have accomplished that they once thought impossible; or (b) imagine that they have done something important for the world which they thought was impossible.

E. B. White testified to the value of keeping a journal:

> When I was young, I began writing about my experiences and keeping a record of my thoughts and desires. If I was worried about something, I wrote about my fears. If I went somewhere, I told where I went, whom I met, and what I did. I found that I liked writing. It exercised my mind and relieved my feelings. I still have my journal — millions of words. I can recommend keeping a diary or journal. It helps you learn to write and it stirs up your mind in a good way.
>
> (Plummer, 1984, p. 38)

As a source of inspiration, White suggested to children that they: (a) think of an animal they'd like to know about; (b) do research in the library to discover what it likes to do and eat, who its enemies are, and other facts; and (c) write an imaginary animal story, using these facts as a basis.

Enslin, a poet, challenged the children to be curious about everything around them, explaining that curiosity is one thing that artists and writers have in common. He encouraged the children to write down a question they would like to have answered, and then write a poem giving all the reasons for their curiosity, beginning the first line with: "I am curious about . . ." Enslin included in his letter a poem he wrote about the ocean using this technique.

Writing to professional authors enables children to learn first-hand the tricks of the writing trade. It also helps to build their concept about authorship, teaching them that the stories they read are written by real people. This is an important step in children's learning to perceive themselves as authors. Just as learning from authors can be an inspirational experience for children, hearing from children can be rewarding for an author as long as children's requests are considerate and their questions sincere. The child-author communication process deserves careful monitoring by the teacher.

■ Book Characters Who Write

Reading stories about heroes and heroines who are avid writers is another strategy for building students' concept of authorship, helping them realize that children, as well as adults, can be authors. In addition, such stories can motivate children to want to be writers. Book characters who are writing enthusiastically for their own purposes demonstrate to children that writing can be important, interesting, and enjoyable.

Whitaker Murphy *(Return to Sender)* and Leigh Botts *(Dear Mr.*

Henshaw) are habitual letter writers whose correspondences create a series of amusing events. The hero of *Zed* writes a breathtaking adventure story based on his experiences as a hostage of Arab terrorists. Daphne and her friend *(Daphne's Book)* write a book together, with one as author and the other as illustrator.

Journal writing is a favorite activity of Anastasia Krupnik *(Anastasia Krupnik* and *Anastasia, Ask Your Analyst)* and several other protagonists in recent children's books. Anastasia uses her journal to help her cope with sixth-grade boys, parents, teachers, and a baby brother, as well as to keep lists of interesting words, ideas to write about, and things she likes and dislikes. Abby Jones *(Loretta P. Sweeny, Where Are You?)* shows how writing in a memo book can be useful in making plans and organizing clues for solving crimes. The young detective records her thoughts and comments on her successes and failures daily in her journal. *The Ramona Quimby Diary* is a personal journal for the reader, containing fill-in sections with blank lined pages. Ramona's experiences are scattered throughout the book to help the owner of the diary think up ideas for writing.

Leigh Botts *(Dear Mr. Henshaw)* demonstrates how a beginning writer can evolve into a confident writer by developing fluency through journal writing. When he wrote to his author-friend complaining that he had trouble thinking what to say in his journal, Mr. Henshaw suggested that he pretend that his entries were letters to someone. Leigh followed the advice and wrote regularly to "Dear Mr. Henshaw" in his journal, until he discovered before long that he no longer needed this crutch. He wrote, "I don't have to pretend to write to Mr. Henshaw any more. I have learned to say what I think on a piece of paper."

An annotated list of selected trade books about children who write, including all those discussed above, can be found in the "Recommended Children's Book" feature at the end of this chapter. The books listed are appropriate for children in the third grade and above.

After fifth-grade teacher Sonja Sandeno used *Dear Mr. Henshaw* as a model in her classroom to introduce her students to journal writing, she observed:

> Since I read *Dear Mr. Henshaw* to my class, the students really understand what journals are all about. They realize that this isn't just something I made up. They saw how important Leigh's diary was to him, how it helped him express and clarify his feelings of frustration, excitement and anger. Many of my students now take their journals home over the weekend to write stories simply for their own pleasure.
>
> I have only a few students now who get stuck when I ask them to write something. We have a long way to go with punctuation and spelling, but the output is extensive and the children are putting themselves into their writing. *Dear Mr. Henshaw* made it all come together for them.
>
> This not only applies to the writing, but to the reading as well. They beg me for time each day to share what they've written with the class. And, my two

copies of *Dear Mr. Henshaw* are making a tour through the room. They all want to read it for themselves.

(Noyce, 1985, pp. 45–46)

The strategies we have presented in the above section implement the theories of Smith, Krashen, and others by providing ways for teachers to make their classrooms "communities of writers." Involvement in these activities enable children to identify with other writers through reading.

A SOURCE OF PATTERNS AND MODELS

■ ■ Reading can expose students to models of different types and styles of writing. This can occur incidentally during the reading of children's literature, basal readers, and content-area texts, or intentionally during instructional lessons in which the teacher selects model pieces of writing for children to study and imitate. The latter is actually one of the oldest means of teaching writing, dating back to ancient Greece and Rome (Ryan, 1986).

The research cited at the beginning of this chapter attests to the incidental effects—both good and bad—that reading can have on children's writing. The studies cited by Krashen (1984) showed that children who do large amounts of recreational reading tend to be better writers. This extra reading exposes the children to models of writing and subconsciously builds their writing competence. As Flower and Hayes explain, "a well-read person simply has a much larger and richer set of images of what a text can look like" (1980, p. 28). Eckhoff's (1984) study pointed out that what is being read—the models themselves—is very important. If children's reading repertoires consist mainly of basal reader stories, their writing is likely to reflect the simple style modeled in the stories. On the other hand, if children's reading diets include large amounts of good literature, their writing will tend to contain the complex sentence patterns and mature style typically found in high-quality children's literature. Taken together, these findings suggest the need for teachers to provide frequent opportunities for children to read trade books in the classroom.

In his extensive review and meta-analysis of writing research, Hillocks (1986) reported that the results of studies investigating the intentional use of models to teach writing were mixed. His meta-analysis showed that models were more effective than grammar study but somewhat less effective than the average of all methods of writing instruction. He cautioned, however, against interpreting these findings to mean that the study of models is an ineffective way to teach writing. There are many different ways in which models can be used in composition instruction—entire works can be studied, short passages differing in a single characteristic can be analyzed, models of good and poor writing can be contrasted; the effectiveness of these different types of models may vary among students, depending on their age and ability. Furthermore, models can simply be studied and analyzed, or they can be used as tools to help students accomplish their own writing purposes. Current research is not sufficiently refined to discriminate between these different types and uses of models.

We believe that the "use" factor is of utmost importance. Most of the studies reviewed by Hillocks used model pieces of writing in a traditional, analytic way. As a result of this traditional approach, students learned to describe the components and characteristics of a given type of writing but not how to produce their own versions. In this respect, the traditional use of models is very similar to grammar study, which teaches students how to describe and analyze different syntactic constructions. Since there is over-whelming evidence that grammar instruction has little effect on students' writing, it is hardly surprising that the analytic study of model pieces of writing is similarly ineffective.

Models can be used in other, more effective ways to improve student writing. Children can be introduced to models and then given opportunities to use the models in meaningful writing situations. Such instruction will result in procedural knowledge—the knowledge of how to actually produce one's own version of the model. Hillocks (1986) notes: "The [traditional] use of models may be thought of as an attempt to teach declarative knowl-edge about discourse. Such knowledge may be contrasted with the pro-cedural knowledge necessary to the production of structures inherent in a type of discourse " (p. 238). Research has shown that approaches to writing instruction which focus on procedural knowledge are much more successful than those that emphasize analytic knowledge (Hillocks, 1986). This sug-gests that process-oriented uses of models should have a more positive impact on children's writing than the traditional method.

In the sections that follow, we will describe a strategy—the Individual Reading Strand—that can be used to organize the regular reading of chil-dren's literature in the classroom. Then several examples of how model pieces of writing can be used to provide children with procedural knowledge will be presented.

■ Individual Reading Strand

According to the U.S. Office of Education (1986) report, *First Lessons,* there is a need for more reading of literature in our schools at all grade levels. Not only is good literature a source of models of skilled writing, it is also a source of motivation for learning to read. As a result of listening to and reading good literature, many children come to the realization that reading is a worthwhile, enjoyable activity and are therefore willing to put forth the effort and energy necessary to learn to read. Such experiences also build children's writing competence by familiarizing them with the charac-teristics of good writing, provided that children read like writers.

One option for filling this need to bring literature into the classroom is the Individual Reading Strand, in which children read self-selected trade books as part of the regular curriculum. Students keep daily records of their independent reading and respond to the books in a variety of writing assignments such as those described in Chapter 3. Pupil-teacher conferences are held to discuss individual progress in reading and writing. These independent literacy activities and conferences enable teachers to diagnose children's reading and writing skills for small group instruction. Equally important is the enjoyment children derive from reading literature related to their own interests.

Several elements are needed in order to implement the Individual Reading Strand, which is appropriate for use as soon as children have acquired the skills needed for independent reading and writing:

1. A large supply of good children's literature in the classroom library — The more books available, the more likely that children will find books that match their reading interests and abilities. However, quality is as important as quantity. Good literature will spark enjoyment in reading and provide models that will enhance children's writing competence. "Children's Choices," which appears yearly in the October issue of *The Reading Teacher,* is an excellent source of high-quality trade books popular with children. Other reliable sources include the *Bulletin of the Center for Children's Books* and *The Horn Book Magazine.*

2. Regular reading of these books to the class by the teacher — This reading by teachers will acquaint children with the joys of good literature and will motivate them to read the books themselves. The reading that teachers do in their classes will also motivate student writing.

Jim Trelease has compiled a "treasury" of children's favorite read-aloud books, many of which have been recommended to him by teacher friends (*The Read-Aloud Handbook,* Penguin, 1982). Grade levels from Toddler to Young Adult are designated for six categories of books: Wordless Books, Picture Books, Short Novels, Novels, Poetry, and Anthologies. All books listed have been well received by children when read aloud to them and, according to Trelease, they will inspire children to read more books of the same kind. The handbook is a rich resource for teachers at all levels.

3. Ample opportunities for the children to read trade books — One of the best strategies for providing time for the regular reading of literature in the classroom is Sustained Silent Reading (SSR). In this strategy, a certain amount of time (usually fifteen to thirty minutes) is set aside every day for the silent reading of trade books. Silent reading is the only activity permitted during this time. The teacher reads silently along with the students, providing a model of adult recreational reading. In some schools, SSR is done building-wide, with everyone in school, including the principal, secretaries, and custodians, engaging in silent reading. For more information on SSR, see Mc-Cracken (1971).

In addition to SSR time, any unscheduled time throughout the school day is considered free reading time in classrooms where the Individual Reading Strand is flourishing.

4. Frequent writing activities related to the reading of literature — This

writing can take place in journals or can be done in response to specific questions and assignments. For example, when Rose Napoli's sixth-graders complete a book they may write an entry in their spiral notebooks, to which she responds, or they may answer one of her "secret" questions, such as:

    a. What questions would you ask if the author were here?

    b. How might the author answer it?

    c. Select sections of the book in which you think the author has done a particularly good job with description. What makes these sections effective? Be specific and refer to the text. (Calkins, 1986, p. 71)

In classrooms where independent reading is a regular activity, a writing workshop can prevail, with writing experiences springing from reading. Macrorie (1973), for example, asks his students to write freely in their journals for a short period of time every day. After they have written five or six journal entries, he asks them to choose one to revise into a finished piece of writing, carrying it through the entire process to the publishing stage. In this approach, students are not limited to writing about their independent reading. However, if surrounded by literature, they will often choose to do so.

Donna Carrara's fourth-grade classroom (Jaggar et al., 1986) is an example of the rich literary environment that can be created by the Individual Reading Strand:

> When you walk into the room, the first thing you notice are the books, hundreds of them, on shelves, on tables, in boxes. The bulletin boards are covered with drawings, diagrams, and book jackets, all centered around class discussions of story elements, such as character, setting, plot, problem, and resolution. The same richness is reflected in the daily activities of the children. They are read to every day; they are all involved in whole class reading; they do Sustained Silent Reading (SSR); they have individual conferences with Donna on their reading and they talk about books with their classmates. In addition, they write every day, sharing their writing with the class and conferencing with Donna about it. Every day they write in learning logs, answering questions aimed at helping them reflect on their reading and writing.
>
> (p. 297)

The Individual Reading Strand, as proposed here, is hardly a new strategy. It is actually a version of Individualized Reading, popularized decades ago by progressive educators such as Veatch (1966). Individualized Reading was very popular in the 1960s but quickly fell out of favor with the advent of the back-to-basics movements in the 1970s and 1980s, as witnessed by such recent articles as "What Ever Happened to Individualized Reading?" (Bagford, 1985). A major reason for the decline of Individualized Reading was that basal readers offer a more systemic approach to teaching the type of isolated skills assessed by reading-achievement tests. As a result, basal programs have become the predominant approach to reading instruction, taking up most of the time devoted to reading in many schools.

Teachers who wish to implement the Individual Reading Strand may therefore feel constrained by the rigid structure and time demands of their basal programs. One partial solution is to promote the reading of trade books and related writing activities during the language arts period (Noyce & Christie, 1985). Research reviewed at the beginning of this chapter shows that additional reading of literature has as much, if not more, of a facilitating effect on children's writing than the grammar study taught in many language arts textbooks.

As mentioned in Chapter 3, elementary teachers in Berkeley, California, have devised another solution (Buckley, 1986). They decided to use the basal reading system as the core of their reading curriculum. However, in order to provide time for the reading of literature and for integrated reading/writing activities, the teachers evaluated the basal reader lessons, workbooks, and dittos to determine what content was necessary for student growth in reading and what was optional (i.e., activities which provided practice on skills the children already had mastered or which had little relationship to actual reading). The optional content was eliminated, freeing time for reading literature and for writing activities. The teachers found that only three days a week needed to be scheduled for the basal system. The remaining two days could then be devoted to Individual Reading Strand activities.

■ Instructional Use of Models

The Individual Reading Strand provides students with many opportunities to encounter models of skilled writing. Teachers, however, have little control over the models to which the students are exposed or the specific characteristics of the writing upon which students focus. There are occasions when teachers may wish to center students' attention on specific writing skills or styles. The strategies described below are designed for these situations.

□ Blackburn's Modeling Strategy

Blackburn (1985) gives an excellent example of how instruction with models can be incorporated with process-oriented writing experiences. She first exposed the students in her first-grade class to several of Bill Martin's pattern books, stories that contain repetitious but entertaining events and sentence patterns. The books were read to the class and placed in the book corner so they could be read by the children. Children were also given many opportunities for free writing.

One of the books, *The Haunted House* (Holt, Rinehart & Winston, 1970), caught the attention of a boy named Shawn. In this book, the main character goes through each room of an old house and discovers it is empty. In the last room, the attic, the protagonist is surprised by his reflection in a mirror, exclaiming, "I went into the attic . . . I was there!" During one of the free writing periods, Shawn wrote his own version of the story:

> I came upon a haunted house.
> I opened the door.
> I saw a goblin. A-A-A-A-A
> I went in the T.V. room.
> I saw a devil. A-A-A-A-A
> I went in the kitchen.
> I saw Daddy Frankenstein. A-A-A-A-A
> I went upstairs.
> I saw a witch. She went E-E-E-E-E
> I thought they were bad,
> but they were good. (p. 4)*

This was the longest, most sophisticated story Shawn had written to date. The predictable sequence of events and sentence patterns borrowed from the model book made it much easier for Shawn to compose a story of his own. Note, however, that it is not an exact imitation of the Bill Martin story. The rooms are occupied by menacing creatures instead of being empty, and Shawn departs from the basic sentence pattern by adding noises made by the creatures.

Blackburn distinguishes between her use of models and more traditional approaches:

> Many approaches to writing encourage the use of adult models for children's writing. Usually the model is presented several times to the children and then they are directed to write their own story based on that model. What is different in this case is that Shawn did not try to craft a piece of writing around an adult model. He chose the model because it was appropriate for the piece of writing that he was conceiving. The conception of his own story came first, then he selected a model.
>
> (p. 5)

After writing a rough draft of his story, Shawn revised and refined during peer-editing sessions (more on this topic below in the Revising/ Editing section). It ultimately was published in book form and placed in the reading corner. Blackburn relates how, after hearing Shawn's story during an editing session or after reading the finished book, several students in the room then used *Shawn's* book as a model for other stories about haunted houses. So child-authored as well as adult-authored books can serve as models for children's writing.

Blackburn's strategy for using literary models is a simple one:

---

*Excerpts on pp. 110–111 from E. Blackburn, *Breaking ground: Teachers relate reading and writing in the elementary school.* Copyright © 1985 Heinemann. Used with permission.

1. Expose children to a wide variety of literature by reading books to children, having a large number of children's books in the classroom library, and providing ample time for children to read these books in class.

2. Provide ample opportunities for free writing and use a workshop approach (rough draft, peer editing, publishing) to help children write their own books.

3. Place the child-authored books in the classroom library so the children can read each other's stories.

In the process of writing their own stories, children will naturally use their favorite library books and peer-produced books as models. Once children have decided on the type of story they wish to write, the teacher can assist by suggesting books or child-authored stories to use as models. This strategy is a natural companion to the Individual Reading Strand procedure described above.

☐ *The Integrated Sentence-Modeling Cycle*

We have developed a more structured approach for using literary models: the Integrated Sentence-Modeling Cycle (ISMC). This strategy is designed to help acquaint primary-grade students with complex sentence patterns. Research has shown that one of the greatest limitations of young children's writing is lack of syntactic flexibility (Hunt, 1965). Children's written syntax trails considerably behind the syntax used in their oral language. When writing, they tend to be overly reliant on short, choppy simple sentences or on run-on compound sentences (see Figure 4.1). The ISMC is designed to familiarize children with more advanced sentence patterns so they will have a greater selection of word orderings to use while writing.

Like Blackburn's strategy, the ISMC utilizes children's literature and peer-produced books. The ISMC, however, is more selective in the trade books used and in the writing activities that follow from the books. Four types of children's books are utilized:

1. Books repeating complex syntactic structures, e.g., *If I Found a Wistful Unicorn,* by Ann Ashford (Peachtree, 1978).
2. Books containing repeated happenings which can be used as the basis of patterning activities, e.g., *Find the Cat,* by Elaine Livermore (Houghton Mifflin, 1973).
3. Wordless books for which a patterned text can be written, e.g., *The Bear and the Fly,* by Paula Winter (Crown, 1976).
4. Books containing simple, kernel sentences which can be expanded into complex structures, e.g., *At Mary Bloom's,* by Aliki (Greenwillow, 1976).

A list of books in the first category, those that repeat complex sentence patterns, are presented in the second part of the "Recommended Children's Book" section at the end of this chapter. The books in this list are appropriate for use with children in the primary grades. For an annotated listing of the other three types of books used in the ISMC, see Noyce and Christie (1981).

FIGURE 4.1   Sample of a Third-Grader's Choppy Syntax

The Hardest Problem I Ever Faced
One day I had a really hard math
problem I didn't now what to do. Then
I told my teacher about it then
she made it easyer. I still coudent
get it. She made it easyer again. The
last time, I got it. Then it was time
to go home at last, And at home, I had
a nother problem I didn't go home I
went to my freind michel's house, I
knocked on the door, Nobody was home so
I found my house It boked like
michel's house but it wasn't. My mom
and Dad were home I went into my bedroom
I rested I was very very tierd. And when
I was just about to lay down my sister
came in my bed room,

                        Jamie

The children's books are used in a four-step cycle to acquaint students
with a variety of complex sentence patterns. The following cycle is used:

Step 1. *Listening.*   The children listen while the teacher reads children's
         books that repeat a target syntactic structure.
Step 2. *Speaking.*   The children engage in oral games and activities in which
         the target pattern is repeated.
Step 3. *Writing.*   The children write stories in which they are encouraged to
         use the target sentence pattern. A workshop approach with peer
         editing and publication is employed.
Step 4. *Reading.*   The children read trade books (from Step 1) and child-
         authored books (from Step 3) which contain repeated examples of
         the target structure.

The Strategy Example illustrates how the ISMC could be used to give children experience with subordinate clauses beginning with *when.*

———————————— **STRATEGY EXAMPLE 4.1** ————————————

An Example ISMC Lesson

The following is an example of how the Integrated Sentence-Modeling Cycle can be used to acquaint primary-graders with subordinate clauses beginning with *when:*

1. Listening
Several trade books which contain repeated *when* constructions are read to the entire class. Titles include *Old Mother Middle Muddle,* by Bill Martin, Jr. (Holt, Rinehart & Winston, 1970); *That Makes me Mad,* by Steven Kroll (StarStream, 1980); and *The Shopping Basket,* by John Burningham (Crowell, 1980).

2. Speaking
Sentences containing *when* clauses (from the books that have just been read) are charted on the board, and the children take turns making their own oral sentences which follow the pattern. Next, the entire wordless picture book, *Pancakes for Breakfast,* by Tomie de Paola (Harcourt Brace Jovanovich, 1978), is shown on overhead transparencies. This acquaints the class with the sequence of the story. Then words are written for the story by having students contribute sentences orally, using as many *when* clauses as possible. The teacher writes the sentences on the transparencies as they are spoken. Once completed, the entire story is read out loud by the class. The story can be copied onto a copy of the actual book (use a paperback version), and this modified book placed in the reading corner. Below is one third-grade class's version of the story:

PANCAKES FOR BREAKFAST

Once upon a time there lived an old lady named Linda. Linda woke up, and the dog stretched and yawned. When she got up, she thought about eating pancakes for breakfast. When she got to the kitchen, she put on her apron, got out her recipe book, and thought of pancakes. She looked the recipe up. Then she got out a bowl and some flour. Linda sifted the flour. When she went to the refrigerator, she found she was out of eggs. She walked to the hen house and plucked the eggs. When she looked in the pitcher of milk, she found that it was empty. She went out the door and milked the cow. She poured the milk in a pitcher. Linda stirred the batter, and she churned some butter. The butter looked good! When she went to get the syrup bottle, she found that it was empty. She went to the neighbor's to borrow some syrup. She dreamed of pancakes all the way home. When she walked through the door, she was shocked! The pets had made a mess. Sadly she walked back to the neighbor's house. They fed her pancakes! Linda and her pets lived happily ever after.

The End

3. Writing

The events in *Pancakes for Breakfast* are reviewed from the previous lesson. Next, the writing topic "Cake for the Party" is introduced. The class brainstorms ingredients and other items needed to make a cake, and these words are recorded on the chalkboard. Then the children are given the following assignment: (a) write a story entitled "Cake for the Party"; (b) pattern it after the book *Pancakes for Breakfast;* and (c) use as many *when* sentences as possible. After writing their first drafts, the students meet in editing groups to revise and proofread their stories. The final drafts are published in several class books, which are placed in the reading corner. An example of a third-grader's story is presented in Figure 4.2.

4. Reading

The children are given an opportunity to read the trade books used in Step 1 and the peer-produced books from Step 3. In another activity, the children are divided into small groups, and each child is given a paper headed "When ____, that makes me mad." The children fill in the sentence, telling what makes them mad, and then illustrate their sentences in cartoon form. They read each other's cartoons as the session progresses.

The results of a pilot study showed that the ISMC led to significant gains in third-graders' writing fluency and use of complex sentence patterns (Noyce & Christie, 1983). Teachers reported that the children responded enthusiastically to the ISMC's varied activities, such as listening to children's books, writing cartoon captions and stories of their own, and reading peer-produced books. These positive experiences may have resulted in improved attitudes toward writing, which in turn were responsible for the ISMC students' gain in writing fluency. The interrelated nature of the activities also undoubtedly contributed to the program's effectiveness.

☐ ***Rhetorical Imitation***

Lodge (1984) has described a related strategy that can be used to introduce students to the syntax and style of adult authors. This strategy, known as Rhetorical Imitation, enables students to combine the skilled writer's syntax with their own ideas and language. Several steps are involved:

FIGURE 4.2 Kimberly's "Cake for the Party" Story

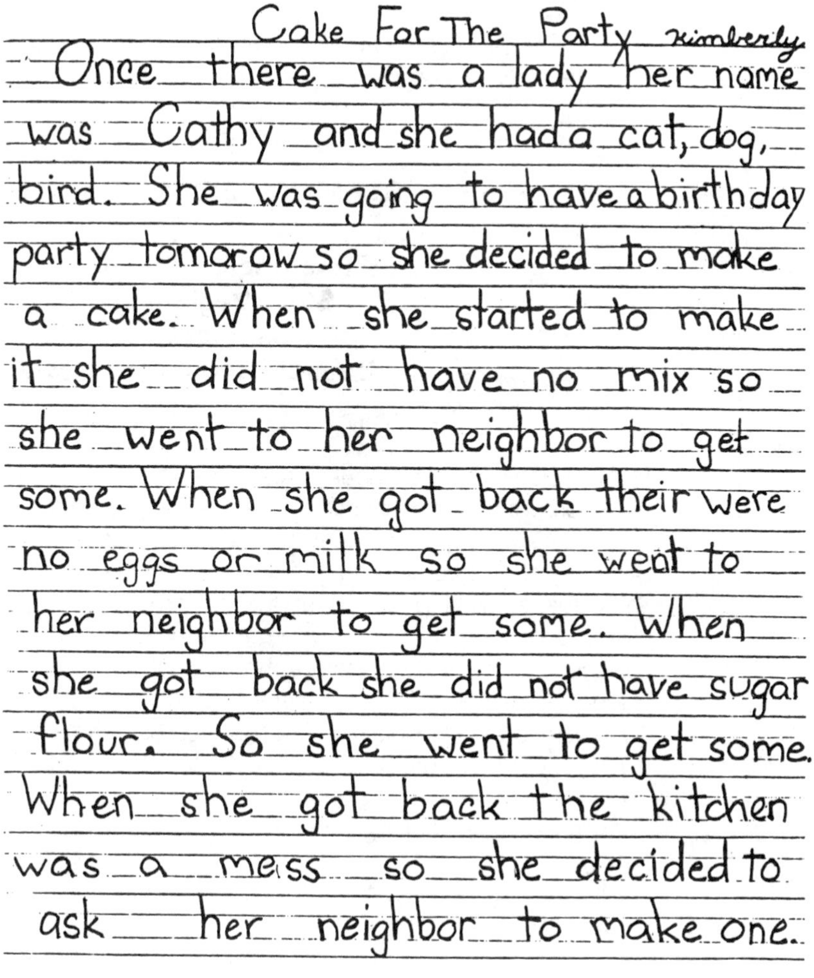

Cake For The Party   kimberly

Once there was a lady her name was Cathy and she had a cat, dog, bird. She was going to have a birthday party tomorow so she decided to make a cake. When she started to make it she did not have no mix so she went to her neighbor to get some. When she got back their were no eggs or milk so she went to her neighbor to get some. When she got back she did not have sugar flour. So she went to get some. When she got back the kitchen was a mess so she decided to ask her neighbor to make one.

1. A passage from a book appropriate for the age group is selected to illustrate a particular type of writing. For example, the first paragraphs of *Bunnicula,* by Deborah and James Howe (Avon, 1979) could be used to model story beginnings with intermediate-grade students. *Freaky Friday,* by Mary Rodgers (Harper & Row, 1972) would be a good choice for the upper grades.

2. The teacher helps the students note the organization and style of the original text.

3. The students then make lists of related details that could be used in their own stories.

4. The students are given a worksheet containing the original text on one side and a text frame on the other. This frame contains the important structure words—articles, tense indicators, connectives, and key phrases—which constitute the style the students will try to use. The students then fill in

the frame, using their own words. The Strategy Example illustrates a frame for *Bunnicula*.

5. The students are then given a composition assignment in which they are to write a story beginning of their own.

——————————— **STRATEGY EXAMPLE 4.2** ———————————

Rhetorical Imitation
Story Beginning:
Bunnicula,
by Deborah and James Howe

The book you are about to read was brought to my attention in a most unusual way. One Friday afternoon, just before closing time, I heard a scratching sound at the front door of my office. When I opened the door, there before me stood a sad-eyed, droopy-eared dog carrying a large, plain envelope in his mouth. He dropped it at my feet, gave me a soulful glance and with great, quiet dignity sauntered away.

Inside the envelope was the manuscript of the book you now hold in your hands, together with this letter:

Gentlemen:

The enclosed story is true. It happened in this very town, to me and the family with whom I reside. I have changed the names of the family to protect them, but in all other respects, everything you will read here is factual.

Allow me to introduce myself. My name is Harold. I come to write

The _____ you are about to read was brought to my attention in a most unusual way. _____ _____, just before _____, I heard _____ at the front door of my office. When I opened the door, there before me stood _____ ___ carrying a _____ _____. He dropped it _____ _____ and _____ _____.

Inside the _____ was ___ _____ _____, together with this letter:

Gentlemen:

The enclosed story is true. It happened _____, to _____ _____. I have _____ _____, but in all other respects, everything you will read here is factual.

Allow me to introduce myself. My name _____. I _____

merely by chance. My full-time occupation is dog. I live with Mr. and Mrs. X (called here the "Monroes") and their two sons: Toby, aged eight and Pete, aged ten. Also sharing our home is a cat named Chester, whom I am pleased to call my friend. We were a typical American family—and still are, though the events related to my story have, of course, had their effect on our lives.

I hope you will find this tale of sufficient interest to yourself and your readers to warrant its publication.

Sincerely,

Harold X.

_____. My full-time ___
_____. I live _____
_____
_____
_____. Also sharing our home is _____
_____, whom I _____
_____. We were _____
_____, though the events related to my story have, of course, _____.
I hope _____
_____
_____
___.

Sincerely,

_____

Source: Deborah Howe, "Editor's note from Bunnicula." Copyright © 1979 James Howe. Reprinted with the permission of Antheneum Publishers, an imprint of Macmillan Publishing Company.

Exercises similar to our *Bunnicula* example, which enables students to immitate accomplished writers by using their own ideas within the experts syntax, have been used successfully in both elementary and secondary classrooms. Excerpts from Laura Ingalls Wilder, William Manchester, John Steinbeck and Bruce Cotton have been recommended by Northridge Writing Project Teachers (Lodge, 1984) as sources of descriptions for more mature writers to emulate. Story beginnings are particularly effective texts to immitate because writers are likely to make maximum use of rhetorical devices and sensory description at this point to capture readers attention.

Lodge tells how one class of inner city fourth-graders immitated E. B. White's description of the comfortable barn in *Charlotte's Webb* (Harper & Row, 1952) while writing descriptions of their own classrooms, "The inner city children who wrote following this model described their school room using the same structure to convey the same sense of security and desirability of the barn in *Charlotte's Web.*" One of the most important aspects of the immitation experience is the satisfaction young writers feel as they compose interesting sentences patterned after those of their favorite writers.

Rhetorical Imitation has been found to increase the maturity of students' written syntax. Lodge reported that, as a result of this procedure, students tended to use longer sentences and more complex syntax in their own writing. She commented, " 'Wading around in someone else's syntax' has benefits for these students in discovering that they can use resources in syntax of which they were unaware" (1984, p. 6).

This strategy is compatible with a workshop approach to writing instruction. After writing the rough drafts peer editing groups meet to revise and refine their writing. In these groups, the students are exposed to each other's variations of the model. The final drafts are then published and read by the students.

The writing situations in the ISMC and Rhetorical Imitation are not as authentic as those in Blackburn's less structured strategy. In Blackburn's approach, the students first come up with their own ideas and purposes for writing and then choose a model that will help them accomplish their goals. In the ISMC and Rhetorical Imitation strategies, students are given writing assignments involving the imitation and extension of models. These latter approaches, however, are still process oriented, and have the advantage of being able to focus students' attention on particular characteristics and features of writing. It has been our experience that, while some children will take full advantage of an unstructured curriculum such as Blackburn's and independently seek out and become familiar with many types of writing, other students require more structured approaches. An ideal arrangement would be to rely primarily on the Individual Reading Strand coupled with Blackburn's process-oriented writing activities. Procedures such as the ISMC and Rhetorical Imitation can be used when needed (and perhaps only with selected children) to focus on particular types of literature or characteristics of writing.

☐ **Choose Your Own Adventure**

Another use of models to teach writing skills involves the Choose Your Own Adventure series by Edward Packard and R. A. Montgomery (Bantam Books). These popular multiple-storyline books get children to participate in the reading/composing process as they choose the events that happen in the story.

Packard and Montgomery (1985) have published a booklet that outlines a strategy whereby children can make up their own stories following the Choose Your Own Adventure pattern. The strategy involves three stages:

1. *Planning.*   Students are guided to make decisions about:
   a. the main theme of the story
   b. the type of story (realistic fiction, science fiction, historical fiction, or fantasy)
   c. the main character(s)

    d. the setting

    e. the main goal or challenge

    f. the plots (different things that might happen as the main characters try to obtain their goals)

    g. the choices that will occur

2. *Outlining.* Students are shown how to make a flowchart diagram of the story (see Figure 4.3).

3. *Writing.* Students are given tips for filling in the details of their outline and writing the multi-plot story.

A good way to use this strategy in the classroom is to first stock the class library with a good supply of Choose Your Own Adventure books. The teacher sparks interest in the books by reading one or two to the class, letting the students make choices about the course of the story. Then the students are given an opportunity to read the books. Students who are particularly attracted to this type of story are introduced to the Packard and Montgomery booklet and work as a small group to make a multi-storyline book of their own. Then students could write their own stories and use peer-editing groups to publish child-authored books for the class library. This same strategy can be used to acquaint students with a variety of literary

FIGURE 4.3 Sample Outline with Plot Summary for a Choose Your Own Adventure Story Source: Original conception by Edward Packard and R. A. Montgomery. Reprinted by permission of Bantam Books. All rights reserved.

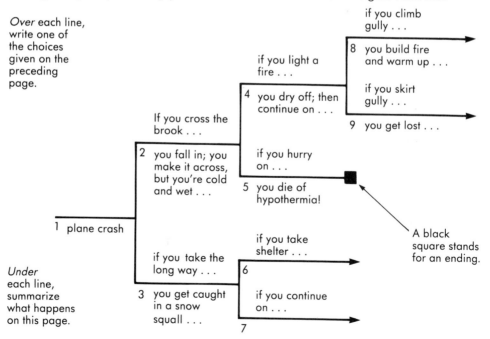

genres by simply using a different series of multi-storyline books, such as Choose Your Own Mysteries.

REVISING/EDITING

■ ■   Reading is more than just a source of models of writing; it is an indispensable part of the writing process. As Goodman and Goodman (1984) have pointed out, writers must be "their own readers, in fact, it's impossible to write without reading" (p. 156). This is because writers must constantly reread in order to review what they have written, to make sure they are accomplishing their writing goals, and to make revisions. Research has revealed that reviewing and revision are important parts of the writing process. Proficient writers have been found to reread and revise their writing more than less skilled writers (Bridwell, 1980; Sommers, 1980). In addition, good writers tend to focus their revisions on content and organization, whereas poor writers usually concentrate on mechanical features such as spelling and punctuation (Krashen, 1984).

Monitoring—the reading and evaluating of what one has written—plays a key role in reviewing and revision. In order for revision to occur, writers must first review (reread) their writing and realize that there are problems with an existing text that are blocking the attainment of writing goals. Aulls (1985) explains that, in order to activate revision, "there must be a spontaneous click of awareness within the learner that a problem in meaning construction exists" (p. 42). This "click" is the result of monitoring. Writers can then reword, expand, or reorganize the ideas they are attempting to communicate.

Donald Graves's (1983) research has shown that children focus their revising efforts on five types of problems: (a) spelling; (b) motor aesthetics (handwriting and appearance); (c) conventions (capitalization and punctuation); (d) topic and information; and (e) major revisions (reorganization, addition or deletion of information). Graves discovered that beginning writers tend to focus most of their attention on the mechanics of writing (spelling, motor aesthetics, and conventions). As writers mature, major revisions and revisions involving topics and information become more frequent. Not all children, however, progress beyond mechanical revision. Graves explains, "Some children are soon able to put the mechanical imbalances and discrepancies behind them and get on to information and topic focus. For others, the battle over mechanics is lifelong" (p. 236).

Teachers play an important role in the development of children's monitoring and revision strategies. If teachers attend primarily to mechanical features of students' writing, their students' monitoring and revising will tend to be limited to these surface features. On the other hand, if teachers provide experiences which focus students' attention on the content and organization of writing, their students will begin to make major revisions in order to better achieve their writing goals.

In the sections that follow, we will describe several strategies that can help children become better readers of their own writing and the writing of others. These procedures, which are all connected to the process approach to writing instruction, include Group-Paper Revision, Peer-Editing Groups, and the Press Conference.

■ Group Paper Revision

Before children can effectively evaluate their own writing or that of their peers, they must be trained in the revising/editing process. One approach teachers can use as early as second grade to help students discover the qualities of good writing is group revision of a paper written by the teacher that contains intentional faults. The fact that there is no peer ownership of this paper allows for a completely objective critiquing experience for the class.

Some teachers deliver humorous messages or describe actual events related to the class in their papers for group revision. The example below, which is about *Flat Stanley,* by Jeff Brown (Dell, 1964), illustrates a paper written to provide sentence-combining experiences and practice with the proper use of commas, while announcing that a popular book is available in the library.

THE RETURN OF THE BOY YO-YO

Stanley Lambchop found out that it's not so bad to be four feet tall a foot wide and a half inch thick. He and his mother were walking in the city not long ago. Her ring fell off her finger. It rolled through a sidewalk grating to the bottom of a dark hole. Clever Stanley saved the day! He took off his shoelaces. He tied them together. He tied the end to his belt. He made himself into a human yo-yo. He had his mother lower him through the bars of the grating. He rescued the ring.

Mrs. Clancy our school librarian says that *Flat Stanley* by Jeff Brown is now back in the library where you can check it out. Don't miss this funny book! It's about a boy hero. His bulletin board fell on him. It made him flat. He had a funny adventure.

The teacher, using an overhead projector and assuming the role of writer, reads through the entire paper with the class. The students begin the evaluation process by discussing their positive reactions to its content. Many Bay Area–National Writing Project teachers have experienced success with using the PQP technique (Lyons, 1981) in the evaluation process:

| P | (Praise): | What did you like about my paper? |
| Q | (Question): | What questions do you have about my paper? |

P   (Polish):   What kinds of polishing do you think my paper
                              needs before it can be published?

After several specific elements of good writing have been identified
through the praising process, the teacher asks the group for constructive
criticism and questions about confusing areas. By inviting suggestions from
the students, the teacher is modeling a step in the peer revision process for
later use when the students will ask their own peer groups for help with
parts of their papers. Elbow (1981) recommends that teachers ask two types
of questions at this point: (a) reader-based questions in which students are
asked to discuss the effects on the reader, e.g., "Which words or phrases
affected you most?" and (b) criterion-based questions in which they are
asked to identify certain qualities of writing, e.g., "Are the parts arranged in
proper sequence?" In *Writing with Power,* Elbow (1981) provides lists of
reader-based and criterion-based questions to guide older students in evaluating and revising writing; many are also appropriate for young children.

Students involved in the revising of "The Return of the Boy Yo-Yo"
might be expected to react positively to the title and enjoy the humor of the
brief adventure. It is likely that their first questions would be related to the
two series of short simple sentences. For example, someone might ask if this
was done intentionally to create a certain effect. This question could lead to
group revision through sentence combining. A possible outcome would be
the combining of sentences six through eleven and thirteen through sixteen
to read something like this:

> After making himself into a human yo-yo by taking off his shoelaces, tying
> them together, and tying the end to his belt, he rescued the ring by having his
> mother lower him through the bars of the grating.
>   Don't miss this book of funny adventures about a boy whose bulletin
> board fell on him, making him flat.

After content revisions have been made, proofreading skills needed
for the polishing stage are practiced. The purpose of Group Paper Revision
is to involve students in the diagnosis of particular mechanical errors.
Rather than dealing with the mechanics of writing in isolated exercises,
children have the advantage of encountering errors in a text. This strategy is
consistent with Weaver's (1979) theory that instruction in grammar should
take place at the rewriting stage when there is a felt need on the students'
part, rather than prior to writing. The proofreading of the "Return of the
Boy Yo-Yo" will necessitate reviewing rules for the use of commas following words in series and in apposition.

A notation system for proofreading is taught step-by-step during the
Group Paper Revision exercise. As students read and identify comma faults
in the paper, the teacher marks the errors on the overhead transparency,
using the proofreading symbols agreed upon by the class for peer editing.
The system used is a simplified version of the standard code taken from

Webster's dictionary; therefore, reteaching of the symbols will not be needed as children progress through the grades.

The Editing Marks proofreading system, designed for *Language for Daily Use* (Harcourt Brace Jovanovitch, 1983), is a good example of a code appropriate for primary-grade children, yet compatible with the standard code. This system is illustrated in Figure 4.4.

During the group-editing process, the sentences with comma omissions in "The Return of the Boy Yo-Yo" are marked as follows on the overhead:

> Stanley Lambchop found out that it's not so bad
> to be four feet tall∧ a foot wide∧ and a half inch thick.
> Mrs. Clancy∧ our school librarian∧ says . . .

Group paper revising/editing exercises have been adapted by teachers in a number of ways, ranging from the "daily edit" to "mixed drill." In the daily edit, one sentence containing a mechanical error appears each day on the chalkboard. As the first task of the day, students read this sentence and revise it in their journals. The teacher then leads a discussion about the rule which applies. Mixed drill is a more comprehensive exercise in which a paper containing a variety of errors is used as the basis of a grammar lesson. The end result of experiences in Group Paper Revision is competence in peer revising/editing and, eventually, in self-editing.

■ Peer-Editing Groups

Children in the second grade and above, who have been trained in revision and proofreading techniques, possess the necessary tools to begin peer-group editing/revising activities. Groups of three or four children are structured by the teacher, taking into consideration varying abilities, so that students with the capability to spot errors are included in each group. The teacher and several pretrained children model the process for the class through role playing a peer-group session. In addition to the techniques they have learned through experiences with Group Paper Revision (see the previous section), children require procedural guidelines to follow as they engage in the task of revising and/or editing each other's papers. They are given specific instructions that remind them to make useful, constructive suggestions for improving the compositions. In order to facilitate the process, teachers often provide written forms which guide and structure the students' responses.

Crowhurst (1979) maintains that having children give feedback in writing during initial editing sessions lessens the likelihood of negative interaction or argument between writers and responders. Oral responses are effective after children have become comfortable with the peer-group process.

FIGURE 4.4 The Editing Marks Proofreading System   Source: Excerpt from *Language for Daily Use,* Phoenix Edition, Level 7, Silver, by Dr. Dorothy S. Strickland. Copyright © 1983 by Harcourt Brace Jovanovich, Inc. and reprinted by permission of the publisher.

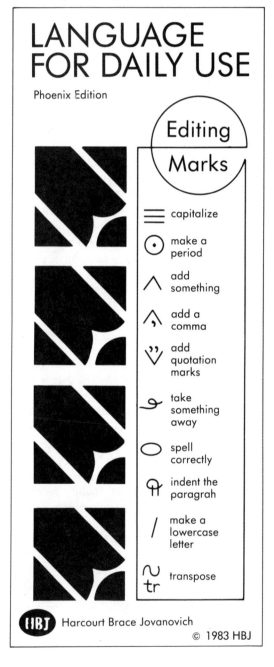

Crowhurst (1979) conducted a writing workshop experiment with third- and fifth-grade peer groups in which children read each group member's paper and wrote comments on a form that had three sections for responses: (a) encouraging responses; (b) comments on content; and (c) suggestions for improvement. The following sets of comments, written by fifth-graders who responded to the same composition about a shipwrecked character on a tropical island, illustrate the advantages of peer feedback on writing:

> Very well worded. Lots of expression. I liked the parts about the bear and how he acted. Where did you get all the stuff from like the gun and shells? How did Lorrie get there. What did you feed the bear? Why didn't you make another camp?

> That bear part was good. So was the barrel part. When you met Lorrie was another good part in your diary. Bad points: First, spelling mistakes. It was sort of mixed up. One day you were on the other side of the island, the next day you were in Toronto. Who is J. J.? Where did you get the shells for the gun?

> Who's Lorrie? How did you get home to Toronto in the last entry? What happened to Lorrie? Why was it quite a task to get to shore? Why did you take the baby cub home? Is Lorrie the cub or a Human? I felt sorry for you and Lorrie being the only ones on the island with not much food and water. A few words I couldn't understand because spelt wrong like freind. What does J. J. stand for? (Crowhurst, 1979, p. 760)

Notice the consistency in their comments on the good aspects of the story and the way in which weaknesses in the story line, organization, and mechanics were pointed out. This type of criticism is much more constructive than the "red pencil" editing traditionally done by teachers. If the author of the "Island" story did act on some of these suggestions, the result would have been a much better composition. In addition, the three reviewers benefited from the Peer-Editing Group experience, being more likely to spot the same problems when reviewing/editing their own writing.

Crowhurst reported that the children in her experiment enjoyed both writing for their peers and responding to them. Several commented that they got ideas for writing from their friends' stories, and many asked the teacher to let them write more often. It was concluded that peer-group experiences motivated the children to do their best writing.

☐ ***Crowhurst's Circle Strategy***
The peer-group format used in Crowhurst's writing workshop requires students to pass their stories around in a circle so that each child's paper is

read by everyone in the group. The children write their comments on a form attached to the paper; therefore, each writer receives independent feedback from each individual in the group. An appropriate form for use with elementary-grade Peer-Editing Groups is presented in Figure 4.5.

☐ *Donaldson's Triad Strategy*

Donaldson (1982) describes success using a similar approach with upper-grade students. Students are grouped in triads to read each other's writing. Each writer's paper is read by two peers, for the purpose of offering constructive comments about content and mechanics. The readers mark specific lines on the paper on which they wish to comment, one reader using letters on the left-hand side of the paper and the other using numbers on the right-hand side. The readers then write their comments on a blank piece of paper, using the same numbers or letters to key their responses to specific lines in the writer's paper (see Figure 4.6). This approach has the advantage of calling the writer's attention to the exact location of technical errors without defacing the composition. In addition, it provides two independent sets of feedback.

FIGURE 4.5 PQP Form for Peer-Group Editing

Writer _____
Editor _____
Title _____

PQP = Praise, Question, Polish

1. PRAISE: These are the things I particularly liked about the paper —

2. QUESTION: I have these questions about this paper —

3. POLISH: I have these suggestions to make the paper better —

FIGURE 4.6   Donaldson's Triad Editing Strategy

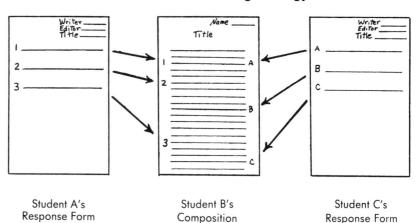

| Student A's | Student B's | Student C's |
| Response Form | Composition | Response Form |

☐ *Separate Revising and Proofreading Groups*

Teachers of primary- and intermediate-grade children may prefer to separate the revising of content from the editing/proofreading process by using response groups for feedback on content only (i.e., revision), and assigning the final proofreading of all papers for mechanical errors to special editorial committees. This not only simplifies the peer-group process to accommodate shorter attention spans but also provides an excellent vehicle for teaching grammar and mechanics. As children take their turns being the "experts" on proofreading committees, they are responsible for finding errors, reviewing or learning the rules, and applying their knowledge.

Cramer (1977) recommends that teachers appoint "specific skills" groups for a designated period of time. For example, one group is responsible for spelling, one for punctuation, another for syntax. All the children in the class serve, in turn, on groups dealing with the various proofreading functions, gaining experience with conventions of writing through editing experiences. Each group has a leader, or consulting editor, who can perform the task accurately, providing a model for less skilled students. Cramer urges teachers to place a proofreading chart in a prominent place in the classroom to help children edit their own material as well as that of others. Questions to appear on the chart include:

> Is my paper headed correctly?
> Did I capitalize the correct words?
> Did I indent for each paragraph?
> Do I have margins?
> Is each word spelled correctly?
> Did I use correct punctuation?
> Did I tell my story in sequence?
> Did I use new and interesting words?

Have I said what I wanted to say?
Do all the parts of the story fit together?
Do I have a good beginning and ending? (p. 84)

Follow-up evaluation of peer-group sessions is essential to the development of good revision procedures. Teachers of older students have reported success with individual feedback forms on which each student rates the performance of the group as Extremely Helpful, Helpful, or Somewhat Helpful. Each student also responds to such questions as, "What two specific suggestions did your group make about improving your paper?"; "What particular strengths did your group point out about your paper?"; and "How well did your group listen to the oral reading of your paper?" This feedback, combined with the teacher's observations made while circulating among the groups as they worked, are the basis of follow-up discussions on procedures. The tape recorder is a useful device for gathering information about peer-group functioning; examples of activity that is worthy of notice can be played back for the class during evaluation sessions.

■ Press Conference

The five-minute Press Conference, held regularly (weekly or biweekly) during writing workshops and independent reading time, is an effective means for improving reading and writing skills. The purpose of this kind of conference is for teacher and student to talk together about writing and reading currently in progress. Instead of conferring after a completed paper has been evaluated by the teacher, they meet to discuss writing at various stages, from first draft to nearly final version. The emphasis of the conference is on communicating ideas and clarifying content, as well as helping the students achieve mastery of the conventions of writing. Reading skills are practiced through the writers' oral reading of passages from their papers as the teacher listens. By seeing samples of the students' writing and by hearing them read regularly in the Press Conference, teachers can diagnose skill needs and provide appropriate follow-up practice for individual children.

The conference usually begins with the writer reading his or her paper while the teacher listens. This reading often enables students to discover some of their own errors, giving them experience in reviewing (monitoring) their writing through reading. It also allows the writer to take responsibility for the initial direction of the conference by asking the first question or making the first comment. The teacher's role is to provide feedback on the content of the paper, to help the child improve it through revision, and to assist in locating problem areas. The instructional aspect of the discussion may focus on one or two particular features of the writing or on errors the student identifies. With first drafts, the emphasis is on content. Mechanical skills are dealt with later, as the paper progresses toward its final version. In some classrooms a Press Conference follows peer-group revising/editing as another step in the writing process. Both the writer and teacher take notes during the conference, the writer jotting down suggestions for revision and the teacher recording diagnostic information related to both reading and writing.

Graves (1983) urges teachers to allow children to do most of the talking during a conference by encouraging them to take charge as authors, initiating questions and comments. According to Graves, the questions teachers ask should be predictable, process-oriented questions which facilitate children's thinking about how they function as writers. Talking to children as fellow writers lets them know that their point of view is important. By discussing the processes writers use, children develop a writer's vocabulary, which helps them to talk clearly with each other and with their teacher about writing. The understanding and use of precise terms like "draft," "lead," and "tighten" eventually have an effect on the quality of the students' writing. Students should be instructed in the use of arrows, asterisks, and numbering to insert material, and shown how to "cut and paste." As Krashen (1984) and Smith (1983) point out, these technical aspects of the writing/revising process cannot be learned through reading; they must be taught to students.

Sixth-grade teacher Connie Russell (1983) found that the following list of questions was helpful as a guide for conferencing with her young writers:

1. What is your favorite part?
2. What problems are you having?
3. Which part are you having trouble with?
4. How did you feel?
5. Does your writing end abruptly? Does it need a closing?
6. Do you show feelings or events with specific examples or do you only tell about them?
7. Does your lead sentence "grab" your audience?
8. Do your paragraphs seem to be in the right order?
9. Is each paragraph on one topic?
10. Can you leave out parts that repeat or that fail to give details about your subject?
11. Can you combine some sentences?
12. Can you use precise verbs such as "sprinted" instead of "ran quickly" in places?
13. What do you plan to do next with this piece of writing? (p. 335)

Teachers are reminded that these are scaffolding questions intended to provide a supporting structure for Press Conferences. They facilitate the teacher's "leading from behind." Effective conferences progress rapidly beyond the generic questions of the teacher to the individual skill needs of each writer.

SUMMARY

■ ■   This chapter has examined three ways in which reading can contribute to the acquisition of skills needed in the composing and revising/editing stages of the writing process. First, reading provides opportunities for children to identify with other writers through such strategies as the Author's Chair, Getting Inside the Author's Head, Professional Writers Tell Them How, and Book Characters Who Write. Such experiences can ultimately lead to children's realization that they belong to the author's club—a necessary prerequisite for reading like a writer (Smith, 1983). Once children think of themselves as authors, they begin to unconsciously learn about the technical and stylistic features of the texts they read, which leads to enhanced writing competence.

Reading also provides children with models of skilled writing which they can assimilate through wide reading (as a result of reading like a writer) or purposefully imitate through strategies that focus on particular models. We suggested the Individual Reading Strand as an effective way to provide for the abundant reading of trade books in the classroom. We also described several instructional strategies, including Blackburn's Modeling Strategy, The Integrated Sentence-Modeling Cycle, and Rhetorical Imitation, that teachers can use to model specific writing skills and conventions.

Finally, reading plays an important role in the revising/editing stage of the writing process. In order to polish and refine initial drafts into publishable works, writers must be able to read and evaluate their own writing, both in terms of content/organization and mechanical errors. We described several strategies for helping students become better reviewers and revisers of their own and other people's writing. Teacher-guided Group Paper Revision is a good starting point for teaching children the basics of the reviewing/editing process. Next, Peer-Editing Groups can be used to teach students how to make constructive comments and criticisms about other children's writing. The teacher-child Press Conference can be used, separately or in conjunction with peer editing, to help children monitor and revise their own writing. These strategies not only enhance children's ability to read and revise writing, but are also a context in which teachers can directly teach or review specific writing skills (e.g., the instruction about punctuation that occurred in the Group Paper Revision of "The Return of the Boy Yo-Yo"). Such instruction, done in connection with a real piece of writing, is often more effective than isolated skill drills.

As was the case in Chapter 3, the strategies described in this chapter contribute to growth in reading as well as in writing. The sharing that occurs in the Author's Chair can be a powerful motivator for recreational reading. Children want to read books so they have something to share in the Author's Chair, and the reading that takes place in the chair acts as an advertisement for the books being read, leading other children to want to read the same books. The extensive recreational reading that takes place in the Individual Reading Strand will, of course, also benefit students' reading by allowing them to practice and consolidate skills learned in isolated skill exercises. In addition, many skills such as sight vocabulary, phonics, and knowledge of word meanings will be learned inductively in the process of wide reading. Similarly, most of the modeling strategies involve reading practice. In the Integrated Sentence-Modeling Cycle, for example, children read both trade and peer-produced books that repeat complex syntactic structures. Our research with third-graders found that the ISMC not only resulted in improved writing performance but also in higher scores on a standardized reading-comprehension test. Finally, the reviewing/revising strategies offer opportunities for students to improve their oral reading abilities.

RECOMMENDED CHILDREN'S BOOKS

Part 1
Trade Books about
Children Who Write

Blos, Joan W. *A Gathering of Days.* Scribner's, 1979.

> This is the fictitious two-year journal of a New England girl, who was thirteen in 1830 when she started writing it. It is an informative, moving, and sensitive book for the mature reader. (Ages 13 and up)

Cleary, Beverly. *Dear Mr. Henshaw.* Dell (Yearling), 1984.

> Leigh Botts learns to enjoy writing through his relationship with an author. This is a funny book to read to a class. (Ages 11–14)

Cleary, Beverly. *The Ramona Quimby Diary.* Morrow, 1984.

> Ramona's experiences, sprinkled throughout the pages, help the owner of this personal journal to think of things to write about. This spiral-bound diary contains fill-in sections to get the writer started, blank pages with wide lines for easy writing, and "Ramona" stickers to mark special days. (Ages 8–12)

Giff, Patricia Reilly. *Loretta P. Sweeny, Where Are You?* Dell (Yearling), 1983.

> Abby and Potsie of Giff's *Have You Seen Hyacinth Macaw?* try to solve another mystery. Abby's memo books add humor throughout the story of their search for a possible victim of the dangerous Loretta P. Sweeny. (Ages 12–15)

Hahn, Mary Downing. *Daphne's Book.* Clarion, 1984.

> Jessica, the best writer in her class, and Daphne, the best artist, are assigned the task of writing a book for the seventh-grade "Write a Book" contest. They decide to write a fairy tale about Jessica's stuffed mouse collection. Jessica develops a close friendship with the not-so-well-liked Daphne in the process. (Ages 10–14)

Harris, Rosemary. *Zed.* Faber, 1984.

> In response to a request from his teacher, Zed writes an exciting story about being held hostage by Arab terrorists as a child. (Ages 12–15)

Henkes, Kevin. *Return to Sender*. Greenwillow, 1984.

When Whitaker Murphy writes a letter to his television hero, Frogman, he gets an answer from Barney, the mail carrier, and an entertaining story of their correspondence follows. (Ages 10–14)

Hess, Lilo. *Diary of a Rabbit*. Scribner's, 1982.

Written in diary form, this book is an informative source about rabbits and a good model for helping students keep observational journals. (Ages 9–14)

Hunter, Mollie. *Hold On to Love*. Harper & Row, 1984.

Bridie McShane's love for writing helps her endure some trials and opens the door to her friendship with Peter McKinley and a love story. (Ages 12 and up, mature readers)

Klein, Robin. *Penny Pollard's Diary*, illustrated by Ann James. Oxford/Merrimack, 1984.

Penny, a horse lover who regularly writes complaints about people in her diary, develops a friendship with a fascinating, nonconforming eighty-one-year-old woman while visiting a nursing home, and loses her biases against old people. (Ages 10–14)

Klein, Robin. *Penny Pollard's Letters*. Oxford/Merrimack, 1984.

Penny writes regularly to both friends and enemies, expressing her dislike for boys and babies and demonstrating her sense of humor. (Ages 10–14)

Lowry, Lois. *Anastasia Krupnik*. Houghton Mifflin, 1979.

Anastasia's father is a writer, and she is a "chip off the old block." She claims that she would never have made it to age eleven without the green spiral notebook in which she keeps her journal. This is one of a series of *Anastasia* books, all of which are hilarious. (Ages 10–15)

Lowry, Lois. *Anastasia, Ask Your Analyst*. Houghton Mifflin, 1984.

Anastasia is involved in a science fair project, recording her observations of two gerbils in a journal, along with her comments about her family and Sigmund Freud. (Ages 12–15)

Springstubb, Tricia. *Which Way to the Nearest Wilderness?* Little, Brown, 1984.

Two girls open a "poison pen" letter business, writing "When You Care Enough to Send the Very Worst" cards and selling them to their friends. This is a funny, yet touching, family and friendship story. (Ages 11–14)

Part 2:
Children's Books That Repeat Complex Sentence Patterns

If Clauses:

Ashford, Ann. *If I Found a Wistful Unicorn*. Peachtree, 1978.

Graham, John. *I Love You, Mouse*. Harcourt Brace Jovanovich, 1976.

Higgins, Don. *Papa's Going to Buy Me a Mockingbird*. Seabury, 1968.

Mayer, Mercer. *If I Had . . .* Dial, 1968.

Mizamura, Kazue. *If I Were a Mother*. Crowell, 1968.

_____. *If I Built a Village*. Crowell, 1971.

Most, Bernard. *If the Dinosaurs Came Back*. Harcourt Brace Jovanovich, 1978.
Paterson, Diane. *IF I Were a Toad*. Dial, 1977.
Silverstein, Shel. *Where the Sidewalk Ends* (Poems: "One Inch Tall" and "If I Had a Brontosaurus"). Harper & Row, 1974.
Vogel, Ilse-Margret. *The Don't be Scared Book*. Starstream, 1980.
Waber, Bernard. *"You Look Ridiculous," Said the Rhinoceros to the Hippopotamus*. Houghton Mifflin, 1966.
Williams, Barbara. *If He's My Brother*. Prentice-Hall, 1976.
Young, Miriam. *If I Flew a Plane*. Lothrup, 1970.

That Clauses:
Carrier, Lark. *There Was a Hill*. Picture Book Studio, 1985.
Zolotow, Charlotte. *It's Not Fair*. Harper & Row, 1976.

When Clauses:
Burningham, Jon. *The Shopping Basket*. Crowell, 1980.
Kellogg, Steven. *Much Bigger than Martin*. Dial, 1976.
Kroll, Steven. *That Makes Me Mad*. Starstream, 1980.
Martin, Bill, Jr. *Old Mother Middle Muddle*. Holt, Rinehart & Winston, 1970.
Miller, Edna, *Mousekin Takes a Trip*. Prentice-Hall, 1976.
Rylant, Cynthia. *When I Was Young in the Mountains*. E. P. Dutton, 1982.

Where Clauses:
Baten, Helen, and von Molnar, Barbara. *I'm Going to Build a Supermarket One of These Days*. Holt, Rinehart & Winston, 1970.
Keats, Ezra Jack. *Over in the Meadow*. Four Winds, 1972.

Who Clauses:
Aardema, Verna. *Why Mosquitoes Buzz in People's Ears*. Dial, 1975.
Brown, Ruth. *The Big Sneeze*. Lothrup, 1985.
Kuskin, Karla. *A Boy Had a Mother Who Bought Him a Hat*. Houghton Mifflin, 1976.
Preston, Edna. *One Dark Night*. Viking, 1969.
Raskin, Ellen. *Ghost in a Four-Room Apartment*. Atheneum, 1969.
Wescott, Nadine. *I Know an Old Lady Who Swallowed a Fly*. Little, Brown, 1980.

REFERENCES

Aulls, M. W. (1985). Understanding the relationship between reading and writing. *Educational Horizons, 64* (1), 39–44.
Bagford, J. (1985). What ever happened to individualized reading? *The Reading Teacher, 39,* 190–193.
Blackburn, E. (1985). Stories never end. In J. Hansen, T. Newkirk, & D. Graves (Eds.), *Breaking ground: Teachers relate reading and writing in the elementary school* (pp. 3–13). Portsmouth, NH: Heinemann.
Bridwell, L. S. (1980). Revising strategies in

twelfth grade students' transactional writing. *Research in the Teaching of English, 14,* 197–222.

Buckley, M. H. (1986). When teachers decide to integrate the language arts. *Language Arts, 63,* 369–377.

Butler, A., & Turbill, J. (1984). *Towards a reading-writing classroom.* Portsmouth, NH: Heinemann.

Calkins, L. M. (1986). How reading can inspire writing. *Learning, 14*(5), 68–72.

Charlton, J. (Ed.) (1985). *The writer's quotation book.* Wainscott, NY: The Pushcart Press.

Cramer, R. L. (1977). Pass out the red pencils. *Instructor, 87*(1), 80–84.

Crowhurst, M. (1979). The writing workshop: An experiment in peer response to writing. *Language Arts, 56,* 757–762.

Donaldson, C. (1982). The O'Hare method, or how to grade 90 papers in 31 minutes. In P. S. Taylor, F. Peitaman, & J. McCuen (Eds.), *In the trenches* (pp. 67–71). Los Angeles: University of California Press.

Eckhoff, B. (1984). How reading affects children's writing. In J. M. Jensen (Ed.), *Composing and comprehending* (pp. 105–114). Urbana, IL: ERIC/RCS.

Elbow, P. (1981). *Writing with power.* New York: Oxford University Press.

Flower, L., & Hayes, J. (1980). The cognition of discovery: Defining a rhetorical problem. *College Composition and Communication, 31,* 21–32.

Goodman, K., & Goodman, Y. (1984). Reading and writing relationships: Pragmatic functions. In J. M. Jensen (Ed.), *Composing and comprehending* (pp. 155–164). Urbana, IL: ERIC/RCS.

Graves, D. (1983). *Writing: Teachers and children at work.* Exeter, NH: Heinemann.

Graves, D., & Hansen, J. (1984). The author's chair. In J. M. Jensen (Ed.), *Composing and comprehending* (pp. 69–76). Urbana, IL: ERIC/RCS.

Hansen, J. (1983). Authors respond to authors. *Language Arts, 60,* 970–976.

Hillocks, G., Jr. (1986). *Research on written composition: New directions for teaching.* Urbana, IL: ERIC/RCS.

Hunt, K. W. (1965). *Grammatical structures written at three grade levels.* Champaign, IL: National Council of Teachers of English.

Jaggar, A. M., Carrara, D. H., & Weiss, S. E. (1986). The influence of reading on children's narrative writing (and vice versa). *Language Arts, 63,* 292–300.

Krashen, S. D. (1984). *Writing: Research, theory, and applications.* New York: Pergamon.

Lodge, H. C. (1984, Fall). Responsive writing: Connecting literature and composition. *Los Angeles Basin Writing Council Newsletter,* pp. 1–7.

Lyons, B. (1981). The PQP method of responding to writing. *English Journal 70*(3), 42–43.

Macrorie, K. (1973). *Telling writing.* New York: Hayden.

McCracken, R. A. (1971). Initiating sustained silent reading. *Journal of Reading, 14,* 521–524, 582–583.

Noyce, R. M. (1985). Book children who write. *Kansas Journal of Reading, 1*(1), 45–47.

Noyce, R. M., & Christie, J. F. (1981). Using literature to develop children's grasp of syntax. *The Reading Teacher, 35,* 298–304.

Noyce, R. M., & Christie, J. F. (1983). Effects of an integrated approach to grammar instruction on third graders' reading and writing. *Elementary School Journal, 84,* 63–69.

Noyce, R. M., & Christie, J. F. (1985). R/X for better reading and writing: Read like a writer. *Kansas Journal of Reading, 1*(1), 3–6.

Packard, E., & Montgomery, R. A. (1985). *How to write a book like a Choose Your Own Adventure book.* New York: Bantam.

Plummer, J. (1984). A gift from Maine. *Instructor, 94*(4), 36–39.

Russell, C. (1983). Putting research into practice: Conferencing with young writers. *Language Arts, 60,* 333–340.

Ryan, S. M. (1986). Do prose models really teach writing? *Language Arts, 63,* 284–290.

Smith, F. (1983). Reading like a writer. *Language Arts, 60,* 558–567.

Sommers, N. (1980). Revision strategies of student writers and experienced adult writers. *College Composition and Communication, 31,* 378–388.

Stotsky, S. (1983). Research on reading/writing

relationships: A synthesis and suggested directions. *Language Arts, 60,* 627–642.

U. S. Department of Education. (1986). *First lessons.* Washington, DC: U. S. Government Printing Office.

Veatch, J. (1966). *Reading in the elementary school.* New York: Wiley.

Weaver, C. (1979). *Grammar for teachers: Perspectives and definitions.* Urbana, IL: National Council of Teachers of English.

5

Combining Writing with Traditional Reading Activities I

Prereading Readiness and Guided Reading

Comprehension is dependent on the schema available to the reader, and writing is a schema building process.
—Marino, Gould, & Haas, The effects of writing as a prereading activity on delayed recall of narrative text

Chapters 3 and 4 described how reading can promote writing by supplementing the prewriting, composing, and revising/editing stages of the writing process. Given the reciprocal and mutually enhancing relationship between reading and writing, it is hardly surprising that the converse is also true: writing can facilitate reading. This the topic of the next two chapters.

In describing strategies for using writing to promote growth in reading, we have used the Directed Reading Activity (DRA) as an organizer. The DRA, first recommended by Betts (1946), is the basic lesson format used by most basal reader series. Since basal readers comprise the predominant approach to reading instruction in the elementary grades, we believe that structuring writing for reading strategies in this manner will simplify the incorporation of writing into regular reading activities.

The DRA traditionally has four stages: (a) prereading readiness; (b) guided reading; (c) skill building; and (d) enrichment. The *prereading readiness* stage is used to prepare students for reading a passage. This usually includes introducing new vocabulary and relating students' past experiences to the topic of the passage. If a topic is totally new to students, an effort is made to build their background knowledge about it prior to reading.

The *guided reading* phase is when the story is actually read by the students. The teacher begins by setting purposes for reading so students will focus on important elements in the story. Then the students read the passage (or a portion of it) silently. A discussion of the reading ensues, with the teacher asking questions which focus on the purposes set forth prior to reading. Oral rereading, which Betts designated as a separate step, is often used in conjunction with these postreading discussions. In the primary grades, this cycle of setting purposes, reading, and discussion is often repeated every few pages of the story. As children progress through the grades, the amount of text in each cycle increases until finally entire stories are read without interruption.

Skill-building activities are used to teach and practice the many sub-skills which a basal series considers necessary for proficient reading, including sight vocabulary, word meanings, word-attack skills such as phonics and contextual analysis, basic and higher-order comprehension skills, and study skills. These activities usually take the form of small group lessons, workbook pages, and loose-leaf ditto exercises.

Finally, most basal lessons include an *enrichment* section, which provides opportunities for children to extend their experiences with stories through related readings, writing activities, dramatization, and art projects. As explained in Chapter 3, this is the part most often neglected because of pressure to cover all the skill activities included in each basal lesson.

This chapter describes how writing can be incorporated into the prereading readiness and guided reading stages of the DRA. In particular, it focuses on strategies that use writing to activate and build students' prior knowledge of story topics and that helps students set their own purposes for reading. A strategy that uses writing to promote high-quality postreading discussions is also included.

Strategies for incorporating writing into the other stages of the DRA are covered elsewhere in this book. Using writing to supplement basal skill-building activities is the topic of Chapter 6. We have already presented strategies for using writing with basal enrichment activities in Chapter 3. Some of the drama activities in Chapter 8 can also be used to enrich basal stories.

The Strategies described in these next two chapters are not restricted to use with basal readers. Most of the activities can also be used with content area passages and, as several of our examples illustrate, with shared reading experiences involving children's literature.

PREREADING READINESS

■ ■   The prereading readiness phase of the Directed Reading Activity (DRA)
commonly includes vocabulary instruction and teacher-initiated discussions
to assess and activate students' prior knowledge about the topic of the
passage to be read. These readiness activities are almost always oral in
nature. There may be some writing, but it is usually done by the teacher on
the chalkboard, chart paper, or overhead transparency. Students rarely
write, and if they do, their writing is usually limited to writing vocabulary
words in sentences.

As an example, we will use the prereading readiness activities from
"Bears Aren't Everywhere," a lesson focused on in Chapter 3. This story,
which is in the Ginn 720 series third-grade reader, *How It Is Nowadays,* is
about how a boy named Danny hears a noise in the woods and imagines it is
caused by a bear. The teacher's edition instructs teachers to establish
students' background for the story: "Ask the children if they have ever
heard noises that frightened them or thought they saw something that
frightened them. Have the children describe the kinds of noises they heard,
what they thought caused the noise, and what actually caused the noise"
(p. 154). This type of discussion is intended to activate the children's prior
knowledge about imaginary fears.

In our discussion of schema theory in Chapter 1, we explained why
activation of text-relevant prior knowledge or schemata is an important
prerequisite to reading comprehension. In order to understand text information, readers must assimilate that information into their prior knowledge, the schemata they already possess. Readers must also make use of
their store of prior knowledge in order to make inferences. Research has
shown that accurate, text-relevant prior knowledge facilitates recall of text
information (Bransford & Johnson, 1973; Langer, 1982). It should be
noted, however, that prior knowledge is not always beneficial. Lipson
(1984) found that erroneous or contradictory prior knowledge can interfere
with learning new information while reading. It is very important, therefore, that teachers assess students' knowledge of text topics prior to reading,
help them to activate relevant schemata, and assist them in resolving conflicts between existing knowledge and new information in the text.

Oral discussions, such as the one recommended for use with "Bears
Aren't Everywhere," are one means for teachers to activate and assess
students' prior knowledge. Writing activities are another. We explained in
Chapter 1 that writing involves the use of the same schemata used in
reading. In order to write on a topic, the writer must activate and build
relationships between schemata relevant to that topic. Thus, writing can be
an excellent means of getting students to generate text-related schemata
during the readiness phase of the DRA. Prereading writing activities have

the additional advantages of: (a) providing teachers with a permanent record of students' prereading knowledge about passage topics; and (b) giving students valuable writing practice.

Little research has been done on the effectiveness of writing as a prereading activity, but the findings of one recent study are quite encouraging. Marino et al. (1985) gave one group of fourth-graders a writing assignment related to a text about pioneers on the Oregon Trail. They were asked to pretend that they were living during the pioneer days and were on the way to Oregon. They were then asked to write a letter describing their experiences. Control subjects were given a non-text-related writing assignment which involved writing about something interesting which happened to them. Both groups then read the pioneer passage, and their recall was assessed twenty-four hours later. The results showed that subjects who did the text-related writing assignment, the letter about pioneer experiences, scored significantly higher on the recall test than controls. The facilitative effect of the prereading writing assignment was particularly strong for below-average readers. The researchers speculated that the text-related writing assignment may have contributed to the students' reading comprehension both by activating prior knowledge about pioneers and by arousing personal interest in the topic. They concluded, "The assignment to write before reading appeared to elicit the kinds of behavior that good readers experience spontaneously: make predictions, ask questions, and create an investment in 'want to know' " (Marino et al., 1985, p. 203). In other words, the writing assignment made the students more active readers.

In the sections that follow, we present three strategies that use writing as a means for activating prior knowledge and arousing students' interest in passage topics: Semantic Mapping, Prereading Writing Assignments, and Brainwriting. These activities are not intended to completely replace traditional prereading discussions. The writing activities have the disadvantage of taking more time than oral discussions, and such discussions are valuable in their own right. However, the strategies described below can be used on an occasional basis to take advantage of writing's schema-activating potential and to provide students with additional writing practice.

■ Semantic Mapping

Semantic maps are graphic representations, taking the form of a flow chart, which illustrate concepts and relationships between concepts (Pearson & Johnson, 1978). Semantic maps have a strong link with schema theory, having been used initially in theoretical articles to graphically illustrate the nature of schemata (see Figure 1.3). Educators quickly recognized the instructional value of these devices, and soon semantic maps became widely advocated as a way to teach the meanings of key vocabulary terms (e.g., Johnson & Pearson, 1984). Usually, the teacher begins by writing a key

FIGURE 5.1   Semantic Map for "Avalanche"

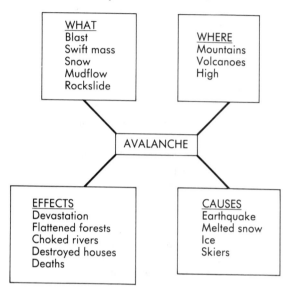

vocabulary term on the chalkboard and then asks students to suggest other words that are related to the key term. These words are written in a list, and then a map is constructed, with help from the students, showing how the words are related to the key term. Figure 5.1 gives an example of a semantic map for the term "avalanche."

Semantic Mapping has been found to be an effective means of teaching word meanings (see, for example, Johnson, Toms-Bronowski, & Pittelman, 1982). Several factors appear to be responsible for this effectiveness. The map diagrams help to illustrate how concepts are related to each other, making these relationships more concrete and accessible to children. Semantic maps also serve as a catalyst for group discussion of vocabulary terms, getting students to think more actively about word meanings (Stahl & Vancil, 1986).

Semantic Mapping's usefulness is not limited to vocabulary instruction. When children add concepts to a semantic map, they are activating their prior knowledge connected with the key term or topic. The teacher can then, through discussion and use of the map, show how their existing concepts fit with the new concept. McNeil (1987) explains: "The making of a semantic map is a procedure for building a bridge between the known and the new. The map provides the teacher with information on what the pupils know about a topic and gives the pupils anchor points to which the new concepts they will encounter can be attached" (p. 7). Semantic maps therefore provide a promising means for assessing and activating students' background knowledge prior to reading. Research has found that semantic maps, used as a prereading activity, result in better story recall in low-ability readers than traditional Directed Reading Activity readiness activities (Sinatra, Stahl-Gemake, & Berg, 1984).

Semantic Mapping exercises traditionally have been oral in nature, with maps used as stimuli for discussion. McNeil's (1987) strategy is an excellent example of how oral Semantic Mapping activities can be used as a prereading activity. This strategy uses teacher-led discussions to activate students' prior knowledge relevant to text topics.

While quite effective when used in this oral manner, semantic maps can also be combined with writing to create valuable prereading readiness experiences. Take, for example, our modification of McNeil's (1987) mapping strategy in which we have added activities that involve student writing. These writing activities were added to encourage more active processing of the concepts in the map. The modified strategy proceeds as follows:

1. The teacher begins by writing on the chalkboard the topic that the students are going to read about.

2. The teacher asks students to brainstorm all the ideas they can think of related to the topic, and these ideas are listed on the board in categories. This step informs the teacher as to what the students already know about the topic. It also makes the students aware of their own prior knowledge.

3. The teacher helps the students label each category by getting them to focus on what the words have in common.

4. The students are asked to write a brief composition, using the map as a guide, in which they tell what they know about the topic.

5. The students then read the original passage to find out more about the topic.

6. After reading the selection, the students are asked to add new ideas acquired from reading to each category of the map. This helps to link new concepts with the students' prior knowledge.

7. The students then revise their prereading compositions, adding the new information they have learned.

Our "Space Shuttle" semantic map in Figure 5.2 illustrates how our modification of the McNeil strategy can be used to prepare intermediate-grade children for reading Sally Ride's *To Space and Back* (Lothrup, Lee, & Shepard, 1986). The map categorizes children's prior knowledge in graphic form and provides material to help them write a short piece on space shuttles prior to reading the book. This writing exercise is intended to generate interest in the content of the book and to prepare students to understand space travel concepts.

After reading *To Space and Back,* students can extend the semantic map with newly learned concepts such as "jet pack," "g-suit," "robot arm," and "Snoopy Cap." As they revise their original papers, they will link these new concepts with their prior knowledge about space shuttles, increasing their understanding of the book.

FIGURE 5.2   Semantic Map for Sally Ride's *To Space and Back*

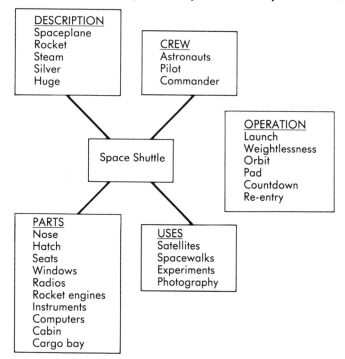

Buckley (1986) has described another way in which Semantic Mapping can be used in conjunction with writing as a prereading activity. It uses the same type of semantic maps as McNeil's strategy, but differs in that students work in pairs rather than in teacher-led groups and make their own semantic maps. The strategy, which has been used successfully with children in grades three through six, involves the following steps:

1. Partners discuss the passage title and brainstorm ideas connected with the title. One student acts as scribe and writes the ideas down.
2. The students use different color crayons to underline, in one color, all the words that belong to the same conceptual category (e.g., in our Space Shuttle example, all the "description" words might be underlined in blue, the "operation" words in red). They then decide on names for each of the

different colored groups of words. These category names are written at the bottom of the page.

3. The partners make a map of their ideas, placing the title of the passage in a circle in the middle and extending as many lines from the circle as there are categories. At the end of each line they write the category name and list all the related ideas under these names.

4. Using the map as a guide, each partner writes a composition, incorporating as many of the ideas on the map as possible.

5. The partners read each others' compositions and discuss similarities and differences.

6. The students then read the original passage silently and discuss how it compares with their own compositions. As an option, students could revise their stories, incorporating new information obtained from the text.

The two mapping strategies described above have the potential to facilitate comprehension in several ways. First, they both use writing to help activate students' text-relevant prior knowledge. Second, the students' prereading maps and compositions can inform the teacher of gaps or conflicts which exist between the students' existing schemata and the concepts in the text. This can allow the teacher to take remedial action (e.g., correct student misconceptions) prior to reading. Finally, the maps and writing activities may spark interest in the passage topic, motivating the students to become more active, attentive readers. Of course, they both have the additional advantage of providing valuable writing practice.

■ **Prereading Writing Assignments**

As described earlier in this chapter, Marino and associates (1985) found that text-related Prereading Writing Assignments significantly improved fourth-graders' recall of a passage about pioneers. The following is the writing assignment used in the Marino study:

> Pretend you are a young person in 1845. You are a pioneer heading for the Oregon country. You and your family have stopped to make camp for the night on the Snake River when you meet a group of young orphans. The oldest is a 13-year-old boy who tells you of his determination to carry on with his father's plan to take the family to Oregon. John, you learn, is a very brave and clever boy who has just saved his sister from drowning. Write a letter home to your grandparents describing this boy and the story he has told you.
> (p. 204)

This assignment has two features that may have promoted the students' comprehension. First, it focused on key elements in the story to be read—pioneers, the main character (John), and the central problem (getting to Oregon)—triggering relevant prior knowledge. "Pioneer," for example, probably brought to mind images of wagon trains, horses, frontier clothing, and rugged living, for many of the students. This schema activation may have made it easier for them to assimilate and understand the story. Second, the assignment asked the students to "put themselves into the story" and encounter the main character, John Sager. This resulted in many of the students becoming personally involved—so much so that some disregarded the instructions to write a letter about John and the story he told. Instead, these students wrote about their relationship with John (e.g., " 'I invited him to stay overnight' and 'We became very close' ") or made predictions about what might happen to John in the story (" 'I bet he'll have to fight off Indians' "). Apparently the writing assignment led many of the students to personally identify with John Sager, resulting in intense personal involvement and interest in the story.

We suggest the following guidelines for preparing these kinds of Prereading Writing Assignments:

1. The assignment should involve major concepts in the story about to be read. Focus on concepts that are crucial to the understanding of the story. Possibilities include the geographical setting, the historical period, character traits of the protagonist, major activities in which the characters engage or problems they encounter.
2. If possible, the assignment should encourage students to become personally involved with the story's plot and characters. Assignments that have students make-believe that they are part of the story are especially effective in this regard.

The Strategy Example presents Prereading Writing Assignments for several well-known children's books intended for students in grades three through six.

———————— STRATEGY EXAMPLE 5.1 ————————

Prereading Writing Assignments

Ida Early Comes Over the Mountain, by Robert Burch (Avon, 1960). Imagine that one of your friends tells you he met some "hillbillies" while he was on a vacation trip. Picture in your mind the type of people he was referring to and list your ideas. What do you think they looked like? (Perhaps you can draw a hillbilly.) How do you think they talked? What do you think they did for entertainment? Pretend that you took such a trip and made a hillbilly friend. Write a conversation you and your friend might have had about life in the Tennessee mountains.

The Amazing Bone, by William Steig (Farrar, Straus, and Giroux, 1976).
Some people believe if a black cat crosses your path or you break a mirror you will have bad luck, and if you find a four-leaf clover or knock on wood you will have good luck. Think about some of the superstitions talked about by people in your family or by your friends. List objects that have been said to have magic powers to bring good luck. Pretend you have found one of these things and write a letter to a pen pal describing the good fortune it brought you.

Superfudge, by Judy Blume (Dell, 1980).
Some people are given nicknames because of certain physical characteristics they have. For example, someone called "Freckles" probably has a freckled face and someone called "Red" most likely has red hair. Others are nicknamed for a variety of reasons, including the shortening of given names for the convenience of family and friends. Why do you think a boy might be called "Fudge"? Write a short description of this boy as you imagine him and explain why he has been given this unusual nickname.

Through using Prereading Writing Assignments which require intermediate-grade students to role play characters in basal reader stories or children's books, teachers can help activate students' story-relevant prior knowledge and, at the same time, increase their personal involvement in the stories.

■ Brainwriting

Brainstorming is frequently used by teachers to stimulate productive thinking for reading and writing. By encouraging students to freely build on each other's thoughts, the Brainstorming technique awakens prior knowledge and facilitates the generation of ideas. The approach is not without drawbacks, however. Rodrigues (1983) reminds teachers that dominant students can sometimes control the process by directing the flow of thoughts and by inhibiting shy students. In his opinion, the major weakness in the Brainstorming technique is the lack of time it provides for incubation of the ideas already contributed. The rapid pace does not allow students enough time to critically analyze the ideas created by their peers. While Brainstorming does promote ideational fluency, an important aspect of creativity, it does not develop critical-thinking skills. Rodrigues recommends Brainwriting as an alternative strategy for use with students of all ages.

In a Brainwriting activity, the class is divided into groups of four or five students. Each student is directed by the teacher to write his or her own ideas about an assigned topic on a sheet of paper. When they have written several ideas, each member of the group places her or his paper in the center of the group and takes another student's list, adding more ideas to it. The process of adding to each others' lists continues until the teacher stops it, at which point each group constructs one list to share with the class by combining their individual lists and building on them.

The following Strategy Example illustrates how Brainwriting can be used to get readers in third grade and above to use higher-order thinking skills in connection with the children's book *Wilfred Gordon McDonald Partridge.*

STRATEGY EXAMPLE 5.2

Brainwriting Example

The following illustrates how Brainwriting can be used to get third-grade and older readers to employ higher-order thinking skills in connection with the children's book *Wilfred Gordon McDonald Partridge,* by Mem Fox (Kane/Miller, 1985). Brainwriting is first used as a prereading activity to activate prior knowledge. After the story has been read, the lists generated in the prereading activity are used as the stimulus for a discussion in which students critically analyze "memory," a major concept in the story.

1. Groups of students are given the topic "What is a memory?" for the Brainwriting activity. After they have individually listed three or four ideas on their papers about what a memory means to them, they exchange lists and add more ideas to the lists of others.

2. After the teacher directs the groups to stop their individual Brainwriting, the students work together as groups to select and combine ideas, constructing a group list to read to the class. A teacher-directed session follows, during which the various groups share their ideas about the meaning of a memory.

3. The reading of *Wilfred Gordon McDonald Partridge* follows the Brainwriting activity. The story concerns a young boy who overhears his parents discussing a "poor old" woman in the old people's home next door. The woman, according to the parents, is losing her memory. Wilfred Gordon becomes concerned about this because Miss Nancy, the lady in question, is his favorite person. He asks various people to tell him what "a memory" is, hoping that he can help her find hers, and he receives an assortment of answers: "Something you remember"; "Something warm"; "Something from long ago"; "Something that makes you cry"; and "Something as precious as gold." He

looks for things at home which, in his mind, meet each of these definitions of a memory (shells, a puppet, a medal, a football, and an egg) and takes them to his ninety-six-year-old friend. Together they enjoy one-by-one the recollections awakened in Miss Nancy by Wilfred Gordon's objects.

4. In postreading discussion, students can: (a) compare their own ideas about a memory with those of the book characters interviewed by Wilfred Gordon; (b) discuss the various definitions of a memory and develop one definition the entire class agrees upon; and (c) draw inferences about things Wilfred Gordon might have selected for his basket if he had heard their definitions of a memory.

Among the advantages of this strategy, according to Rodrigues, are:

First, every student contributes, even the most shy. Second, students have time to contemplate other students' ideas, and that will stimulate them to think of new ideas. Third, the total class is producing ideas, eliminating the difficulty of one person having to take down many ideas in brainstorming. (1983, p. 60)

The major weakness of Brainwriting is that it is slower than Brainstorming, and smaller groups reduce the size of the "brain pool" available for generating ideas. It is therefore not intended to be a replacement for oral Brainstorming activities, but rather a strategy that can be used occasionally to enrich the Brainstorming experience.

GUIDED READING

■ ■ The second step of the Directed Reading Activity is often referred to as guided reading. During this step, the students read the passage silently, usually with some guidance from the teacher. This guidance usually entails having the teacher set forth purposes for reading the passage. It is assumed that these teacher-set objectives will help focus students' attention on the most important aspects of the passage and will also create interest and motivation for reading, all of which should facilitate reading comprehension.

In "Bears Aren't Everywhere" in the third-grade reader, *How It Is Nowadays* (Ginn Reading 720), for example, the guided reading cycle is repeated every two or three pages. The teacher's edition recommends that the teacher set the following goal for reading the first three pages: "Find out what starts Danny thinking about bears." After the students have read the three pages silently, the teacher initiates a discussion by asking questions such as: "What started Danny thinking that bears were everywhere?" "What kind of bears did he think were there?" "Did Danny really see the bears?" and "What did he do to send the bears away?" (p. 154). This cycle of teacher-set aims, silent reading, and teacher-led discussion is repeated three more times during the ten-page story.

Research has established clearly that purposes for reading do affect comprehension. In an oft-cited study, Pichert and Anderson (1977) had several groups of subjects read a passage about what two boys did at home while playing hooky. The passage described the various rooms in the house as it described the boys' activities. One group read the passage from the perspective of a potential home buyer, whereas another group read the story from the point of view of a burglar. These different perspectives resulted in the two groups setting different goals for reading. The home buyers' reading objective was to discover the good and bad points about the house, whereas the burglars' was to discover if there was anything in the house worth stealing. Results showed that the subjects tended to have better recall of information related to their perspectives and purposes. For instance, more of the home buyer group recalled that the house had a leaky roof, whereas the burglar group had better recall of the fact that the house contained a valuable color television set.

The theory of selective attention helps to explain the mechanisms through which purposes affect comprehension. According to this theory, readers tend to gauge the importance of upcoming text elements in terms of their reasons for reading and then focus most of their attention on the elements deemed to be most important. As a result of the extra attention these important elements receive, they tend to be learned and recalled better than less important elements (Anderson & Pearson, 1984).

While it is well established that purposes for reading are important, the value of the traditional practice of teachers setting objectives for students is open to question. In the guided reading portion of a typical basal lesson, the *teacher* sets several goals for reading, the students read a portion of text, and then the *teacher* leads a discussion focusing on the targets set prior to reading. While this type of structure can initially make comprehension easier for children, the danger exists that students may become overly dependent on it. If teachers always set the goals for their students' reading, it may become difficult for students to establish their own reasons for reading. Stauffer (1981) points out that when teachers do all the purpose-setting and ask all the questions during postreading discussions, "The pupils learn to wait for specific instructions. The process they learn is to study the teacher and know what pleases or displeases. Little if any pupil thinking or initiative is required. Their performance is that of intellectual puppets" (p. 65). While stated a bit strongly, Stauffer makes the point that the traditional guided reading does little to promote independent reading habits or active involvement in reading.

Recently, several strategies have been developed to be used as alternatives to the guided reading portion of the DRA. These strategies, which involve self-questioning and prediction, can be used to help students learn to establish their own purposes for reading.

Self-questioning strategies teach children to ask their own prereading questions. Mason and Au (1986) explain the value of self-questioning:

> To be able to ask questions, students must be actively thinking about and working with the text. In asking their own prequestions, that is, questions about material not yet read, students decide what the selections might be about and what they might want to learn from it. This gives students the chance to set their own purposes for reading.
>
> (p. 157)

Thus, self-questioning can enhance comprehension both by encouraging active involvement and by giving students experience with setting their own reading purposes. Research has shown that teaching students to construct their own questions can improve retention of both narrative and expository material (Singer & Donlon, 1982; Balajthy, 1983).

Prediction is another source of purposes for reading. If students make predictions prior to reading, they have a purpose: read to see if their predictions are confirmed or disproved in the passage. If students share and discuss their prereading predictions, this often leads to controversy about whose predictions are correct, adding additional motivation for reading (Tierney, Readence, & Dishner, 1985). Students will want to read the passage in order to prove that their predictions are right and that those of their fellow students are wrong.

Self-questioning and making predictions have the additional benefit of fostering self-monitoring, an important metacognitive reading skill. Self-monitoring involves continually checking to see if what one is reading conforms to prior expectations and makes sense. If something read does not conform to expectations, the reader is alerted that something may have been misread or misinterpreted, and rereading usually occurs. If self-monitoring is not taking place, these interpretations slip by unnoticed and comprehension suffers. The strategies discussed below help students set expectations for reading and, in so doing, facilitate self-monitoring. Other strategies for promoting metacognition, the conscious awareness of comprehension processes, are discussed at the end of Chapter 6.

In the sections that follow, we describe several strategies that use writing to promote self-questioning and making predictions. The goal of all of these strategies is to help students become more proficient at setting appropriate purposes and expectations for reading. We have also included a strategy, Save the Last Word for Me, that uses writing to promote more student-centered postreading discussions. All of these strategies can be used as substitutes for traditional, teacher-dominated guided reading activities.

■ **Question-Eliciting Questions**

Singer (1978) has proposed a clever strategy for promoting self-questioning: teachers ask questions which elicit questions from students in return. Following Singer's suggestion, Lori Wegley developed a question-eliciting strategy for use in her third-grade classroom. She based her approach on Singer's three components for guiding comprehension instruction:

1. *Modeling Behavior.* Teacher-posed questions precede student-posed questions as models.
2. *Phase-in/Phase-out Strategy.* After taking students through a question-asking demonstration, teachers proceed to teach students to ask their own questions, phasing themselves out and phasing the students in as questioners.
3. *Active Comprehension.* Students learn to guide their own thinking through self-generated questions about the text.

To encourage active involvement in the story to be read, she also included a prereading writing assignment based on the self-generated questions.

Wegley started her strategy by reading the title and first two paragraphs of a basal reader story to the class. In the example that follows, the story was "The Alligator Under the Bed," by Joan Lowery Nixon *(Hidden Wonders;* Scott, Foresman, 1981):

THE ALLIGATOR UNDER THE BED

"Mama!" Jill called. "Mama, come here!" Her mother sped into her bedroom. "What's wrong? It's past your bedtime," she said. "You should be asleep."

Jill tugged her blanket up to her neck. "There's an alligator under my bed," she said softly.

After this, Wegley asked her first question-eliciting question, *"What questions could you ask from the title alone?"* Students responded with such questions as:

"Was there really an alligator under the bed?"
"Is the alligator really dead?"
"Did they find the alligator?"
"Was the alligator under the covers or under the bed?"
"How did the alligator get under the bed?"

Wegley's second question, *"What would you like to know about Jill?"* brought these questions from students:

"Did Jill have a Dad?"
"How old is she?"
"Is she scared of the alligator?"

"Do Jill's parents believe her?"
"Does Jill get hurt by the alligator?"
"Does Jill ever get to sleep?"

Other questions Wegley asked elicited similar questions in return from students. For example, she asked, *"Is there anything you would like to ask the author about this story?"* The students responded with:

"Do the people in the story get rid of the alligator?"
"Was it really an alligator or was it something else?"
"What comes next?"
"How did she choose the title?"
"Where did she get the idea for her story?"

After the question-generating session, Wegley involved her students in a writing activity to build greater interest in the story. Each student chose one of the questions to answer as an author. When these written answers were read to the class, the children became highly motivated to read the story in order to see if their answers were confirmed by the story. Melanie's explanation of "What comes next?" in Figure 5.3 is typical of the responses written by the children in Wegley's class.

FIGURE 5.3   Melanie's Answer to "What Happened Next?"

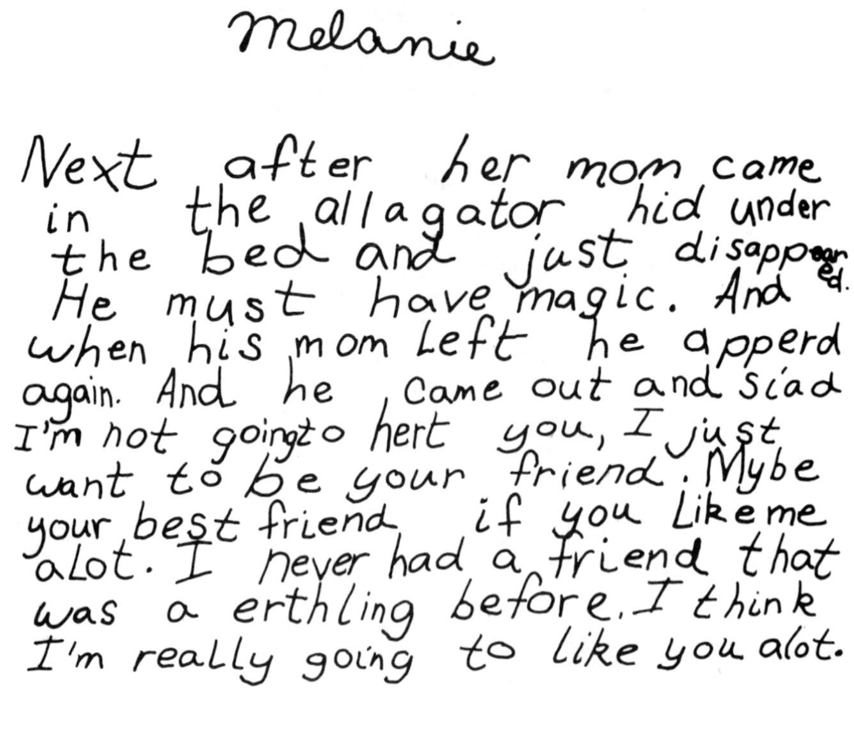

Melanie

Next after her mom came in the allagator hid under the bed and just disappeared. He must have magic. And when his mom Left he apperd again. And he came out and siad I'm not goingto hert you, I just want to be your friend. Mybe your best friend if you Like me alot. I never had a friend that was a erthling before. I think I'm really going to like you alot.

■ **Directed Reading and Thinking Activity**

Stauffer (1969) developed the Directed Reading and Thinking Activity (DRTA) as an alternative to the typical Directed Reading Activity (DRA) format used in most basal reader series. The major difference between the two strategies is who sets the purposes for reading. The teacher establishes the reading purposes in the DRA. In Stauffer's DRTA, on the other hand, students are helped by the teacher to set their own purposes for reading. This is done by encouraging students to make predictions about what is going to happen in the story and to read to see if their predictions are correct.

The DRTA strategy involves a cycle of three steps which can be repeated several times during the reading of a passage:

> 1. *Purpose Setting.* The teacher helps students survey the section of the passage to be read, focusing their attention on the title, headings, illustrations, and/or first-page clues. The teacher then encourages the students to make predictions about the passage by asking questions such as "What do you think will happen to _____ (main character)?" or "What do you think the section on _____ (heading) will be about?" The students are also asked to justify and support their predictions.
>
> 2. *Reading.* The students read silently to a stopping point specified by the teacher. While doing so, they actively search for evidence to support their predictions.
>
> 3. *Proving.* The teacher leads a discussion in which students are asked to present evidence confirming or disproving their earlier predictions. The other students judge whether or not the evidence is valid. The students are then asked to predict what comes next in the passage, and the cycle is repeated.

We recommend that teachers occasionally modify the DRTA strategy by having students write down their predictions and supporting evidence. This can be done on a regular piece of paper or on a ready-made form such as the one illustrated in Figure 5.4. The sequence of the three major steps — purpose setting, reading, and proving — remains the same. The major changes are:

1. During the *purpose setting* stage, students write down their predictions. They also write a justification for each prediction. Putting predictions and justifications down in writing encourages students to think carefully about their hypotheses. It also provides a permanent record, ensuring that students will not forget their predictions while reading.

2. During the *reading* stage, students jot down evidence supporting or disproving their predictions. This encourages them to monitor their reading and provides a record of the evidence to be used in postreading discussions.

3. In the postreading *proving* discussions, students take turns reading their predictions, evidence, and revisions (if any). The group then evaluates the evidence presented.

FIGURE 5.4   Blank DRTA Record Form

PREDICTION # 1: _____

_____

_____

Justification: _____

_____

_____

Read to page _____
EVIDENCE
  Confirm: _____

_____

_____

Disprove: _____

_____

_____

PREDICTION # 2: _____

_____

_____

Justification: _____

_____

_____

Read to page _____
EVIDENCE
  Confirm: _____

_____

_____

Disprove: _____

_____

_____

By adding writing to the already effective DRTA strategy, teachers will encourage their students to make thoughtful predictions about the passages they are going to read and to monitor their reading closely to see if their predictions are confirmed.

■ Buckley's Basal Reader Prediction Strategies

Buckley (1986) has developed several procedures that use writing to help students make predictions about basal reader stories. These strategies have been implemented successfully in Berkeley, California schools. Since they are described rather briefly in Buckley's article, we have elaborated on each in the descriptions presented here.

The first is a self-questioning strategy in which pairs of students begin by surveying a basal reader story, examining its title and illustrations, and then reading the first paragraph or page. Students then write two questions they want to have answered from reading the passage. The partners then share their questions and make guesses about possible answers. Following reading of the passage, the partners discuss the answers to each other's questions.

The second strategy involves having students write their own prereading versions of stories about to be read. As in the preceding strategy, students are first paired with partners. The following steps are then carried out:

1. The partners take turns carefully describing each illustration in the basal story. After each illustration is described, students predict what they expect to happen in that part of the story.

2. When all the illustrations have been examined, each partner writes a story, based on the information in the pictures, predicting what will happen in the basal passage.

3. Partners then read and critique each other's predictions.

4. The original basal reader story is then read by both partners.

5. When finished reading, the partners have a discussion in which they compare their predictions with the actual story line.

The second strategy has much in common with the DRTA. Students are encouraged to think carefully about what is going to happen in the story they are about to read, they make predictions, and then they read to see if their predictions are confirmed. Both strategies motivate children to want to read basal reader stories, help them to set their own purposes for reading, and encourage them to monitor their reading. Buckley's strategy is more time consuming than the DRTA but has the advantage of giving students practice in story writing.

■ Other Self-Questioning Strategies

Fitzgerald (1983) describes a method that uses writing to increase students' awareness of the importance of asking themselves questions as they read. Pairs of students read the first section of an assigned story and together write three questions about important content from that section. They continue this process for each of the remaining sections of the story, developing a feel for the importance of questioning themselves while they read. When the reading and question writing have been completed, the partners exchange their list with another pair and write answers to the questions on the new list, without referring to the story. The written answers are then returned to the pair who wrote them, and the pairs discuss the acceptability of each other's answers. The teacher finalizes the experience by emphasizing to the students the value of asking similar questions of themselves when they are reading, explaining that "you have to be aware of what you know and don't know in order to form the questions" (Fitzgerald, 1983, p. 253).

Several other approaches which focus on writing to develop self-questioning skills are described by Devine (1986):

1. Use the news reporter's approach with young children, explaining that reporters try to answer the questions, "Who? What? Why? Where? and How?" in their stories. Then instruct children to read a text and write six questions a reporter might ask. For example, "Who is the most important person in the story? What is he or she doing? Why are they doing it? When does all this happen?" (p. 263).

2. Ask students to anticipate possible test questions over the material to be read. One approach is to have them skim the text and write questions they think the teacher might ask. An alternative is to have them write questions as they read. This exercise develops the habit of asking questions of a text and checking comprehension while reading.

3. Tell students in advance of their reading that they will be writing a summary as a postreading activity. This will encourage them to "read to detect trivial or redundant material, to think of general rather than specific terms, and to watch for possible main idea sentences" (p. 265).*

Each of the strategies described in this section demonstrates how writing adds an important ingredient to the teaching of self-questioning skills for reading. By integrating the writing of questions with reading, these strategies have several advantages over oral formats. Written questions promote retention of ideas by affording students the opportunity to reread; they help focus the students' attention and keep them on task; and they facilitate communication between students by providing a visual base from which to operate.

■ Probable Passages

Wood's (1984) Probable Passages is a strategy for integrating writing with the reading of basal reader passages, featuring a unique merger of story grammar and prereading prediction. It assumes the students have some knowledge of Mandler and Johnson's (1977) six story elements (setting, beginning, reaction, attempt, outcome, and ending). It is recommended that the story template and story diagram activities described in the "Text Structure" section of Chapter 6 be used to familiarize students with these elements prior to using the Probable Passage strategy.

*From Thomas G. Devine, *Teaching Reading Comprehension: From Theory to Practice.* Copyright © 1986, and reprinted by permission of Allyn & Bacon.

The strategy is divided into four stages, described below, with an example of how the strategy could be used with Elizabeth Shub's "The White Stallion" (in *Caravans,* Houghton Mifflin, 1986):

1. *Preparation Stage.*

　　a. The teacher analyzes the basal reader story and selects key terms basic to the plot.

　　b. These terms are written on the chalkboard in a simple list:

the West	galloped
Gretchen	frightened
white stallion	Anna (Gretchen's horse)
lost	lifted
alone	wagon train
back	return

　　c. A blank story frame is written on a second section of the chalkboard. This frame consists of story elements appropriate to the story being read. In some stories, it is best to separate the setting category into two elements (characters and location) and to combine others (e.g., combine beginning and reaction into a problem category).

　　d. On a third portion of the board, an incomplete probable passage is presented, corresponding to the story frame structure:

BLANK PROBABLE PASSAGE

The story takes place _____
_____. _____ is a
character in the story who _____.
A problem occurs when _____. After
that _____. Next _____
_____. The problem is solved when
_____. The story ends _____.

2. *Prereading Stage.*

　　a. Read the list of key words and ask the students to repeat them.

　　b. Tell students to use the words to make up a story mentally. Then help the students put the words into the appropriate slots in the story frame (see Figure 5.5). Emphasize that some of the words on the board may fit in several slots and that students may add other words that belong in their predicted stories.

　　c. Have students use the words from the story frame to complete a logical probable passage. For example, they might develop the following passage using the story frame in Figure 5.5:

FIGURE 5.5   Completed Story Frame

SETTING		PROBLEM	SOLUTION	
Location	Characters	Beginning/Response	Attempt/Outcome	Ending
the West	Gretchen	lost	return	back
wagon train	Anna (Gretchen's horse)	frightened	lifted	wagon train
	white stallion	alone	find*	galloped

*Word added by students

PREREADING PROBABLE PASSAGE

The story takes place in the West on a wagon train trip. Gretchen is a character in the story who has a horse named Anna. A problem occurs when Anna, the horse, gets lost. After that Gretchen is alone and frightened that she will never see Anna again. Next Gretchen meets the white stallion. The problem is solved when the white stallion helps Gretchen find her horse. The story ends when Gretchen gallops back to the wagon train on Anna.

3. Reading Stage. The students read the basal reader story.

4. Postreading Stage.

a. The students discuss how their probable passage compares with the actual plot of the story.

b. The class makes any necessary changes in the way that words are categorized in the story frame.

c. Students modify the probable passage to reflect the actual story plot.

REVISED PROBABLE PASSAGE
Actual Plot

The story takes place in the West on a wagon train trip. Gretchen is a character in the story who has a horse named Anna. A problem occurs when Gretchen and Anna get lost. After that the white stallion leads Anna away, leaving Gretchen all alone and frightened. Next Anna comes back, but Gretchen can't get up on her back. The problem is solved when the white stallion helps Gretchen get on Anna's back. The story ends with Gretchen returning to the wagon train on Anna and the white stallion galloping away.

Wood recommends that, after several teacher-directed experiences with this strategy, students work in small groups to compose their own Probable Passages. The groups can then share and compare their predictions. The reconstruction of the actual plot in the postreading stage can be done in this same manner.*

■ Save the Last Word for Me

Because DRA postreading discussions are totally controlled by the teacher, students' enthusiasm and participation is often minimal. As pointed out earlier in the quotation from Stauffer (1981), students are often content to merely respond to teacher questions as they believe the teacher wants them to respond, putting little effort or thought into their answers.

Burke and Harste (cited in Vaughan & Estes, 1986, pp. 160–161) have designed a strategy to get students more personally involved in postreading discussions by encouraging them to express their own opinions about the stories they read. This strategy, called Save the Last Word for Me, requires students to locate and write down statements in their reading about which they wish to make a comment, to invite the opinions of other students about these statements, and then to tell their own thoughts about the statements. This strategy can lead to much richer postreading discussion than the traditional, teacher-centered guided reading approach.

The Save the Last Word for Me strategy follows these rules:

1. Students read a selection from a basal reader or trade book (each student must have a copy).
2. Each student finds three to five statements in the reading that are of special interest and writes each statement on an index card.
3. After recording the statements on the fronts of index cards, students write their own views about the statements on the reverse sides.
4. One student reads a statement to the class and locates it in the text, enabling others to see the context or focus of the topic.
5. Next, students discuss the statement for a reasonable length of time, giving their own opinions in a session moderated by the teacher.
6. Last, the student who wrote the statement on the card has the last word on the issue, expressing either the opinion written on the back of his or her card or a changed opinion resulting from hearing the thoughts of others.

Vaughan and Estes (1986) recommend that teachers modify the rules to make the strategy appropriate for their classrooms. They suggest that, in some instances, teachers extend the discussion briefly by asking for student responses after they have given their "last word." It is possible, too, that misinformation may arise in the discussions, in which case a correction by the teacher would be allowed. They advise that if such rule changes are to be

*From Wood, Karen D. (1987). Probable passages: A Writing Strategy. *The Reading Teacher, 37,* pp. 496–499. Reprinted with permission of the International Reading Association and Karen D. Wood.

FIGURE 5.6 Save the Last Word for Me Index Cards from *The Cat Ate My Gymsuit*

FRONT   BACK

"Middle class kids have problems, too."
p. 1

No one is free from problems. It's just hard to see the problems of others sometimes because of our own.

"It sure gets tough when you get older. It's much easier to be a little kid whose big problem is learning to tie shoelaces."
p. 52

The teenage years are complicated. It's hard to feel comfortable about yourself.

"That'll teach the school to group all the smart kids in one class. We were indestructible."
p. 8

Ability grouping is not always good. It isn't fair to the kids in the lower-level classes.

"She (Ms. Finney) really listened."
p. 17

When teachers listen, they show that they care. They invite students to communicate with them.

"Mom always made me go to tap and ballet lessons. She said that they'd make me more graceful."
p. 1

We often "grow" from doing things that parents and teachers tell us are good for us, even though we may not want to do them.

made, teachers should make them before starting the activity and maintain them throughout the class period.

The sample cards in Figure 5.6 illustrate the use of the Save the Last Word for Me strategy with *The Cat Ate My Gymsuit,* by Paula Danzinger (Dell, 1974), which is appropriate reading for students in grades five through eight. All of the statements quoted on the front side of the index cards were made by Marci Lewis, the teenage heroine of the book, who complains about everything and everyone except her favorite teacher, Ms. Finney.

The Save the Last Word for Me format works well with reading groups of five or six students, allowing all group members an opportunity to interact through discussion with others who have read the same book or story. In addition to encouraging rich postreading discussion, the strategy also promotes higher-level cognitive skills. When students write their own viewpoints about statements they read, they enter a transactional relationship with the text to become critical readers. Discussing these opinions with others furthers the transactional process by requiring students to use inferencing and problem-solving skills as they formulate their thoughts. During the final step, they engage in the evaluation process as they decide whether or not to change the opinion they originally wrote on their cards.

SUMMARY

This chapter has dealt with ways in which writing can be incorporated into the first two steps of the Directed Reading Activity: prereading readiness and guided reading. We decided to focus on the DRA strategy since it is the lesson format used in most basal reader series, the predominant method of reading instruction in this country.

We began the "Prereading Readiness" section by explaining why prior knowledge plays such a crucial role in reading comprehension and why writing is an ideal means to activate that knowledge. We then presented three prereading strategies that can be adapted to take advantage of writing's schemata-activating potential. The first strategy, Semantic Mapping, uses diagrams as stimuli for text-related writing assignments. The diagrams and resulting student writing serve to activate prior knowledge about the text topic and can inform the teacher of misconceptions that need to be corrected prior to reading. After the text has been read, the semantic maps and student compositions are altered to accommodate new information learned from the passage. The second strategy, Prereading Writing Assignments, uses writing involving role playing to activate text-related knowledge and to encourage personal involvement in stories. The third strategy, Brainwriting, incorporates writing into the familiar Brainstorming process as a means to improve its effectiveness as a prereading activity.

We prefaced the "Guided Reading" section with a brief discussion of why purposes and perspectives for reading are another important factor in reading comprehension. We pointed out that the traditional guided reading is teacher-centered, with the teacher both setting the purposes for reading and directing postreading discussions. Overuse of this strategy has the potential danger of making students overly dependent on teacher guidance. We then presented several strategies in which writing is used to help children set their own goals for reading. The Question-Eliciting Questions procedure accomplishes this by getting students to ask themselves questions prior to reading. Several other strategies encourage purpose setting by having students make predictions about stories and then reading to determine if their predictions were correct. All of the strategies in this section have the extra advantage of fostering self-monitoring of comprehension, an important metacognitive skill discussed further in Chapter 6. We ended this section with the Save the Last Word for Me strategy, which can be used to increase student involvement in postreading discussions.

The prereading readiness and guided reading suggestions in this chapter are intended to be used as occasional substitutes for traditional DRA activities. These writing activities will not only prepare and motivate students to read stories but have the additional advantage of providing them with valuable writing practice.

REFERENCES

Anderson, R. C., & Pearson, P. D. (1984). A schema-theoretic view of basic processes in reading comprehension. In P. D. Pearson (Ed.), *Handbook of reading research* (pp. 255–291). New York: Longman.

Balajthy, E. (1983, April). *The relationship of training self-generated questioning with passage difficulty and immediate and delayed retention.* Paper presented at the American Educational Research Association, Montreal.

Betts, E. A. (1946). *Foundations of reading instruction.* New York: American Book.

Bransford, J. D., & Johnson, M. K. (1973). Consideration of some problems of comprehension. In W. G. Chase (Ed.), *Visual information processing* (pp. 383–438). New York: Academic Press.

Buckley, M. H. (1986). When teachers decide to integrate the language arts. *Language Arts, 63,* 369–377.

Devine, T. G. (1986). *Teaching reading comprehension: From theory to practice.* Boston: Allyn & Bacon.

Fitzgerald, J. (1983). Helping readers gain self-control. *The Reading Teacher, 37,* 249–253.

Johnson, D. D., & Pearson, P. D. (1984). *Teaching reading vocabulary* (2nd ed.). New York: Holt, Rinehart & Winston.

Johnson, D. D., Toms-Bronowski, S., & Pittel-man, S. D. (1982). *An investigation of the effectiveness of semantic mapping and semantic feature analysis with intermediate grade level children* (Program Report 83-3). Madison: Wisconsin Center for Educational Research.

Langer, J. A. (1982). Facilitating text processing: The elaboration of prior knowledge. In J. A. Langer & M. T. Smith-Burke (Eds.), *Reader meets author/Bridging the gap* (pp. 149–162). Newark, DE: International Reading Association.

Lipson, M. Y. (1984). Some unexpected issues in prior knowledge and comprehension. *The Reading Teacher, 37,* 760–764.

Mandler, J. M., & Johnson, M. S. (1977). Remembrance of things parsed: Story structure and recall. *Cognitive Psychology, 9,* 111–151.

Marino, J. L., Gould, S. M., & Haas, L. W. (1985). The effects of writing as a prereading activity on delayed recall of narrative text. *Elementary School Journal, 86,* 199–205.

Mason, J. M., & Au, K. H. (1986). *Reading instruction for today.* Glenview, IL: Scott, Foresman.

McNeil, J. D. (1987). *Reading comprehension: New directions for classroom practice* (2nd ed.). Glenview, IL: Scott, Foresman.

Pearson, P. D., & Johnson, D. D. (1978).

Teaching reading comprehension. New York: Holt, Rinehart & Winston.

Pichert, J. W., & Anderson, R. C. (1977). Taking different perspectives on a story. *Journal of Educational Psychology, 69,* 309–315.

Rodrigues, R. J. (1983). Tools for developing prewriting skills. *English Journal, 72*(2), 58–60.

Sinatra, R. C., Stahl-Gemake, J., & Berg, D. N. (1984). Improving reading comprehension of disabled readers through semantic mapping. *The Reading Teacher, 38,* 22–29.

Singer, H. (1978). Active Comprehension: From answering to asking questions. *The Reading Teacher, 31,* 901–908.

Singer, H., & Donlon, D. (1982). Active comprehension: Problem-solving schema with question generation for comprehension of complex short stories. *Reading Research Quarterly, 17,* 166–186.

Stahl, S. A., & Vancil, S. J. (1986). Discussion is what makes semantic maps work in vocabulary instruction. *The Reading Teacher, 40,* 62–67.

Stauffer, R. G. (1969). *Teaching reading as a thinking process.* New York: Harper & Row.

Stauffer, R. G. (1981). Strategies for reading instruction. In M. P. Douglass (Ed.), *45th Claremont Reading Conference Yearbook* (pp. 58–73). Claremont, CA: Center for Developmental Studies.

Tierney, R. J., Readence, J. E., & Dishner, E. K. (1985). *Reading strategies and practices* (2nd ed.). Boston: Allyn & Bacon.

Vaughan, J. L., & Estes, T. H. (1986). *Reading and reasoning beyond the middle grades.* Boston: Allyn & Bacon.

Wood, K. D. (1984). Probable passages: A writing strategy. *The Reading Teacher, 37,* 496–499.

6

Combining Writing with Traditional Reading Activities II:

Skill Building

As the children I observed wrote, rewrote and conferred, they selected and reselected their main ideas, organized their supporting details, adjusted and defended their sequence. They reached toward inference, they discovered cause and effect, they developed and challenged conclusions. In a sense, everything that happened during writing time related to skills traditionally viewed as reading skills
—Calkins, Making the reading-writing connection

In the previous chapter, we described how writing can be incorporated into the prereading readiness and guided reading stages of Directed Reading Activity, the format used for most basal reader lessons. Now we shift our attention to how writing can be used in the third stage of the DRA: skill building. This stage involves lessons and practice activities which focus on skills deemed necessary for proficient reading.

The skill-building stage receives ample attention in basal teacher manuals, often requiring more time than all of the other stages of the DRA put together. In our oft-used example of the "Bears Aren't Everywhere" lesson from *How It Is Nowadays,* the third-grade reader in the Ginn 720 reading series, there are no less than seventeen different skill activities. Six of these are brief, teacher-led lessons, and the remainder consist of four workbook pages and seven pages of ditto exercises for independent practice. Among the skills taught or practiced are: (a) the meanings of new words; (b) recognition of topic sentences; (c) the *lt, pr,* and *spr* letter-sound correspondences; (d) recognition of consonant digraphs and consonant blends; (e) the *ful* suffix; and (f) identifying key words in written instructions. These skill activities were not randomly selected; rather, they were chosen as a result of an elaborate scope and sequence organization which insures that each subskill is introduced in what the basal authors believe to be the optimal sequence and that repeated practice is provided for each skill in at least several levels of basal series.

If basal reading series have an outstanding strength, it is that they do a thorough and systematic job of teaching isolated reading skills, particularly those related to word recognition. However, the value of this extreme emphasis on isolated skill development is debatable — some reading experts even argue that it is one of the basal approach's greatest weaknesses. Goodman (1986), for example, has compiled a list of "What is Wrong with Basals," which includes a number of items related to skill instruction, including:

1. They put undue emphasis on isolated aspects of language: letters, letter-sound relationships, words, sentence-fragments, or sentences. Often, particularly in workbooks, there is no cohesive, meaningful text and no situational context.
2. This leads learners to put inverted value on the bits and pieces of language, on isolated words and skills, and not enough on making sense of real, comprehensible stories and expository passages.
3. They introduce arbitrary sequences of skills which involve readers in abstract exercises instead of reading to comprehend.
4. They isolate reading from its use and from other language processes.
5. They often create artificial language passages or text fragments by controlling vocabulary or by building around specific phonic relationships or word attack skills.
6. They minimize time spent on reading while monopolizing school time for skill exercises.

(excerpts from pp. 361–362)

One way to solve these problems is for teachers to become discriminating users of basal teacher manuals. Rather than following every suggestion and direction like a recipe in a cookbook, teachers can select those activities that will help specific children's reading development and supplement the basal by adding needed activities that are not included in the manual. Durkin (1983) explains:

When a school (or school system) chooses a certain series, it commits itself to the overall goals of that program. . . . What is important to note about such a commitment is that it does not bind any teacher to manual suggestions for each lesson. In fact, the responsibility of the truly *professional* person is to select from the manual recommendations (a) only what will advance reading ability and (b) only what is needed by a particular group of students to whom the lesson will be directed. At any given time, therefore, what is suggested may be used, altered, shortened, lengthened, or skipped. What is important but *not* in a manual will have to be added by the teacher.

(p. 360)

Durkin's recommendations suggest a way in which writing can help to supplement and improve basal skill instruction. Writing is a natural context in which many reading skills can be learned, often more effectively than in contrived instructional situations. Chapter 2 gave examples of how beginning readers could be encouraged to learn the principles of phonics through writing experiences rather than through drill on isolated letter-sound relationships and completion of workbook exercises. It is possible, therefore, to replace some of the less desirable skill exercises in basal manuals with writing experiences which use the same skills.

The purpose of this chapter is to demonstrate how writing can help students develop reading skills, replacing or supplementing traditional basal reader skill activities. We have grouped the writing-for-reading strategies according to the main skills on which they focus: (a) word recognition and vocabulary knowledge, which are necessary for the comprehension of individual text words; (b) syntax or word ordering, which is an important factor in sentence-level comprehension; (c) text structure, which has an important role in understanding paragraphs and passages; (d) paraphrasing and text condensation, which assist in literal comprehension by promoting the active processing of text information; (e) higher-order reading skills, which involve critical and creative thinking; and (f) metacomprehension, which refers to the conscious awareness of comprehension processes. Several of these skill areas—syntax, text structure, and metacomprehension—play an important role in reading comprehension but receive little attention in current basal skill programs. Using writing to build competence in these areas is a good example of the supplementation to which Durkin was referring in her above quotation.

The strategies we describe below have one thing in common. They all link writing activities with texts that the students are reading. This linkage is crucial, since research suggests that isolated writing practice, not connected to reading, has little effect on students' reading skills. This has been reported for a number of different types of "isolated" writing programs, ranging from Sentence-Combining exercises (Straw & Schreiner, 1982) to process-oriented writing workshops (Ferris & Snyder, 1986). Such programs do facilitate students' writing (and are worthwhile for that reason), but they appear to have little impact on students' reading abilities, at least as measured by standardized reading tests. On the other hand, when writing activities are connected to passages that children read, gains have been found in reading as well as writing (Noyce & Christie, 1983). So it is crucial that writing activities aimed at enhancing reading skills be linked to reading experiences.

WORD RECOGNITION AND
VOCABULARY KNOWLEDGE

■ ■ Word recognition—the ability to recognize the oral equivalents of words represented by written language—and vocabulary knowledge—knowing the meanings of words—are given much attention in basal reader skill programs. Much emphasis is given to building students' sight vocabularies—the stock of words that can be recognized instantly—and to teaching phonics and contextual and structural analysis, which can be used to figure out the identities and/or meanings of words which are not instantly recognized in students' sight vocabularies.

There is good reason for emphasizing these word-level reading skills. Gough (1984) contends that word recognition is the "foundation of the reading process" (p. 225). He points out that, while many other factors are involved, reading comprehension cannot occur unless words in the text are recognized. He uses the following example to make his point:

A WOMAN NEEDS A MAN LIKE A FISH NEEDS A BICYCLE.

In order to understand this sentence a reader must: (a) recognize grammatical relationships among the words (e.g., that man is a noun rather than a verb); (b) activate prior knowledge about key terms (e.g., men, women, bicycles, and fish); and (c) take into account the discourse context in which the sentence occurs. However, before any of the above can occur, the words in the sentence must be recognized. "The reader must see that the sentence contains MAN, not FAN or MAT, and NEEDS, not FEEDS or NEARS, or the sentence will be misunderstood" (Gough, 1984, p. 225).

As discussed in the preceding chapter, readers' prior knowledge, particularly knowledge of word meanings, is essential for comprehension. One cannot possibly understand a text unless the correct meanings of most of the words are already known. In schema theory terms, comprehension cannot occur unless the words in the text are linked with preexisting schemata (meanings). Not surprisingly, vocabulary knowledge has consistently been found to be strongly related to reading comprehension ability. In fact, some researchers contend that knowledge of word meanings is the most important component in the comprehension process (e.g., Davis, 1972).

Word recognition and vocabulary knowledge are both important factors in reading comprehension. With this fact in mind, Stotsky (1982) recommends that teachers employ some less frequently used writing activities, including copying and dictation, to improve students' skills in these areas. Both copying and dictation are tied to an actual sample of written language and are likely to be more meaningful than isolated word recognition and vocabulary exercises.

■ Copying

Copying involves having students write down, verbatim, selected text passages. Studies have shown that, by simply copying the material they are reading, students can increase their ability to understand that material (Corbett, 1971). There are several possible ways in which such activity can facilitate comprehension. Copying encourages active engagement with the vocabulary in the passage, resulting in enhanced word recognition. The copied passage can also serve as a stimulus for the discussion of word meanings.

The effectiveness of copying for building word recognition and vocabulary knowledge has been observed by primary-grade teachers. Cutter (1979) relates her experiences with a low-achieving boy in her third-grade class who had poor word recognition skills and was almost a nonwriter, unable to participate in journal writing. She required him to copy from a variety of reading materials (brochures, textbooks, newspapers) at journal-writing time, and allowed him to continue to practice copying until his word recognition skills had improved to the extent that he could read better and write down his own thoughts with confidence. Hunter and Beaty (1981) urged students to copy poems as they read them, for better understanding and greater enjoyment. In Stotsky's view, copying the writing of accomplished writers focuses students' attention on elements of style and syntactic structures, in addition to building vocabulary.

Second-grade teacher Suzy Kline (1987) described a copying activity particularly suited for use with younger children. She discovered that daily conversations about events she and her students experienced could be the basis for a powerful tool—a classroom diary. Each morning after class discussions, children dictated those incidents they wanted to remember, while she recorded them on the chalkboard. Then the children dated a page in their individual composition books, copied the paragraph, and finally read it aloud together. Each entry contained new words for children to reread and explore with their dictionaries. Kline commented: "Kids wrote about events that were important to them: Chuck's mom got a new water bed. Chris's brother sleepwalks. Brett's kitten throws up when it smells garbage. Charlie's mother advertised her old kerosene heater on the 'swap shop' " (p. 80).

Through the classroom diary experience, Kline's students increased their word recognition skills, discovered the meanings of new words, learned to write good topic sentences, recalled punctuation and capitalization rules, and discussed their concerns. Kline encouraged careful handwriting by alerting her students that the diaries would go home for parents to read after twenty entries. She found that the activity reinforced spelling and grammar skills while stimulating the children's interest in reading and writing.

A note of caution is in order concerning copying. It should not be overused or it will turn into a boring chore rather than a meaningful learning experience. It is important that the material copied is of interest to students. The success of the classroom diary is due in large part to children's natural interest in their own activities. Favorite passages from literature are also appropriate and motivating for copying activities.

■ Dictation

Dictation requires students to copy down an orally presented text. The teacher reads a passage, and students copy it down verbatim. A popular teaching technique in European schools, dictation is seldom used in America for purposes other than testing spelling and handwriting ability. However, proponents of dictation in the elementary school consider it an appropriate instructional tool for developing children's reading and writing skills at all grade levels. Dictation provides a contextual method for building word knowledge, and when increasingly complex sentences are used, it equips children to deal with larger units of language.

For example, dictated passages from literature can provide the basis of intermediate- and upper-grade students' paraphrasing and free-writing activities. Squire (1983) notes that British children in the equivalent of our grades three through nine study dictated "Prose Paragraphs" regularly, looking at the relationships of words to other words, words to sentences, sentences to other sentences, and so forth. Both narrative and expository passages are used. The period of instruction ends with a writing exercise in which students paraphrase the passages. In all, British students receive close to six hundred hours of such instruction over a six-year period. The knowledge they gain about vocabulary, syntax, and prose structure is considerable.

☐ *Self-Edited Dictation*
Stotsky (1983) describes a dictation strategy in which students take dictation from prose selections and then compare their versions with the original, correcting any errors. Selection of interesting passages from the regular basal reading program ensures that the vocabulary and content are appropriate for most students in the class. Stotsky advises teachers to choose third-person narrative or informational passages without dialogue for dictation purposes, and to begin with short, three- or four-sentence passages at first. When longer passages are used, she recommends breaking them up into units according to the ability and attention span of the children in the class. Of course, this strategy is not limited to use only with basal reader selections. Excerpts from the books of recognized children's authors — such as Madeline L'Engle, Mark Twain, E. B. White, Roald Dahl, and Scott O'Dell — provide excellent models for elementary and middle school students, familiarizing them with literary language and the techniques of accomplished authors.

Stotsky advises teachers to clearly describe the procedure before starting the first dictation exercise. The Strategy Example illustrates the types of directions which should be given to children. The grading procedure is especially important. Stotsky explains: "Students have a powerful incentive to improve their handwriting and to proofread carefully if they are graded only for the number of errors they do not find themselves. In this way, only unwillingness to proofread carefully is penalized. Careful proofreading usually involves rereading a passage many times" (1982, p. 332).

STRATEGY EXAMPLE 6.1

DIRECTIONS FOR DICTATION

1. Observe margins and skip every other line.
2. The passage will be read three times:
   a. The purpose of the first reading is to allow you to hear the entire passage without writing, in order to get the meaning. Listen and do not write. Difficult and unusual words will be written on the board.
   b. The second reading will be done slowly in phrases, without repetition, while you write. Remember: nothing will be repeated.
   c. The third reading will be at normal speed, allowing you to check for omissions, punctuation, and errors.
3. Proofread your paper using the copy of the dictated passage provided to you. You will be graded on the number of errors you do *not* find in your paper.

Source: From S. Stotsky. Dictation: Building listening, writing, and reading skills together. Reprinted from *The Leafet,* Journal of the New England Association of Teachers of English, 82:2 (Spring 1983), pp. 6–12. Reprinted with permission.

Proofreading will naturally focus students' attention on the spelling of words, enhancing their word recognition abilities. Follow-up activities can be used to focus students' attention on the meanings of key words in the passage, building their vocabulary knowledge. In addition, dictation exercises can equip students to read complex syntax by providing practice in the transcription and reading of succeedingly more difficult constructions in connected discourse.

☐ *Prereading Dictation*

Sullivan and Thompson (1985) report that the reading comprehension of their upper-grade students improved noticeably after their participation in a series of dictation experiences designed as a variation of the usual "read-discuss-write" model of instruction. Prior to giving a reading assignment, the teacher dictated a few brief passages from it as the students copied them. The primary purpose in using dictation in this way was to focus the students' attention on the reading that would be assigned to them and build interest in the passage. Sullivan and Thompson claim:

> Students compelled to write down a part of what they will later be expected to read and analyze seem later to read with more concentration and appreciation. The physical act of writing out a passage makes these students more intimately involved with material which they might otherwise merely scan. Furthermore, taking down dictations seems to help them discover that there is an infinity of forms, techniques, and styles of the written word.
>
> (1985, p. 89)

They advise teachers that, while it would be "tedious and impractical" for students to write down everything they read as a regular practice, selected Prereading Dictation exercises are likely to increase their comprehension.

SYNTAX

■ ■ English is a positional language that relies heavily on word ordering to communicate meaning. For example, "Sue hit the ball" has a considerably different meaning than "The ball hit Sue." In this simple illustration, word ordering determines whether Sue or the ball is the active agent responsible for the hitting and which is the recipient of the action. In order to fully understand written sentences, students must not only be able to recognize and know the meanings of individual words; they must also realize how the meanings of the words are affected by their position in the sentence.

While most children come to school knowing most of the basic English sentence patterns, they begin to encounter a number of complex syntactic constructions in upper-grade and high school content-area texts which, if unfamiliar, can interfere with reading comprehension (Devine, 1986). In addition, research has shown that there are large individual differences in children's rates of syntactic development. Loban (1976), for example, found that some primary-grade children were six years behind other children in their ability to use and interpret sentence patterns. Such children may have difficulty understanding some of the more basic syntactic constructions.

There is ample evidence that sentence-combining activities, which require students to combine several simple sentences into one sentence while retaining important information, are effective in developing the syntax of intermediate-grade and older students' writing (Stotsky, 1975). Sentence-modeling exercises, requiring children to write sentences similar to model patterns, have been recommended for younger children, and several studies have reported that such exercises improved the writing of primary-grade students (Noyce & Christie, 1983; Odegaard & May, 1972).

Because familiarity with the syntactic patterns used by writers is essential to readers as they strive to make meaning from the text, it is logical to assume that sentence-manipulation practice would indirectly facilitate students' reading comprehension by familiarizing them with advanced syntactic structures. Research on the effects of sentence-combining programs on reading has had mixed results, with most studies (e.g., Neville & Searls, 1985; Straw & Schreiner, 1982) reporting that such programs produce significant gains on informal cloze tests of comprehension but not on standardized reading tests. The only studies reporting gains on standardized tests featured sentence-manipulation activities which were integrated with reading (Noyce & Christie, 1983; Obenchain, 1971). In these latter studies, the sentences manipulated came from material that the students had read or were to read later. The subjects had experience not only in constructing complex sentences but also in reading such sentences.

Sentence-combining and modeling exercises can indirectly promote reading comprehension in several ways. Over time, such exercises can equip readers to process complex units of text more efficiently. Such exercises can help word-bound readers learn to cluster groups of words into phrases and clauses, building larger units. This "chunking" process enables them to remember better what they have read. Authors use complex syntax to specify relationships between the ideas in a sentence. Sentence-manipulation activities can help readers recognize these relationships, enabling them to reconstruct more fully the meaning encoded in the text.

"Open," or nondirected, sentence-combining exercises encourage students to explore multiple ways to combine kernel structures, with no single correct solution (Strong, 1976). For example:

Kernel sentences:

Harry was a magician.
Harry was clever.
He made himself disappear.
The audience was delighted.

Possible combinations:

Harry was a clever magician who delighted audiences by making himself disappear.
By making himself disappear, a clever magician named Harry delighted the audience.
To the delight of the audience, Harry, the clever magician, disappeared.

In open sentence combining, a variety of sentence transformations and combinations can be explored. Any of the kernel sentences can serve as the base clause, and there is no predetermined correct result.

"Signaled," or directed, sentence-combining activities, in which students use parenthetical clues to develop predetermined structures, require right answers. For example, in the following exercise the student must use *that* in combining two sentences:

Kernel sentences:

Julie discovered *something.*
Her reading contest badge was missing. (*that*)

Correct combination:

Julie discovered that her reading contest badge was missing.

Strong (1976) encourages teachers to use both signaled and open approaches to ensure that students experience the advantages of each format — "the discipline of attending to increasingly complex transformations, the freedom of exploring a personal style" (p. 63).

Lawlor (1983) reports that there is no agreement in textbooks about the sequencing of sentence-combining instruction, raising the issue of which constructions should be taught early and which should be postponed until students are more mature. He notes the speculation of some experts that sentence combining should merely ask children to apply their oral skills to written language. For example, Hailey (1978) advises teachers to introduce syntactic patterns present in children's speech, presenting the constructions one at a time in sequence. On the other hand, we have studied children's writing at different grade levels to determine the frequency with which they use different sentence patterns in their written language (Noyce & Christie, 1985). We found that third-graders rarely use subordinate clauses introduced by *what, who, where, until,* or *after* in their narrative writing. Exercises in which complex sentences are built with these connectives would appear to be appropriate for these students. Upper-level students, having already developed facility with the preceding structures, could profit from exercises involving less frequently used connectives such as *while, unless, since, before, although, whenever, whom,* and *as.*

Whichever sequence or type of sentence-combining activity is used, it is important to link the exercises to reading. As mentioned earlier, the only studies reporting consistent gains in reading comprehension have featured integrated reading and writing activities. It is important that students not only have experience writing complex syntactic structures but also have practice reading the structures. The strategies that follow are examples of how sentence-manipulation activities can be successfully integrated with reading.

■ Basal Sentence Combining

The basal reader can be an excellent vehicle for linking reading and writing. Reutzel (1986) describes basals as a rich source of material for sentence-combining exercises, pointing out that basal readers contain syntactically simple constructions which students can combine in varied patterns to make interesting longer sentences, reinforcing their reading skills as they write. He points out that basals have the additional advantage of being easily accessible to teachers and can save time by making it unnecessary for them to make up their own sentences to be combined.

Reutzel recommends the teaching of four basic sentence-combining techniques in the primary and intermediate grades:

1. *Addition.* Two or more simple sentences are joined with *and.*
2. *Embedding.* Modifiers from one sentence are inserted into another sentence.
3. *Coordination.* Two equally important sentences are joined by a coordinating conjunction (*and, but, for, or*), a semicolon, or a correlative conjunction (*either . . . or, neither . . . nor*).
4. *Subordination.* Two or more sentences are combined, with one made dependent upon another through the use of a subordinating conjunction (*when, because, if, who, after, that*).

Students need to be taught a signaling system to denote which of the four techniques they are to use and to designate the positioning of suggested changes. Strong (1981) has developed four useful symbols for this purpose: the arrow, umbrella, margin signal, and footnote (see Figure 6.1). The examples in Figure 6.2 illustrate the use of the four sentence-combining techniques and their signaling devices. The sentences, extracted from several different basal series, are syntactically identical to the originals; however, the content has been revised.

Reutzel cautions teachers about trying to teach too many sentence-combining techniques to children at one time. Ample practice should be provided for learning each procedure before new techniques are introduced. We also recommend that teachers make an effort to follow up sentence-combining exercises with reading experiences focusing on similar syntactic structures. For example, if children have just practiced the subordination strategy using *if* and *because,* have them search for similar constructions in the books they are reading. Children's literature, with its uncontrolled syntax, will usually be a better source of complex structures than basal readers.

■ Sentence Reconstruction

Variations of nondirected sentence combining have been used successfully to reinforce students' abilities to process discourse by improving their syntactic skills. The reconstruction of sentences in material students are

FIGURE 6.1   Strong's (1981) Sentence-Combining Signals

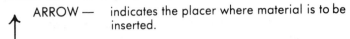

ARROW — indicates the placer where material is to be inserted.

UMBRELLA — designates a cluster of words to be embedded.

MARGIN SIGNAL — denotes that a coordinating or correlative conjunction is to be added.

FOOTNOTE — points to sentences to be combined through subordination.

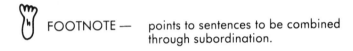

preparing to read is one such variation. In this strategy, complex sentences are first decombined—separated into simple , kernel sentences. After grasping the meaning in the simple sentences, students then recombine the kernels back into complex structures. Experimentation has led teachers to recommend this strategy for use with both elementary-grade disabled readers and normal high school students.

As a result of their observations of tutored children in grades one through nine, Nutter and Safran (1984) concluded that sentence reconstruction exercises can improve the reading comprehension skills of learning-disabled children. In their experiment, tutors decombined complex sentences from the textbooks the children were reading into simple sentences. Prior to reading the material individually, children were asked to recombine the kernel sentences by manipulating them into various patterns. After discussing their versions of the sentences, they read the original story. The tutors reported that the prereading sentence reconstruction activities made the students more confident with reading material beyond their present reading levels and improved their understanding of complex structures.

When Sharon Austin's (1986) high school students complained about the length and complexity of the sentences of major writers, particularly Faulkner and Poe, she decided to involve them in the decombining of sentences in paragraphs taken from literature, followed by the recombining of the simple sentences in their own combinations. In the process, the students discovered that syntax is used by writers to produce a desired effect. Austin observed that the sentence reconstruction took her students

FIGURE 6.2   Sentence-Combining Examples

1. ADDITION:
   I hurried out to the garage.
   I turned on the water to clean the floor.
   S-C Rewrite: I hurried out to the garage <u>and</u> turned
   on the water to clean the floor.

2. EMBEDDING:
   Once there was a boy who lived in New Mexico.

   He lived in an adobe house.

   The house had two rooms.

   S-C Rewrite: Once there was a boy who lived in a
   two-room adobe house in New Mexico.

3. COORDINATION:
   therefore ── Debris flew everywhere.
   The boy and his friends ran for cover.
   S-C Rewrite: Debris flew everywhere; therefore, the
   boy and his friends ran for cover.

4. SUBORDINATION:
   although Becky likes to play soccer.
   She didn't join a team this year.
   S-C Rewrite: Although Becky likes to play soccer,
   she didn't join a team this year.

beyond traditional sentence-combining exercises to experimentation with techniques of established writers and analysis of their styles. Students discovered that the techniques authors use are determined by their purposes. As a result, they developed new appreciation for the literature they were reading and increased their understanding of it.

In one exercise, Austin had her students recombine the sentences in the first paragraph of Faulkner's famous short story, "The Bear." The original is as follows:

He was ten. But it had already begun, long before that day when at last he wrote his age in two figures and he saw for the first time the camp where his father and Major de Spain and old General Compson and the others spent two weeks each November and two weeks again each June. He had already inherited then, without ever having seen it, the tremendous bear with one trap-ruined foot which, in an area almost a hundred miles deep, had earned for itself a name, a definite designation like a living man.

One of Austin's students reconstructed this paragraph to read:

He was ten. But it had already begun. It was long before that day when he wrote his age in two figures. It was long before he saw the camp for the first time where his father, Major de Spain, old General Compson, and the others stayed. They stayed at that camp two weeks each November and June. He had inherited a tremendous bear. He had never seen the bear. The bear had one trap ruined foot. The bear had earned a name. It was a definite designation like a living man. It was known in an area almost a hundred miles deep.

(p. 6)*

Students found this simplified rendition to be boring and childish. They recognized that Faulkner's story-telling style made the original passage sound as though a person were actually talking.

After similar experiences with reconstructing passages from Poe, Austin's students commented that they sometimes preferred their own versions, although they credited Poe for using repetition and phrasing skillfully for dramatic purposes.

We recommend that teachers of children try the reconstruction technique within one-sentence contexts, using excerpts from appropriate classical literature. Kenneth Grahame's *The Wind in the Willows* is a suitable book for this purpose. We have chosen two sentences from the book to illustrate the process. Each exercise becomes more challenging than the previous one as students are given longer and more complex sentences to reconstruct.

In each exercise, students are required to recombine a list of simple sentences into one sentence. The following is the result of decombining one complex sentence from *Wind in the Willows*:

Toad sat straight down.
He sat in the middle of the road.
The road was dusty.
His legs stretched out before him.
He stared fixedly.
He stared in the direction of the motor car.
The motor car was disappearing.

After writing their own sentences, students compare them with the original sentence in the book:

Toad sat straight down in the middle of the dusty road, his legs stretched out before him, and stared fixedly in the direction of the disappearing motor-car.

*From S. Austin (1986). Beyond sentence combining. *Quarterly of the National Writing Project and The Center for the Study of Writing, 8*(3), pp. 5–7, edited by Gerald Camp.

Repeated reading, comparison, and discussion encourages students to become critical readers of Grahame's sentences.

These exercises can increase in complexity with each experience, until students are presented with such challenging lists as this one to incorporate into one sentence:

Toad talked big.
He talked about what he was going to do in the days to come.
The stars grew fuller.
The stars grew larger.
The stars were all around them.
A moon appeared.
It appeared suddenly.
It was yellow.
It appeared silently.
It came from nowhere in particular.
The moon came to keep them company.
It came to listen.
It came to hear them talk.

Grahame's original sentence is:

Toad talked big about what he was going to do in the days to come, while stars grew larger and fuller all around them, and a yellow moon, appearing suddenly from nowhere in particular, came to keep them company and listen to them talk.

Sentence reconstruction activities can also help readers cope with the syntax of past eras by creating an awareness of differences in the elements of style between the students' own sentences and those of classical writers. For example, a reconstruction exercise based on the first paragraph of Daniel Defoe's *Robinson Crusoe* (1719), a lengthy novel written in archaic vocabulary and syntax, demonstrates changes in our language and helps students read the classics with interest and proficiency.

TEXT STRUCTURE

■ ■ In addition to the general knowledge and reading purpose schemata discussed in Chapter 5, there is another type of schema which has an important impact on reading comprehension. This type of schema pertains to the reader's knowledge about the structure and organization of different types of written discourse. Research has revealed that the two most common types of text—narrative and expository—have very different structural principles (Mandler & Johnson, 1977; Meyer, 1975; Stein & Glenn, 1979).

Narrative stories are organized around a temporal order of events involving one or more main characters, whereas expository texts are organized around logical relationships between concepts such as ordered listings, cause/effect, problem/solution, comparisons, and contrasts (Meyer & Free-dle, 1984). Through experience, readers develop schemata for different types of texts, and these schemata facilitate comprehension by helping readers to anticipate what is important in a passage and to focus their attention on that content. For example, the schemata for narrative texts will guide readers to pay attention to the goals of the main characters, their attempts to achieve these goals, and the outcomes of these attempts. Expository text schemata, on the other hand, focus the reader's attention on identifying the relationships among the main concepts in the passage. Research has shown that the ability to recognize and utilize text structure leads to better recall of text information (Meyer, Brandt, & Bluth, 1980).

Primary-grade students' knowledge of narrative story structures is typically far ahead of their knowledge of expository structures. This is because they have had less exposure to expository passages, and because the structure of expository texts tends to be more difficult and complex (Drum, 1984). In this chapter we will focus on narrative discourse, saving the discussion of expository structures for Chapter 7, "Writing and Reading in the Content Areas."

Text-analysis research has shown that many simple narrative stories share the same basic structure. Researchers have devised "grammars" to describe this structure. A popular story grammar devised by Mandler and Johnson (1977) has two major elements: (a) a *setting,* which describes the time and location of the story and introduces the main character; and (b) one or more *episodes,* in which the main character sets goals and attempts to achieve them. Each episode has six components:

1. *Beginning.* A problem occurs which starts the "action rolling";
2. *Simple Reaction.* The main character's thoughts and feelings about the beginning;
3. *Goal.* What the main character decides to do about the problem that emerged in the beginning;
4. *Attempt.* How the main character attempts to reach the goal;
5. *Outcome.* Describes whether the attempt is a success or failure;
6. *Ending.* Tells about the consequences of the attempt and outcome. (adapted from Spiegel & Fitzgerald, 1986)*

In addition, there are higher-order components, including the *theme,* which is the story's major idea, and the *plot,* which is how the episodes are organized (Cooper, 1986).

*From Spiegel, D.L., and Fitzgerald, J. (1986). Improving reading comprehension through instruction about story parts. *The Reading Teacher* (39), pp. 676–682. Reprinted with permission.

Most children begin school with some awareness of narrative story structure as a result of a variety of experiences, including the fairy tales and stories that their parents have read to them and the hundreds of stories they have watched on television and in movies (Flood, Lapp, & Farnan, 1986). However, many primary-grade students have been found to have only a partially developed sense of story. Fitzgerald and Spiegel (1983), for example, found that more than 20 percent of the fourth-graders in their study lacked a clear sense of narrative story structure. This lack of story sense undoubtedly inhibited these students' abilities to write their own stories and may have indirectly interfered with their reading comprehension.

Teaching children about narrative structure has been found to improve their writing abilities. Fitzgerald and Teasley (1986), for instance, screened fourth-grade students to identify those who lacked a clear knowledge of story structure. These students were then divided into an experimental and a control group. Results showed that the students who received instruction on narrative structure wrote better-organized and higher-quality stories than control group subjects.

Instruction in story structure has also been found to indirectly improve students' reading comprehension, especially if the instruction includes writing. Research has shown that programs in which children write their own stories that follow model structures (Fitzgerald & Spiegel, 1983) have been much more successful in promoting reading comprehension than programs focused on the mere recognition of story structures (Dreher & Singer, 1980; Sebesta, Calder, & Cleland, 1982). In the unsuccessful programs, students were taught to recognize the structure of *existing* stories. In the successful Fitzgerald and Spiegel (1983) program, students were also taught how to recognize story elements; however, in addition, they were given opportunities to write *their own* stories that followed the story structure. This not only improved low-ability fourth-graders' knowledge of story structure but also significantly enhanced their reading comprehension. Apparently, writing stories to fit structural templates encourages children to consciously attend to story organization and gets them to attempt to control text structure. They learn about story structures by constructing their own. This, in turn, can help them recognize the same structures when reading, facilitating recall by focusing their attention on important story elements.

The following strategies are examples of different ways in which writing can help improve students' knowledge of narrative story structure. These text-structure strategies, like the sentence manipulation in the previous section, do not lead to specific reading activities. Instead, these writing activities can indirectly facilitate reading comprehension by building greater awareness of text structures. Over time, these activities should facilitate both the story writing and reading comprehension of intermediate-grade students, particularly those who have a limited knowledge of narrative structure.

■ **Story Templates**

The Fitzgerald and Spiegel (1983) program mentioned above used Story Templates based on story grammar to acquaint fourth-graders with narrative text structure. These templates featured the seven elements in Mandler and Johnson's (1977) story grammar: setting, beginning, simple reaction, goal, attempt, outcome, and ending (see definitions above). Figure 6.3 shows the "Mrs. Cow" story Spiegel and Fitzgerald used to illustrate each of these components.

Students were first taught to recognize these story parts and then given opportunities to write their own stories containing these parts. Recognition was taught by introducing one new story part at a time, using a chart containing a story with labeled components (similar to the "Mrs. Cow" story in Figure 6.3). Several examples of the "target" story part were elicited

FIGURE 6.3   The Parts of a Well-Formed Story   Source: From Dixie Lee Spiegel and Jill Fitzgerald. Improving Reading Comprehension Through Instruction about Story Parts. *The Reading Teacher,* March 1986, pp. 676–682. Reprinted with permission of Dixie Lee Spiegel, Jill Fitzgerald, and the International Reading Association.

Setting	One day Mrs. Cow was walking around the barnyard on Mr. Brown's farm.
Beginning	All of a sudden she spied Mr. Brown's garden, just outside the barnyard fence. The garden was full of ripe cabbages, tender green beans, juicy melons, and delicious squash.
Simple reaction	Mrs. Cow said to herself, "My, those vegetables and fruits are very tempting. And I am soooo hungry."
Goal	Mrs. Cow decided to get into the garden somehow.
Attempt	So she trotted all the way back across the barnyard, until she was as far away from the garden fence as she could get. Then she lowered her head and ran as fast as she could right at the fence. Wham! She hit the fence hard.
Outcome	The fence was old and it broke into 100 pieces. Mrs. Cow smiled in satisfaction and stepped daintily over the shattered fence, into the garden.
Ending	Mr. Brown, of course, was not very pleased, and tied Mrs. Cow up in the barn for 3 days as a punishment. But Mrs. Cow was sure that it had been worth it!

FIGURE 6.4   Story Template

SETTING: One hot summer's afternoon, Freddie the turtle decided to go to the river for a swim.

BEGINNING _____

_____

_____

SIMPLE REACTION _____

_____

_____

GOAL _____

_____

ATTEMPT _____

_____

_____

_____

OUTCOME _____

_____

_____

ENDING _____

_____

_____

by the students. Then several nonexamples (other story parts) were presented, and the students discussed why these were not examples of the target component.

Once the students were familiar with the story parts, they were given templates on which to write stories. These templates were worksheets with a setting written at the top and labels for each story element written on the left-hand side of the page (see Figure 6.4). The students then wrote their own stories on the templates, composing their own versions of each of the story elements. Once the stories were written, children shared their stories, all of which were based on the same setting.

Several other story production activities were used to give students additional practice with the story elements. Give the Next Part was a gamelike activity in which a group of students were given a setting and then worked together to compose a story, one part at a time:

1. Students were first asked which story part comes next (the beginning), and required to justify their answers.
2. Alternatives for the beginning were elicited from two students, who were then asked to explain why their particular beginnings met the criteria for a good beginning.
3. The group selected one of the two beginnings for use in the story.
4. Steps 1–3 were repeated for each of the remaining parts of the story.

Cumulative Stories was an activity in which students each wrote their own settings and then passed them on to another child. The students read the setting they had been given and wrote a beginning to fit with that setting. These settings plus beginnings were then read and added on to by other children. When finished, the stories were returned to the students who wrote the initial settings. Spiegel and Fitzgerald (1986) reported that the setting authors were usually quite surprised at how the stories turned out.

Piccolo (1986) has developed a strategy that can be used both to acquaint intermediate-grade students with story parts and as a *readiness* activity for the Spiegel/Fitzgerald template exercises. In this strategy, the teacher uses templatelike questions and a story frame to help students compose narratives about their daily school experiences. The teacher's questions are designed to elicit the elements of a well-formed narrative story. The teacher begins by constructing a story framework, asking questions and writing down the students' responses on the chalkboard. The following illustration shows the types of questions that the teacher (T) asks and gives examples of possible class (C) responses:

SETTING

Main character
    T: What's the name of the main character in our story?
    C: Joey.

Time
    T: What time is it?
    C: Friday noon.

Place
    T: Where is Joey?
    C: At the school cafeteria.

EPISODE

Beginning
    T: What event starts the story?
    C: Joey loses his lunch ticket.

Simple Reaction
- T: How does this make Joey feel?
- C: Very bad. He is very hungry.

Goal
- T: What does Joey want to do?
- C: Eat lunch.

Attempt
- T: What does he do?
- C: Borrow a ticket from Sue.

Outcome
- T: What happens?
- C: Sue has one extra ticket. She gives it to Joey.

Ending
- T: How does Joey feel about this?
- C: He is very happy and likes Sue a lot.

The teacher then takes the phrases and sentences on the board and demonstrates how the framework can be used to make a story:

> It is Friday noon, and Joey is standing in the cafeteria line. Joey suddenly discovers that he has lost his lunch ticket. This makes Joey very sad. He is very hungry, and he wants to eat lunch. Suddenly he remembers that Sue, the girl behind him, usually has an extra ticket. Joey asks her if he could borrow a ticket and pay her back on Monday. Sue gives the ticket to Joey. This makes Joey very happy. From then on, Sue and Joey are very good friends.

This can be repeated with stories based on other daily classroom routines such as going out to recess, checking out books at the library, and going to see the school nurse. After watching the teacher write several stories from story frames on the board, the children can begin writing their own stories based on the frames.

Piccolo's strategy has the advantage of being concrete, using stories that come directly from the children's experiences. In addition, the children are given a considerable amount of guidance, modeling, and structure. It would be a good strategy to use prior to having students write their own stories using templates such as the one illustrated in Figure 6.4.

Piccolo (1986) has also devised a more advanced strategy, the Story Organizer, which is a good *follow-up* activity to Story Template exercises. Story Organizers are appropriate for upper-grade students who are already familiar with story parts and who have already mastered the art of writing simple narratives. This strategy is less structured than the Spiegel/Fitzgerald templates and enables students to write more complicated narratives containing a series of connected episodes. Unlike a Story Template, the student does not write an entire story on the form. Instead, students make notes about elements to be incorporated into their stories. The organizer is then used as a framework or outline for writing the story. In her article, Piccolo presents a Story Organizer form for writing fairy tales. Rob Davis adapted this fairy tale organizer for use in a story-writing learning center in his fourth-grade classroom. He revised Piccolo's form to make it appropriate for use with all literary genres. The resulting "generic" Story Organizer is illustrated in Figure 6.5. Note that it differs from the Spiegel/Fitzgerald templates in several respects. The blank lines are shorter, permitting the student to jot down only a phrase or two for each story element. In addition, there are many more prompts and questions, resulting in a more detailed outline for the story.

Story Template and Story Organizer activities allow children to get actively involved in learning the structure of narrative stories. They learn the parts of story grammars by actually producing meaningful narratives containing these elements. It is important that such activities be followed up by having the students read other narrative stories, drawing their attention to the story parts they have been studying. This type of integrated instruction will ensure that students utilize their knowledge of story structure while reading as well as when writing their own stories.

■ **Macro-Cloze Tasks**

Children's knowledge of story structure can be increased through instructional tasks which involve them in examining parts of stories and their relationship to one another. Whaley (1981) points out that the incomplete and scrambled story exercises which have been used in the past take on an added dimension with story grammar terminology. Parts of stories can be labeled and discussed, enhancing children's concept of story. She recommends a macro-cloze task that resembles traditional cloze exercises in that aspects of the story are deleted. However, in the macro-cloze task, the teacher deletes whole story parts, such as setting and beginning, for the students to fill in rather than just single words.

Whaley (1981) describes two applications of the macro-cloze technique appropriate for use with students above the first grade:

1. The teacher draws lines on the printed story to indicate which sentences are to be omitted. The amounts of material removed from the story may vary from several sentences to several paragraphs. After students read the story they supply the missing section, either orally or in writing. Follow-up discussion focuses on comparing the various versions offered by students and centers on judging why certain types of information are appropriate for filling in the missing section and others are not. The teacher can also

FIGURE 6.5   Rob Davis's "Generic" Story Organizer

STORY GRAMMAR ELEMENTS

CHARACTER

Who will be in your story? _____

What are their names? _____

Describe your main characters. _____

_____

SETTING

Where does your story take place? _____

When does your story happen? _____

GOAL

What does your main character want to accomplish in this story? _____

_____

What is going to interfere with your characters as they try to attain their goal? _____

_____

How is the main character going to overcome this problem? _____

_____

PLOT

What does the main character do first? _____

_____

How does your character feel about this? _____

What does your character do next? _____

What results from these actions? _____

RESOLUTION

What happens to the main character at the end of the story? _____

_____

How does your character feel now? _____

How is your story going to end? _____

provide some incorrect answers and ask students to discuss why those answers do not fit in the story.

2. The class is divided into six small groups, each of which receives a copy of the same story. However, a different section of the story has been deleted for each group. Each group is asked to write the missing section of their story. Then the teacher tape records the section each group has written as a member reads it aloud. When the tape is completed and played back, the children hear a whole new story from setting to ending. A discussion critiquing the new story follows, with attention centering on the parts and their relationships to each other. Finally, the teacher reads the original story to the class, after which the students compare their new story parts with the original ones.

(p. 769)*

■ Story Diagrams

Pictures and diagrams are another means for acquainting children with story structures. Illustrations can provide students with concrete visual representations of story parts and their relationships to each other.

Rubin (1980) has developed a strategy, Story Maker, which is ideal for this purpose. A tree diagram is used to represent the relationships among the parts of a multi-setting, multi-episode plot. If used with the Mandler and Johnson (1977) story grammar labels, these tree diagrams are an excellent way to extend students' knowledge of story structure gained through the template activities described in the previous section.

We recommend that teachers begin with a two-episode structure, such as the one illustrated in Figure 6.6. A modification of Smith and Bean's (1983) Story Maker strategy can then be used to acquaint students with this more complex story structure:

1. The teacher prepares a large blank story tree on chart paper and presents it to a small group of students. There is a brief review in which the story parts are related to previous Story Template lessons.
2. The teacher leads a brainstorming session in which students contribute ideas for filling each level of the story tree.
3. The group reaches consensus on each story part; the teacher writes the agreed upon version on the chart.
4. Using the story tree as a guide, the students each write their own version of the story.
5. When completed, the students read their stories orally, sharing them with the group.

Story Maker tree diagrams can be used in conjunction with Story Template activities such as Cumulative Stories to provide students with additional practice. Each student can be given a worksheet with a blank story tree. They each fill in the setting portion of the diagram. Then the tree

*From Whaley, J.F. (1981). Story Grammar and reading instruction. *The Reading Teacher, 34*, pp. 762–771. Reprinted with permission of the International Reading Association and J.F. Whaley.

FIGURE 6.6   Example of a Two-Episode Story Tree

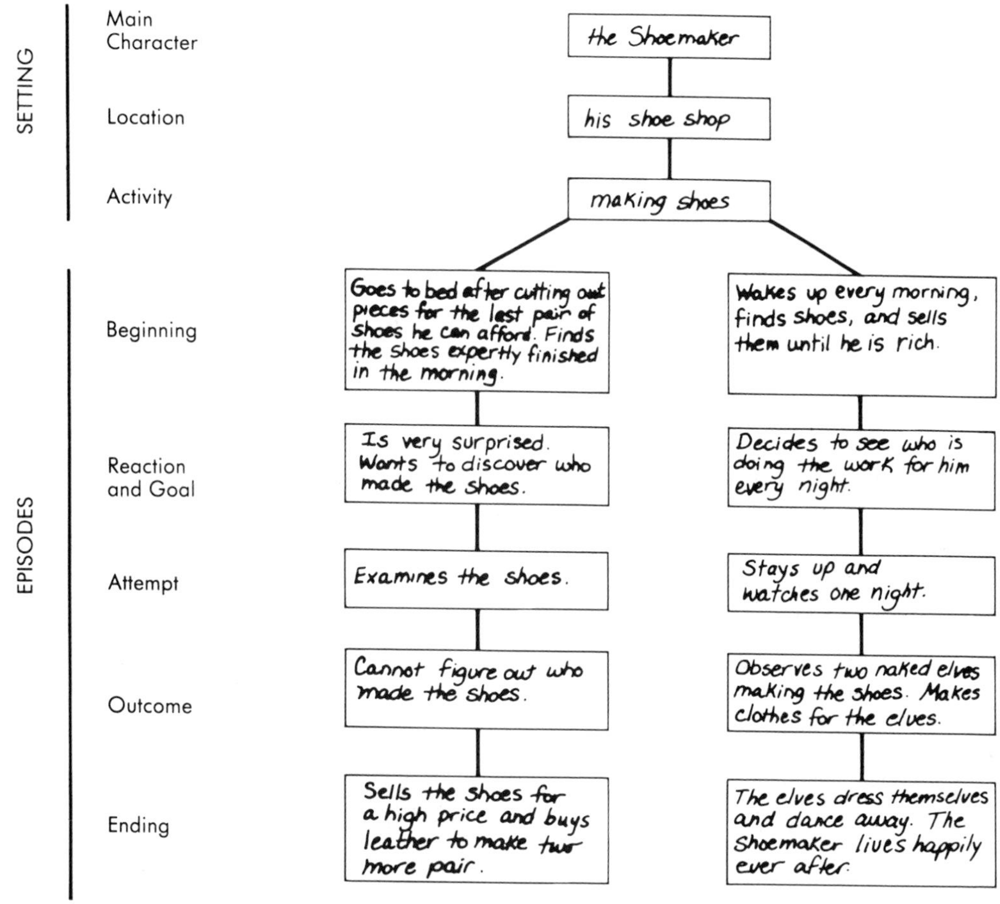

SETTING

Main Character	the Shoemaker
Location	his shoe shop
Activity	making shoes

EPISODES

	Episode 1	Episode 2
Beginning	Goes to bed after cutting out pieces for the last pair of shoes he can afford. Finds the shoes expertly finished in the morning.	Wakes up every morning, finds shoes, and sells them until he is rich.
Reaction and Goal	Is very surprised. Wants to discover who made the shoes.	Decides to see who is doing the work for him every night.
Attempt	Examines the shoes.	Stays up and watches one night.
Outcome	Cannot figure out who made the shoes.	Observes two naked elves making the shoes. Makes clothes for the elves.
Ending	Sells the shoes for a high price and buys leather to make two more pair.	The elves dress themselves and dance away. The Shoemaker lives happily ever after.

diagrams are passed to other students who add parts to the story. The completed stories can then be returned to the setting authors or shared with the group via oral reading.

Once students have mastered two-episode stories, the Story Maker trees can be used to familiarize them with multi-setting stories (see Figure 6.7). Since such stories can be quite long, teachers may wish to begin by having students write group stories. For example, a small group of students can be helped to develop the first three levels of the tree—the main character, two locations, and two activities for each location—together. Then individual students develop plans for one or two episodes for each setting. These episode plans can be shared with the group and critiqued. The revised episode parts are then written onto the large multi-setting chart. Finally, the group can work together to write a story following the plan on the tree diagram.

Story diagrams can also be used to acquaint students with higher-level

FIGURE 6.7 Multi-Setting, Multi-Episode Story Tree

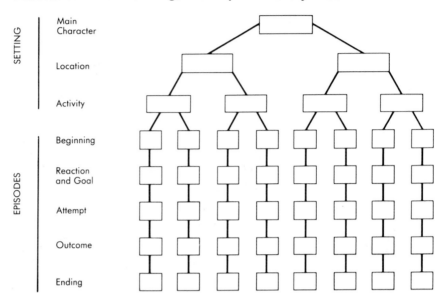

structural features, such as patterns in which the episodes of a story are organized. The plots of folktales, for example, tend to follow several basic patterns:

1. *Circle stories.* The story begins and ends at the same place (*Millions of Cats* and "The Three Poor Tailors").
2. *Cumulative stories.* The events of each episode, plus all the preceding ones, are carried over into the next episode ("The Little Red Hen" and "The Great Big Enormous Turnip").
3. *Rising action stories.* The relating of three events, with increasing action in each succeeding episode ("The Three Billy Goats Gruff" and "The Three Little Pigs").

Recognition of such patterns is an important factor in comprehending and responding to fairy tales. Favat (1977) explains:

> Children's response to the world order and to the hero of the fairy tale, which can be seen as a response to the content of the tale, is probably complemented by their response to the *form* of the tale, and in particular to its unusually regulated patterns, a characteristic that even the occasional reader of the tale soon discovers.
>
> (pp. 51–52)

Pictures have the advantage of being able to concretely represent the relationships between episodes in these different fairy tale patterns, helping students to discover the organization of each type of story. These illustrations can also serve as models to help children write their own fairy tales, further advancing their mastery of the story patterns.

Jett-Simpson (1981) describes a strategy for using pictures to acquaint primary-grade children with the circle story pattern. She uses as her example the book *Millions of Cats.* This tale begins and ends at an old man's house. The story opens with the old man setting out to find a cat for his wife. He eventually stumbles on to millions of cats, and unable to pick the best one, he starts back home with all of them. When they arrive home, the cats fight about who is the prettiest until only one kitten is left. This cat lives happily ever after with the old man and his wife. Several steps are involved:*

> 1. *Presentation of the Model Story.*   The teacher reads the story to the children, encouraging them to become involved in the reading. With *Millions of Cats,* they are invited to join in on the repeat refrain.
>
> 2. *Guidance in Comprehension of Model Story Structure.*   Small groups of students are directed to draw a circle with an illustration of the starting point (the old man's house) at the top. Next, the children are helped to divide the circle into a number of sections corresponding to the number of episodes in the story. *Millions of Cats* can be divided into six episodes: (a) the old man leaves home; (b) he finds the millions of cats; (c) the cats eat all the grass on a hill; (d) the cats drink all the water in a pond; (e) the cats fight over who is prettiest; and (f) only one kitten is left, who is adopted by the man and his wife. Then the children illustrate each scene (see Figure 6.8).
>
> 3. *Discussion of Story Structure.*   The illustrated diagrams are placed on the wall so the class can see how each group interpreted the story. The teacher leads a discussion to focus children's attention on the plot pattern.
>
> 4. *Development of a Group Circle Story.*   A large circle is drawn on the chalkboard by the teacher. A house is put at the top, and the circle is divided into four sections. The teacher tells the students that the story will have four parts: (a) main character leaves home to accomplish a goal; (b) first adventure; (c) second adventure; and (d) third adventure, in which the main character returns home with the problem solved. The teacher then asks a series of questions to help the group plan their story. For example, "Who is going to be our main character?" and "What is going to happen in our first adventure?" After the class has made a choice for each element, a child comes to the board and illustrates that segment of the story. When finished, individual children can take turns telling parts of the story.
>
> 5. *Children Write Circle Stories.*   Individually or in small groups, children plan their own stories using circle diagrams. Jett-Simpson (1981) recommends that initial stories be limited to four episodes. The same guide questions that were used previously can be used to help children decide on the content of each episode. Once the picture stories are complete, the children use them as a plan for writing their own story. As an option, peer groups can be used to revise and polish the stories. The stories can be published and

**FIGURE 6.8   Circle Diagram for *Millions of Cats*   Source: From M. Jett-Simpson.
Writing stories using models structures: The circle story. *Language Arts,* 58, 293–300.
Copyright © 1981 by the National Council of Teachers of English. Reprinted by
permission of the publisher.

placed in the class library. Children should also be encouraged to share their finished stories by reading them aloud to the class.

We recommend adding one additional step to this strategy. After children have written and shared their own circle stories, provide opportunities for them to read other folktales that follow the same pattern. This will give them experience recognizing the pattern when reading. The teacher may initially need to draw children's attention to relationships between the stories they are reading and the stories they have written, but often this recognition will occur spontaneously (Smith & Bean, 1983).

PARAPHRASING AND TEXT CONDENSATION

■ ■ As explained in the introductory chapter of this book, reading comprehension is an active process which involves the reconstruction of meaning embedded in text. Writing, when linked to reading passages, can promote this process by actively engaging students with the ideas contained in a text. Stotsky (1982) explains:

> For anything to be learned or comprehended, it must be worked through completely. Writing may be the most active way of ensuring that process. . . . By requiring students to respond in writing to words and ideas that they are asked to recall, reproduce, restate, select from, generalize, reorganize, integrate, or elaborate on, we may be providing them with the most active comprehension practice possible.
>
> (p. 339)

In this section, we deal with two types of writing activities that require students to review, reprocess, and reconstruct what they have just read. The first of these strategies is paraphrasing, which involves translating texts into one's own words. The second group of strategies consists of summary and précis writing, which require students to rephrase and condense texts at the same time. Both types of writing, when used as postreading activities, can contribute to literal recall by encouraging the active processing of text information.

■ Paraphrasing

Paraphrasing is a postreading strategy in which students translate what they have read into their own words. Paraphrasing has long been used as a testing device to assess comprehension. In fact, Gibson and Levin (1975) report that paraphrasing has been the most widely used measure in comprehension research. The assumption is that accurate paraphrasing requires more than a mere parroting back of the text. To paraphrase, readers must find other words in their vocabulary that match the meanings of the words used in the text. In this sense, paraphrasing forces readers to link the text with their prior knowledge.

Paraphrasing can also be used as a teaching strategy to promote reading comprehension. Having students paraphrase what they read, or "say it in their own words," gives them valuable practice in generating word meanings by requiring them to substitute and reorder words. Hudgins and Spies (1977) concluded, after an experiment in which middle school students were taught to paraphrase dictionary definitions, that practice in translating the meanings of words improves students' vocabulary knowledge. Stotsky (1982) also emphasizes the value of paraphrasing as a technique for learning the meanings of difficult words and syntactic constructions. She points out that, once students have succeeded in putting these words or sentences into their own words, "they have mastered the meaning of the original" (p. 334).

□ *Paraphrasing Pictures*

Stories told with pictures provide satisfying reading experiences for children of all proficiency levels by allowing them to read for meaning without facing word identification problems. Children appreciate the fact that pictures are a mode of writing, symbolizing ideas just as words do. McGee and Tompkins (1983) suggest that older readers often find wordless picture books as appealing as young readers do. Through wordless books, children can practice such generative reading skills as identifying main ideas, sequencing, and making inferences, arriving at their own interpretations of plots and characters through picture reading.

D'Angelo (1979) maintains that writing activities based on wordless books benefit students of all ages. By writing text for wordless storybooks, young children can learn paraphrasing skills to apply later with printed material. This approach can also be used as a remedial strategy with older students who experience difficulty with postreading paraphrasing exercises.

A group experience with an entertaining story told in pictures can lead naturally to a paraphrasing experience for children. The following activity, based on Paula Winter's *The Bear and the Fly* (Crown, 1976), illustrates how the paraphrasing of pictures can help students tell a story as they visualize it, putting it into their own words without having to cope with print:

> 1. Read *The Bear and the Fly* or view the Weston Woods filmstrip of the book together. (Showing the filmstrip eliminates the problem of the small book size.)
> 2. Discuss the hilarious story of the devastation caused by a buzzing fly in the house of a bear family as the father declares war on the fly.
> 3. Review the book or the filmstrip to reinforce the concept of a complete story being told without words, discussing the series of events.

4. Instruct the students to write a journal entry telling the story in their own words as they look at each picture again. Share the writings of any children who volunteer to read them, listing significant details on the board. Ask the class if any important details were omitted in the retellings. Write these on the board also.

5. Work together as a class to write a model paraphrase of *The Bear and the Fly* on the board, using the list of details and the contributions of the students. Edit the pieces together. (See the Strategy Example for a paraphrase of this story written by Rob Davis's fourth-grade class.)

6. Ask the students to copy the edited version in their journals to use in the future as a model paraphrase.

——————————— STRATEGY EXAMPLE 6.2 ———————————

A FOURTH-GRADE CLASS'S PARAPHRASE
OF *THE BEAR AND THE FLY*

Once there was a mother bear, a father bear, and a baby bear. One night they were all eating dinner and father bear was getting hot so he went over and opened the window. Mother bear started to hear a buzzing sound. Mother bear told Father bear that she thought she heard a fly. And she did. Father got up and grabbed his flyswatter and sat back down. Father looked at the fly for a second and then he swang at it. Father spilt everybody's drinks and food over. Then Mother bear and Baby bear started looking at Father bear. Then Dad swung at the fly that was right by Mother's head. When Father bear swung, the fly moved but Mother got hit on the head. Baby bear looked at Mother and the dog. Father started to chase the fly down the hall. Baby bear started looking at the fly that landed on her nose. He smacked her on the nose. He still didn't hit the fly. Then their dog looked at Baby bear. Then the fly landed on the dog's tail. Father hit Grover's tail and Grover began to squeal. Father picked up a chair and got on the dinner table. Mother looked at Papa with one eye opened. Then Papa started to lose his balance. Papa fell off the table head first. The house was a mess! The fly flew out the window.

The End

As a follow-up activity to this lesson, prepare a classroom collection of wordless storybooks (see "Recommended Children's Books"). Direct children to select a book that interests them and read it twice — once for enjoyment of the story and a second time for remembering the story line and important details well enough to be able to write the story in their own words. Allow the children to read the first-draft versions of their stories while the class looks at the pictures in the book, or have them edit their stories in peer groups and post them in a reading corner where other children can read them independently along with the wordless books.

Among the many writers who create wordless picture books, Mercer Meyer, Fernando Krahn, and John Goodall stand out for producing considerable numbers of high-quality books which tell interesting stories. A list of selected wordless books, which are appropriate for use with picture paraphrasing, is located at the end of this chapter.

☐ *Postreading Paraphrasing*

Postreading paraphrasing is often done orally, with the teacher asking students to put some aspect of the story just read into their own words (e.g., "What point was the author trying to make?" or "What happened at the end of the story?"). While such oral activities are valuable, Devine (1986) points out that requiring students to paraphrase in writing has some unique advantages over spoken paraphrases. Writing gives students additional time to think, reread, and organize while constructing their paraphrases and gives them a chance to revise their initial interpretations. If handed in, written paraphrases also provide teachers an opportunity to carefully examine what students understood from a reading assignment.

Shugarman and Hurst (1986) encourage teachers to guide students through the construction of paraphrases in this way:

1. Teachers and students interact after reading the text to be paraphrased, comparing their interpretations with each other and clarifying their understanding of it.
2. The teacher asks the students to write paraphrases of "main ideas, concrete examples, themes, procedures, new ideas, generalizations, and conclusions" (p. 397).
3. Students are permitted to consult with peers, dictionaries, and other resources while writing their paraphrases. Thorough rereading of the text is encouraged.
4. A variety of individual, paired, small group, and class activities for improving reading skills through paraphrasing are used.

The following examples are illustrations of the paraphrasing activities recommended by Shugarman and Hurst:

Give students a short passage and two paraphrases of it, one well constructed and one poorly done. Ask students to discuss the strengths and weaknesses of each. Have them discuss how they could determine meaning and write a meaningful paraphrase.

Give students a short passage and its paraphrase. Discuss the rephrasing as a new, simpler, more concise wording of the same meaning. Ask students to paraphrase a short passage using teacher written guide questions as clues. [See sample questions for expository text in Chapter 7, Figure 7.18.]

. . . Divide the class into teams and one "panel of experts." Assign text pages to be read and paraphrased by each team. The panel decides which paraphrase is best and why.

(1986, p. 398)

Paraphrasing is not an easy undertaking, and many students experience difficulty when attempting it. We suggest that teachers try to simplify the reading task for students in the early stages of teaching paraphrasing in order to avoid some of the complexities that arise with interpretations of words and their meanings.

■ Summary and Précis Writing

The National Assessment of Educational Progress (1981) reports that, although 85 percent of our thirteen-year-olds can complete a multiple-choice comprehension check correctly after reading, only 15 percent can write an accurate one-sentence summary of a paragraph just read. This points an accusing finger at our schools, confirming Durkin's (1978–1979) finding that comprehension skills are more often tested than taught.

Summaries are condensations which retain the gist or essence of a passage. Exercises in summarizing material that has been read promote active processing of text information by requiring students to select the important ideas from a passage and omit the nonessential ones. Summarizing also provides students with practice in recalling information, an essential skill young readers tend to lack. Research on generative reading comprehension confirms that both comprehension and retention of text information can be improved through summary writing (Doctorow, Wittrock, & Marks, 1978; McNeil & Donant, 1982). Summaries restating in abbreviated form what has been read give a teacher useful diagnostic information about students' understanding of reading assignments. In spite of these advantages, summary writing is not widely taught (Hidi & Anderson, 1986), a fact evident in the National Assessment of Educational Progress (1981) findings cited earlier.

Writing a summary involves both paraphrasing and condensing material, requiring students to process text even more thoroughly than they do when paraphrasing it. Whereas a paraphrase is often about the same length as the original passage, a summary is shorter. Summary writing demands that the student be much more selective as to which details to include and which to exclude. This focusing of attention on main ideas may be responsible for some of summary writing's beneficial effect on comprehension.

☐ *Beginning Summary Writing*

In a recent review of summary writing research, Hidi and Anderson (1986)* point out that summary writing is a difficult skill for children to learn, particularly for those below the sixth grade. Primary-grade students often have difficulty in identifying central ideas of a text and in condensing material down into concise capsules. It is important, therefore, to make initial summarizing activities as easy as possible. Hidi and Anderson recommend the following guidelines:

1. Use brief passages at first. Simple narratives are best since young children are most familiar with this genre. Later, expository passages can be used.
2. Texts should be well organized and appropriate in terms of readability level. The vocabulary and content of the passage should be familiar to the students.
3. The text should be in view when younger students write summaries. This reduces the burden of remembering what is in the text, allowing students to focus on summarization. As they become more proficient, they should begin making summaries without the text being present.
4. Initial summaries should be just slightly shorter than the original, involving the retelling of the story with the deletion of only the most trivial details. Once students have mastered the retelling process, shorter and shorter condensations can be required.
5. Initial summaries should be "writer-based" as opposed to "reader-based." This means that the intended audience is the student, not the teacher or the student's peers. These initial summaries should be similar to journal entries, where the main focus is on content rather than mechanics. Once students become proficient at writing summaries for their own use and consumption, they can begin writing more formal, reader-based summaries. Peer-editing groups are a good way to help students revise and perfect summaries prior to publication or grading. Figure 6.9 illustrates a fourth-grader's journal-like summary of Avi's *Night Journeys* (Pantheon, 1979).

☐ *Précis Writing*

A précis is a shortened version of a piece of writing, usually about one-third the length of the original. Due to the strict limitations on length, précis writing is one of the most difficult types of summary writing, but it is also one of the most valuable in terms of its contributions to reading comprehension. Stotsky (1982) maintains that "précis writing is a reading exercise par excellence" (p. 334). It involves reading, reflecting, recalling, understanding, selecting, and summarizing. Because of its length limitations, a précis is a clear indication of the extent to which a reader understands an author's message.

*From Hidi, S., and Anderson, V. Producing written summaries: Task demands, cognitive operations, and implications for instruction. *Review of Educational Research.* Copyright © 1986 by American Educational Research Association. Used by permission.

FIGURE 6.9   Journal-like Summary of Avi's *Night Journeys*

Title - <u>Night Journey</u> Author - Avi

This story takes place in Colonial
Pennsylvania in 1767. A young orphan
boy named Peter York was taken
in by a man named Mr. Everett Shinn

Mr. Shinn was a verry religous man.
He was a Quacker. When Peter was
adopted he really didn't know why Mr. Shinn
adopted him. At the end Peter cried &
Mr. Shinn said he was glad he adopted
him.

By:
 Erica

    Due to the inherent difficulty of précis writing, we recommend that it be delayed until students are in the intermediate grades and until they have had some experience with the simpler summarizing activities outlined above. Once students are able to make accurate summaries involving some condensation of material, they should be ready for précis writing activities.

    According to Gray (1970), the basic process of précis writing involves five steps:

1. Reading the text thoroughly, identifying topic sentences and main ideas;
2. Writing brief phrases capsulizing each topic sentence;
3. Listing other main ideas;
4. Summarizing 2 and 3 in as few words as possible; and
5. Checking the précis for length, and condensing it if it is longer than one-third the original.

    Linking précis writing with paraphrasing is another means for teaching the précis process. Rob Davis has his fourth-graders begin by writing paraphrases of a story. The students then learn précis writing by condensing their own paraphrases by one-third. Their familiarity with the text enables them to focus entirely on the précis writing task. Figure 6.10 shows Erica's précis, based on her class's paraphrase of *The Bear and the Fly* shown earlier:

FIGURE 6.10   Erica's Précis of *The Bear and the Fly*

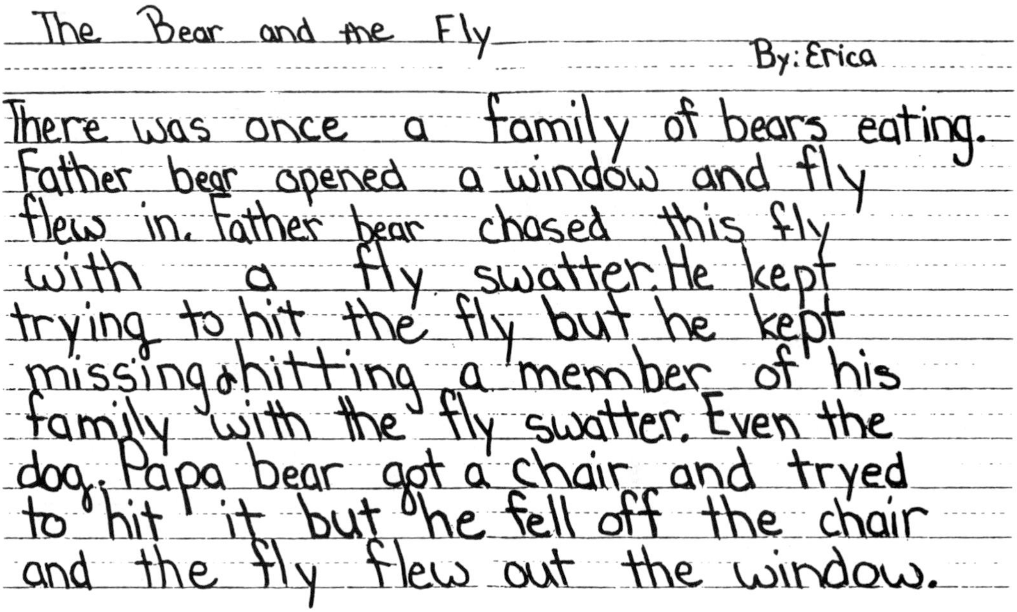

The Bear and the Fly
By: Erica

There was once a family of bears eating.
Father bear opened a window and fly
flew in. Father bear chased this fly
with a fly swatter. He kept
trying to hit the fly but he kept
missing & hitting a member of his
family with the fly swatter. Even the
dog. Papa bear got a chair and tryed
to hit it but he fell off the chair
and the fly flew out the window.

HIGHER-ORDER COMPREHENSION SKILLS

National Assessment of Educational Progress data reveal that children in American schools have shown substantial improvement in reading skills since 1971. However, these gains have been made in basic rather than higher-order skills. La Pointe (1986) reminds educators that instruction must go beyond the level of literal comprehension if students are to become truly proficient readers. They must learn how to read critically, interacting with text by inferencing, analyzing, and evaluating.

Whenever readers' interaction with text goes beyond literal understanding of the message, they are applying higher-order reading skills. These skills include reading between the lines to draw inferences, using knowledge gained from reading to solve problems, critically analyzing text content, putting text ideas together in new ways, and making judgments about what is read. The higher-order cognitive skills encompass the levels of Bloom's (1956) taxonomy from extrapolation (Level 2.3) through evaluation (Level 6.0), as illustrated in Figure 6.11.

The term higher-order reading is generally considered synonymous with critical and creative reading, although some prefer to restrict the definition of creative reading to the synthesis level of Bloom's taxonomy. There is agreement, however, that higher-order reading skills include inferencing, justifying, concluding, hypothesizing, assessing, and evaluating. Readers must examine the text carefully in order to engage in these ad-

FIGURE 6.11   A Definition of Higher-Order Reading Skills Based on Bloom's (1956) Taxonomy

	Level	Cognitive Skill	Reader's Behavior
Higher Order	6.0	EVALUATION	Judging
	5.0	SYNTHESIS	Creating, Putting Together
	4.0	ANALYSIS	Relating, Inquiring
	3.0	APPLICATION	Using Knowledge, Solving Problems
	2.3*	EXTRAPOLATION	Going Beyond What Is Given
Literal	2.2*	INTERPRETATION	Explaining
	2.1*	TRANSLATION	Retelling in Own Words
	1.0	KNOWLEDGE	Recalling

*Subcategories of Level 2.0, COMPREHENSION.

vanced cognitive processes. Writing is often a valuable aid for critical and creative readers as they interact with text. Getting children to critically analyze their own writing and the writing of their peers is an important step in learning to think critically about the texts they read. Responding in writing while reading helps students organize their thoughts and "talk back" to the author.

In the sections that follow, we present a number of ways in which teachers can use writing to help promote higher-order reading skills.

■ **Becoming Insiders**

Atwell (1984) devised her Insiders strategy to create a literate environment, which she describes as "a dining room table with seventy chairs around it" (p. 251). Her purpose was to make her eighth-grade classroom a place where everyone read, wrote, and talked about reading and writing. She integrated her reading program to combine a writers' workshop with reading instruction, predicting that the students' "own writing and the writing they read would intersect" (p. 242).

After stocking her classroom library with a variety of paperback books and collections of her students' own writing, Atwell planned for three or four periods of independent reading each week to allow time for self-selection of books and recreational reading. She gave each student in the class a folder containing blank paper and this letter:

> This folder is a place for you and me to talk about books, reading, authors, and writing. You're to write letters to me, and I'll write letters back to you.
>
> In your letters to me, talk with me about what you've read. Tell me what you thought and felt and why. Tell me what you liked and didn't like and why. Tell me what these books meant to you and said to you. Ask me questions or for help. And write back to me about my ideas, feelings, and questions.
>
> (1984, p. 242)

The students responded enthusiastically to the opportunity to correspond with their teacher about what they were reading. For example, one of her students learned to "write reading" by reading twelve novels and writing thirty-five letters to interact with her about them.

Atwell discovered that this type of writing promoted students' higher-order comprehension skills, causing them to reflect more deeply on what they read than they usually did in oral discussions. She noticed that students began to describe how certain books made them feel. They also began to compare what they did as readers with what she told them she did in her letters to them. Atwell gives an example of how one student's reading process changed in an exchange of letters about L'Engle's *Ring of Endless Night*:

> I think that this book is a good example of describing your surroundings and your thoughts and feelings. What I mean is: I can think back to parts of the story and see pictures of what it looked like. It's great to be able to do that! I really *love* this book! It's one of the *best* I've ever read!
>
> *Tara*

> Dear Tara,
>
> I know exactly what you mean. And the feeling you carry with you is a warm one, a contended one, right? I just reread the novel, *The French Lieutenant's Woman,* and I'm carrying its "feeling" with me today. I suspect I'll go home tonight and re-read its first ending (it has two) as a way to extend the feeling.
>
> What *is* it about good writing that allows us to do this; what makes good books have this effect?
>
> *NA*

> Your right about my feelings—that's what it's like. I sometimes reread parts of books just like you might do. I think it is because the authors

include so many thoughts, feelings and descriptions that we can "lose" ourselves in the books, in the writing.

Tara
(Atwell 1984, pp. 248–249)

Atwell comments that she enjoys the feeling of being "inside" reading and writing as a partner with her students. They too are thriving and developing critical reading skills within the literate environment she has created.

■ Self-Authoring

Children's critical reading skills improve in classrooms where they have the opportunity to write, revise, and share their own texts. Several of the self-authoring strategies described in earlier chapters — the Language Experience Approach, the Author's Chair, Peer Editing/Revising Groups, and Writing Conferences — can promote critical reading by (a) building students' sense of authorship; and (b) encouraging them to revise and critically analyze their own writing and the writing of others.

A sense of authorship can be promoted by the Language Experience Approach. Chapter 2 described how the use of children's own experiences and stories as reading material is an effective approach for teaching beginning readers. Since the children compose the stories they read, they begin to think of themselves as authors as well as readers. According to Calkins (1983a), " . . . writing can generate a stance toward reading which, regretfully is rarely conveyed through reading programs. When children are the makers of reading, they gain a sense of ownership over their reading. As we've seen again and again, owners are different from tenants" (p. 156). By participating in the production of written language, they become what Atwell (1984) calls "insiders" in the reading/writing process. This sense of being part of the process makes children more apt to critically analyze both what they themselves have written and the writing of others.

The concept of authorship can also be encouraged by the Author's Chair strategy (Graves & Hansen, 1984), described in Chapter 4. As children progress through the three-phase authoring process, from replicating a distant author to identifying as an author to questioning other authors, they become critical, assertive readers.

Through revising their own writing, children develop critical judgment to apply to the writing of others. Tierney and Pearson's (1983) composing model of reading, discussed in Chapter 1, stresses that revising skills are as vital for readers as they are for writers, pointing out that readers compose meaning in the same ways writers do. They urge teachers to promote rereading, annotating reactions to text, and self-questioning in order to get students to examine and revise their interpretations of text.

Based on the premise that writing enhances reading, Dionisio (1983) developed a program for teaching reading to sixth-grade reluctant readers that included daily writing activities. Students learned to read for various purposes related to the writing process: (a) collecting information to write about; (b) acquiring style and form; (c) learning how to organize material; and (d) revising and editing. Her most reluctant readers began to read for their own purposes, without being directed to do so, as their needs for reading as a writing tool became evident to them. According to Dionisio:*

> The reasons for reading their own writing apparently had changed in a way that could only increase their comprehension. When students began to interrupt their reading with "Oh, that's not right" and "This is confusing," I became further convinced that the writing and sharing provided them with the opportunity to improve their reading skills.
>
> (p. 747)

Illustrations of reading for each of the four purposes listed above are included here, with examples from Dionisio's classroom.

1. *Reading to collect information to write about*   One student, who wrote a short composition about the sun, complained in a writing conference about not having enough information. The conference stimulated her to go to the library and read for more facts about the sun, which she then incorporated into her revised paper. Dionisio reports that, "In this case the teacher conference generated reading, but in every case the students read for information that was important to them and directly used that information in their writing" (1983, p. 748).

2. *Reading to acquire style*   Reading played a vital role for three students who decided to turn a story into a play before they were familiar with the format of script writing. The teacher suggested they read a play in their basal reader before writing their own. The three students read the play and then held conferences with Dionisio to compare the elements of their play to similar aspects of the play they had read. They critically analyzed their work and revised it into a successful play.

3. *Reading to organize*   The first organizational decision faced by one student, who was trying to write a book about his hobbies, related to dividing the book into chapters. After confusing information on two major topics in one chapter, the writer referred to a book previously read for help in separating the topics, using reading to organize his writing.

4. *Reading to edit*   Students often changed the focus of their reading to edit their papers, using dictionaries and grammar books to correct their mechanical errors. More time was devoted to the critical reading of their own papers and the writings of their peers.

Dionisio's students became voluntary readers through using reading for their purposes as writers. In the process, they developed critical reading skills. Describing one student who had analyzed the writing approach of Laura Ingalls Wilder in an unsolicited report, Dionisio commented:

*Excerpts from pp. 204–205 from Dionisio, M. (1983). Write? Isn't this reading class? *The Reading Teacher, 36,* pp. 746–750. Reprinted with permission of the International Reading Association and M. Dionisio.

Valerie's reading went beyond literal understanding and reflected a kinship with other writers. Furthermore, she had overcome the intimidating notion that written language is unchangeable which Thomas Newkirk . . . calls 'Plato's Challenge.' Valerie had recognized that written language can be questioned and is the result of authors' choices.

(p. 750)

After assessing the impact of her instructional program on her students' reading, Dionisio concluded that writing drove them to read. The students "were using reading and writing as a unified tool for learning; they became willing and able readers and writers."

METACOMPREHENSION

■ ■   Comprehension is understanding; metacomprehension is knowing that you understand. Metacognitive skills enable readers to monitor and evaluate their own comprehension. In addition to knowing a particular reading strategy, they know when and why it works. Brown (1980) defines four important aspects of metacomprehension: (a) knowing when you know and when you don't know; (b) knowing what it is that you know; (c) knowing what you need to know; and (d) knowing the usefulness of trying other strategies when comprehension does not occur. Researchers have found that skilled readers are much more likely than low-functioning readers to use metacognitive skills to control and guide their reading (Baker & Brown, 1984).

Although techniques for teaching self-control of reading have been scarce in teachers' manuals, current research is stimulating interest in how to teach metacognitive reading skills. Fitzgerald (1983)* provides guidelines for teachers, extrapolated from this growing body of research:

1. Use explicit instruction to teach children strategies to use when comprehension goes awry. Don't rely entirely on spontaneous opportunities to teach.

2. Use self-control training. That is, discuss the objectives or reasons for the lessons you do with children, and be sure they are aware that they should apply the strategies when they are reading independently.

3. For training lessons, use materials of moderate difficulty so that some miscomprehension can occur. If materials are too easy, complete or nearly complete understanding is probable. If materials are too hard, little or no comprehension can occur.

4. Provide necessary background knowledge before reading so that the children can use appropriate comprehension strategies. Students can't use metacomprehension strategies if they lack the information from which to construct meaning.

5. Teach students that taking risks and making guesses is good. Students

*From Fitzgerald, J. (1983). Helping readers gain self-control. *The Reading Teacher, 37,* pp. 249-253. Reprinted with permission of the International Reading Association and J. Fitzgerald.

who will guess are more likely to recognize the importance of making an effort to understand the text, that is, they are more likely to use intervention strategies when miscomprehension occurs.

(p. 251)

The teacher's task in metacomprehension instruction is preparing children to use the thinking processes needed to monitor their understanding and to select appropriate reading strategies. Sternberg (1984) identifies these processes or metacomponents as: *plan* (What to do); *strategy* (How I will do it); *monitor* (How I'm doing); and *evaluate* (How well I've done). By modeling and explaining these metacomponents and giving students appropriate feedback when they try to use them, teachers can train "meta-readers." In the plan stage, students need to ask prereading questions to prepare themselves to select the correct strategies for reading. After the strategy is selected, it must be carried out. Choosing and using appropriate strategies are the greatest challenges to readers, because the successful use of strategies depends not only on the difficulty of the text but also on what the student will be required to do after reading (answer questions, summarize, and so forth). To monitor, readers must check their own comprehension and apply other strategies if necessary. When they evaluate, readers judge how successfully they have applied the strategies they chose to use.

The most effective technique for training children to use these steps is teacher modeling. By showing students how they use these metacomponents to control their own comprehension, teachers can help the students to apply appropriate strategies.

Writing plays a vital role in the learning of metacognitive strategies, particularly in the early stages. Written response guides focus students' attention on specific tasks and facilitate their ability to apply new problem-solving strategies to their reading. Writing also gets readers to put their thoughts down on paper, making them more aware of their own thought processes. Teachers also find written response forms useful for monitoring student progress and for providing individual feedback. Self-questioning and reciprocal-questioning strategies recommended for improving meta-comprehension usually require, in addition to oral interaction, the writing of questions and answers. Several strategies that incorporate writing in the teaching of metacomprehension skills are presented below.

■ Quick Writes

A ten-minute period of expressive writing each day, coupled with appropriate teacher guidance, has been reported to improve older students' meta-comprehension skills as well as their attitudes toward reading (Collins, 1985). After participating regularly in free-writing experiences, students in Collins's developmental reading courses were observed to start thinking on paper and to become aware of reading/writing relationships that had previously been abstract or unnoticed. As they began to organize their own thoughts on paper, they were able to understand how other writers organized their ideas. Collins explains:

> This is what reading comprehension is all about and this is what makes expressive writing a powerful teaching tool for reading comprehension. When writing and reading are used together in this way, students soon become conscious of themselves as writers working through a process, then as readers working through the product of another writer's process. In short, students as readers/writers grow in control of their thinking processes. They learn to think as the writer generating text; they learn to think as the reader making meaning from text; and this is what makes expressive writing a metacognitive activity.
>
> (p. 52)*

Teachers who wish to try Quick Writes as a strategy for improving reading comprehension in general and metacognitive skills in particular will find the following suggestions, adapted from Collins's implications for curriculum development, useful:

1. Help students learn to record questions as they are reading a text by using journal writing as a running commentary.
2. Use "expressive" questioning to encourage students to look at what they read from both the standpoint of a reader and a writer. For example:
   a. If you were the writer, how would you express the same thought?
   b. As the reader, do you understand what the writer means?
   c. Does the writer make this point clear?
   d. How could you make the original paragraph clearer?
3. Help students be aware of their purposes for reading and writing by asking:
   a. Why are you reading this story or chapter?
   b. Why are you writing about this topic?
   c. What information are you seeking as you read?
   d. What do you want your reader to know?
   e. What knowledge does the reader already possess about your subject?
4. Train students to become better predictors by showing them the first paragraph and asking:
   a. As a reader, what do you expect will follow this sentence?
   b. As a writer, how would you develop a paragraph with that particular topic sentence?
5. Increase students' critical reading skills by asking:
   a. Is this passage effective? Why or why not?
   b. What would you do to make this passage more effective?
6. Use paired evaluations to determine if students have acquired the skills

*From C. Collins, (1985). The power of expressive writing in reading comprehension. *Language Arts, 62,* pp. 48–54. Reprinted with permission of the National Council of Teachers of English.

you taught. That is, with each writing technique, test to see if students can identify its use by other writers, and with each reading technique, see if students can demonstrate its use in writing for other readers.

■ QARs

Convinced that written practice with a specific technique helps students acquire the competence to apply it, Raphael (1982) developed a method for teaching a question-answering strategy using written response forms to guide students' thinking. The purpose of her Question-Answer Relationship (QAR) program is to teach students how to analyze questions in order to help them find the right answers. The program helps students learn to recognize different types of questions and the kind of reading and thinking demanded by each question type. Her method is based on a procedure developed by Pearson and Johnson (1978) for categorizing questions in terms of the sources of their answers. The three question categories are: text explicit (reading the lines); text implicit (reading between the lines); and script implicit (reading beyond the lines). Script implicit is synonymous with schema implicit, meaning that the answer to the question must be found in the reader's prior knowledge.

Three QARs were used to represent the three question categories:

1. Right There—text explicit questions
2. Think and Search—text implicit questions
3. On My Own—script implicit questions.

The following example illustrates how each QAR works:

KATHRYN HIT HER HEAD ON THE ICE WHEN SHE FELL AT THE SKATING RINK. SHE BRUISED HER FOREHEAD.

QAR #1: Right There
The answer to the question, "Where was Kathryn when she fell and hit her head on the ice?" can be found *Right There* in the sentence. She was at the skating rink. The question-answer strategy is to look at the words in the question and find other words in the sentence that will answer it.

QAR #2: Think and Search
The answer to the question, "How badly was Kathryn hurt?" can be answered by reading ahead and thinking. First, the reader must read beyond the first sentence and realize that "she" in the second sentence refers to Kathryn. The second sentence states that Kathryn bruised her forehead. The reader needs to think about this and realize that bruising one's forehead is not a serious injury. The answer, then, is that she was not hurt very badly— just bruised.

QAR #3: On My Own

"Why did Kathryn fall on the ice?" is a question that requires readers to use their own background knowledge. Since the passage does not give the information, they must determine what they already know that can help them answer the question. Readers with appropriate background knowledge would conclude that, given the fact that Kathryn was at a skating rink, she was on skates and probably lost her balance.

Raphael recommends that students be given a worksheet containing the questions, each of which is followed by the three QARs with blank spaces to record answers. The students then use a three-step procedure to answer each question:

1. Circle the QAR to be used.
2. Find the answer, using the strategy that has been circled.
3. Write the answer in the correct QAR blank.

Figure 6.12 illustrates how students would answer the third question in our KATHRYN example.

Raphael and Pearson (1982) taught QARs to fourth-, sixth-, and eighth-grade students in an attempt to evaluate the effectiveness of this strategy. After practicing with two- and three-sentence passages similar to our KATHRYN illustration, the students practiced using QARs with longer and longer passages, culminating with basal reader passages. Results showed that, following the QAR training, the students could answer questions more successfully than those who had not had QAR instruction.

In a later modification of the model, Raphael (1986) described an easier format for younger students. According to feedback from teachers, middle school students are able to learn the three categories (Right There, Think and Search, and On My Own). However, students in the primary grades need extra help in distinguishing between the two different sources of knowledge—the text and their own background knowledge. Therefore, she revised the model by expanding it to include four types of question-answer relationships: Right There, Think and Search, Author and You, and On My

FIGURE 6.12 QAR Example

Why did Kathryn fall on the ice?
Right There _____
Think and Search _____
(On My Own) _She was skating on ice and probably lost her balance_

Own. The first two types fall into a category called "In the Book" and the second two into "In My Head." The new type, Author and You, refers to questions which require the reader to combine text information with prior knowledge, whereas On My Own questions depend totally on prior knowledge and can often be answered without reading the text.

In this revised QAR format, students would have four answer choices to the question, "Why did Kathryn fall on the ice?" instead of three. The correct QAR choice would still be On My Own because there is no clue to the answer in the text.

■ Think-Alouds

Successful comprehension monitoring requires students to ask the right kinds of questions to plan and evaluate their own reading practices. As mentioned earlier, teacher modeling is one of the most effective ways to develop these active questioning skills (Fitzgerald, 1983; Manzo, 1969; Palincsar & Brown, 1984).

Manzo (1969) recommends a phase-in/phase-out procedure, called ReQuest, that begins with teachers modeling appropriate comprehension questions for a passage of text, continues with reciprocal teaching in which teachers take turns with students asking questions and leading discussion about the text, and ends with individual students asking and answering their own questions. Fitzgerald (1983) describes an approach in which teachers model their own use of self-questioning skills as they read passages aloud to their classes. After explaining the importance of recognizing what we understand or don't understand when we read, teachers demonstrate how to make guesses while reading and how to keep track of what they "Know" and "Don't Know" by listing information in each category on the chalkboard. Palincsar and Brown (1984) experimented with a one-to-one reciprocal teaching game in which children were taught to use two types of comprehension questions: "What is happening now?" and "What will happen next?" Students who learned to use the questions as they read showed increased ability to answer other comprehension questions.

Think-Alouds is a procedure developed by Davey (1983) in which teachers verbalize their own thoughts while reading, enabling them to model the strategies skilled readers use to construct meaning from print. Davey identified five techniques applied by proficient readers: (a) hypothesizing and predicting; (b) organizing images; (c) using prior knowledge effectively; (d) monitoring how well they are understanding as they read along; and (e) knowing what to do to "fix up" their comprehension problems.

The Think-Aloud procedure outlined by Davey teaches the five metacognitive strategies, using these steps:

1. The teacher reads a passage aloud that contains some obvious problems for the readers, such as ambiguities or unfamiliar words, while students

follow along silently.

2. The teacher talks through the thinking processes used as reading difficulties are confronted, modeling the appropriate problem-solving strategies. Students are encouraged to discuss the various strategies as they observe the teacher's use of them. The Strategy Example illustrates how a teacher could model the five techniques with the children's book, *Jumanji*.

3. After several experiences with the teacher modeling strategies, students practice Think-Alouds orally with partners as they read short, teacher-written passages with obvious problems.

4. Students apply the Think-Aloud strategies individually as they read silently, asking such questions as:

a. "What do I predict the book is about after looking at the title and book cover or jacket?"

b. "What picture am I getting at this point?"

c. "What am I reminded of here that I already know about?"

d. "Are my original guesses turning out to be right as I read?"

─────────────── **STRATEGY EXAMPLE 6.3** ───────────────

TEACHER MODELING OF THINK-ALOUDS

The examples which follow illustrate how teachers can model the use of Davey's five metacognitive strategies with Chris Van Allsburg's *Jumanji* (Houghton Mifflin, 1981). Although the text of the book is uncomplicated syntactically, the story line shifts between reality and fantasy, allowing for multiple interpretations. The reader encounters problems which clearly require the use of metacognitive techniques for understanding and enjoyment.

Jumanji tells the exciting story of the adventures of two children as they play a jungle game which comes alive in their living room. Strategies modeled by the teacher while reading the book to children might include:

1. Hypothesizing
Teacher: "Jumanji" sounds like a foreign word. I've never heard it before. I see two monkeys on the front cover and a set of game pieces and dice on the back. I'm predicting that "Jumanji" is the name of an animal game.

2. Organizing Images
Teacher: After Judy read "Lion attacks, move back two spaces," Peter looked behind him and saw a real lion lying on the piano. I'm getting the picture that this part of the story is a dream. I think Peter and Judy will wake up at the end of the game.

3. Using Prior Knowledge (Analogy)

Teacher: This game board reminds me of two games I have played: Candyland and Parcheesi. Both have rules like Jumanji. You roll the dice or take a card to move your game piece along a path, and the game isn't over until someone reaches a goal.

4. Monitoring Understanding

Teacher: As I read, I'm checking on the guesses I made at the beginning. According to the game instructions, "Jumanji" means "golden city." I thought it meant "jungle."

5. "Fixing Up" Problems

Teacher: When Peter gets scared and says he doesn't want to play the game anymore, Judy reminds him that the animals won't go away until the game is over. I don't remember that being in the rules. I'll go back and reread them to see if that's true.

I'm changing my picture about the dream because Peter and Judy aren't waking up. Perhaps they really played the game. The ending makes me think it really happened to them. I'll check back to the start of the story to see if it could have been a dream.

Davey suggests that teachers expose children to a variety of types of reading materials as they practice Think-Alouds. She also recommends that students be provided with a checklist like the one illustrated in Figure 6.13 in order to reinforce their use of the five techniques.

FIGURE 6.13 Self-Evaluation Form for Think-Alouds Source: From Beth Davey. Think Aloud—Modeling the Cognitive Processes of Reading Comprehension. *Journal of Reading,* October 1983. Reprinted with permission of Beth Davey and the International Reading Association.

While I was reading how did I do? (Put an X in the appropriate column.)

	Not very much	A little bit	Much of the time	All of the time
Made predictions				
Formed pictures				
Used "like-a"				
Found problems				
Used fix-ups				

Writing can enhance the Think-Aloud process. Goodman and Burke (1972), for example, have suggested a strategy that can be used to practice Think-Alouds with student-written stories. After the partners have had some experience in identifying and solving problems in teacher-written passages, the students can write their own brief stories containing incongruous or ambiguous information. The students take turns reading their partners' stories, trying to identify and solve the problems. The writers of the passage give feedback as to their partners' success. It has been our experience that students not only identify deliberately created problems but also discover ambiguities that their partners did not intend to write. Thus the students' writing and editing skills are improved along with their self-monitoring abilities.

Teachers can extend the Think-Aloud process by having students write down the difficulties they confronted while reading and the strategies they used to solve them. When finished reading, the students can then share and critique each others' problem-solving strategies. The recording of problems and solutions during the act of reading can encourage active involvement and increase students' conscious awareness of metacognitive processes.

Whether used with or without student writing, the Think-Aloud procedure is an excellent way to promote students' metacognitive reading skills. Davey summarizes the advantages of the technique: "Teacher modeling and student practice of cognitive processes through Think-alouds provides a motivating opportunity for students not only to experience effective reading and problem-solving, but to move these strategies toward independent reading" (1983, p. 46).

The Think-Aloud strategy teaches children to check their own comprehension as they read and equips them with "fix-up" techniques to use when they discover comprehension problems—rereading, scanning, ignoring obstacles, changing reading rate, suspending judgment, and hypothesizing. With practice, students can learn to apply these metacomprehension skills used by proficient readers to increase comprehension as well as to assess their own understanding.

SUMMARY

■ ■   This chapter has described a number of ways in which writing can promote students' reading skills. We began with strategies that facilitate the basic skills of word recognition and vocabulary knowledge. These activities included copying, in which students write down verbatim selected passages, such as a classroom diary, and dictation, which involves students in writing down orally presented texts. The fact that these strategies involve working with actual samples of written language makes them more meaningful than traditional, isolated vocabulary and word recognition exercises.

We then presented sentence-combining and sentence-reconstruction activities, which can be used to enhance students' familiarity with complex syntactic structures. These types of sentence-manipulation activities have been found to increase the syntactic maturity of students' writing. Over time, these strategies should be expected indirectly to facilitate reading by removing syntactic "roadblocks" to comprehension, particularly if the activities are linked with reading experiences.

Next, strategies were presented that use writing to familiarize students with text structure. The Story Template, Macro-Cloze, and Story Diagram activities described in this chapter acquaint children with the structure of narrative stories by helping them learn to make their own stories that follow selected patterns. Research indicates that these types of "constructive" activities are more effective in promoting knowledge of story structure than approaches which merely teach children to recognize the structure of existing texts. Like sentence-manipulation activities, these story structure strategies can be expected to have a direct impact on writing and an indirect effect on reading comprehension. Over time, these activities should have a positive impact on reading comprehension by allowing students to anticipate the structure and organization of different types of texts and to focus their attention on important content.

Paraphrasing and text reduction strategies comprised the fourth set of strategies. These writing activities, when used as postreading activities, can facilitate comprehension by getting students to actively process and reconstruct ideas in a text. Paraphrasing requires that students translate text into their own words, insuring that the ideas in the text are linked with prior knowledge and thoroughly understood. Summary and précis writing are even more demanding, requiring not only translation but also condensation. In order to condense a text, students must make decisions about the relative importance of text concepts, retaining the ones judged to be important and deleting those judged to be less crucial.

The fifth set of strategies use writing to facilitate higher-order reading skills such as inferencing, analyzing, and evaluating. Atwell's Becoming Insiders strategy and self-authoring activities such as the Author's Chair and the Language Experience Approach can help children to become critical readers of their own writing and that of other authors.

Finally, several strategies were presented which use writing to build students' metacognitive or metacomprehension skills. We explained how expressive writing in Quick Writes can increase awareness of the cognitive processes used in reading and writing. QARs focus students' attention on the different types of thinking required by reading questions, and Think-Alouds get students to verbalize the problems encountered during reading and the strategies used to solve them.

Our purpose in this chapter has been to demonstrate that writing is an effective vehicle for improving a variety of different reading skills, ranging from word recognition to higher-order comprehension skills. Our concept of learning to read through writing is based on the premise that writing is a natural context in which reading skills can be learned, and we have emphasized that the kinds of writing experiences which enhance these skills are those linked with the texts students are reading. Properly implemented, the strategies described in this chapter can be excellent replacements for some of the isolated skill drills which abound in most basal reader programs.

RECOMMENDED CHILDREN'S BOOKS

A Selected List of Wordless Story Books

The titles listed here have been recommended as appealing and worth reading by at least one national publication. Only books that tell a story are included.

Bang, Molly. *The Grey Lady and the Strawberry Snatcher.* Four Winds, 1980.
Burton, Marilee. *The Elephant's Nest.* Harper & Row, 1981. (A series of short stories.)
Carle, Eric. *Do You Want to Be My Friend?* Crowell, 1971.
Degen, Bruce. *Aunt Possum and the Pumpkin Man.* Harper & Row, 1977.
dePaola, Tomie. *Pancakes for Breakfast.* Harcourt Brace Jovanovich, 1978.
_____. *Flicks.* Harcourt Brace Jovanovich, 1981. (A series of short stories.)
Goodall, John S. *The Adventures of Paddy Pork.* Harcourt Brace Jovanovich, 1968.
_____. *The Ballooning Adventures of Paddy Pork.* Harcourt Brace Jovanovich, 1969.
_____. *Shrewbettina's Birthday.* Atheneum, 1971.
_____. *The Midnight Adventures of Kelly, Dot, and Esmeralda.* Atheneum, 1973.
_____. *Paddy Pork's Holiday.* Atheneum, 1976.
_____. *Creepy Castle.* Atheneum, 1978.
_____. *Paddy's New Hat.* Atheneum, 1980.
_____. *Paddy's Evening Out.* Atheneum, 1981.
_____. *Paddy Finds a Job.* Atheneum, 1981.
_____. *Shrewbettina Goes to Work.* Atheneum, 1981.
_____. *Lavinia's Cottage.* Atheneum, 1983.
_____. *The Story of a Castle.* Atheneum, 1986.
Hartelius, Margaret. *The Chicken's Child.* Doubleday, 1975.
_____. *The Birthday Trombone.* Doubleday, 1977.
Kent, Jack. *The Scribble Monster.* Harcourt Brace Jovanovich, 1981.
Krahn, Fernando. *April Fools.* E. P. Dutton, 1974.
_____. *Sebastian and the Mushroom.* Delacorte/Lawrence, 1976.
_____. *The Mystery of the Giant Footprints.* E. P. Dutton, 1977.
_____. *Arthur's Adventure in the Abandoned House.* E. P. Dutton, 1981.
_____. *The Creepy Thing.* Clarion, 1982.
_____. *The Secret in the Dungeon.* Ticknor and Fields, 1983.
_____. *Amanda and the Mysterious Carpet.* Clarion, 1985.
Mayer, Mercer. *Frog, Where Are You?* Dial, 1969.
_____. *Frog on His Own.* Dial, 1973.

_____. *Frog Goes to Dinner.* Dial, 1974.
_____. *The Great Cat Chase.* Four Winds, 1975.
_____. *One Frog Too Many.* Dial, 1975.
_____. *Ah-Choo.* Dial, 1976.
Turkle, Brinton. *Deep in the Forest.* E. P. Dutton, 1976.
Winter, Paula. *The Bear and the Fly.* Crown, 1976.

REFERENCES

Atwell, N. (1984). Writing and reading literature from the inside out. *Language Arts, 61,* 240–252.

Austin, S. (1986). Beyond sentence combining. *The Quarterly of the National Writing Project and the Center for the Study of Writing, 8*(3), 5–7.

Baker, L., & Brown, A. L. (1984). Metacognitive skills and reading. In P. D. Pearson (Ed.), *Handbook of reading research* (pp. 353–394). New York: Longman.

Bloom, B. S. (Ed.). (1956). *Taxonomy of educational objectives: The classification of educational goals. Handbook I: Cognitive domain.* New York: David McKay.

Brown, A. L. (1980). Metacognitive development and reading. In R. J. Spiro, B. C. Bruce, & W. F. Brewer (Eds.), *Theoretical issues in reading comprehension* (pp. 453–481). Hillsdale, NJ: Erlbaum.

Calkins, L. M. (1983a). *Lessons from a child.* Exeter, NH: Heinemann.

Calkins, L. M. (1983b). Making the reading-writing connection. *Learning, 11,* 82–86.

Collins, C. (1985). The power of expressive writing in reading comprehension. *Language Arts, 62,* 48–54.

Cooper, J. D. (1986). *Improving reading comprehension.* Boston: Houghton Mifflin.

Corbett, E. (1971). The theory and practice of imitation in classical rhetoric. *College Composition and Communication, 22,* 243–250.

Cutter, M. L. (1979). Journal writing is only the beginning. *English Journal, 68*(6), 68–71.

D'Angelo, K. (1979). Wordless picture books: Also for the writer. *Language Arts, 56,* 813–814.

Davey, B. (1983). Think-aloud—Modeling the cognitive processes of reading comprehension. *Journal of Reading, 27,* 44–47.

Davis, F. B. (1972). Psychometric research on comprehension in reading. *Reading Research Quarterly, 7,* 628–678.

Devine, T. G. (1986). *Teaching reading comprehension: From theory to practice.* Boston: Allyn & Bacon.

Dionisio, M. (1983). Write? Isn't this reading class? *The Reading Teacher, 36,* 746–750.

Doctorow, M., Wittrock, M. C., & Marks, C. (1978). Generative processes in reading comprehension. *Journal of Educational Psychology, 70,* 109–118.

Dreher, M. J., & Singer, H. (1980). Story grammar instruction unnecessary for intermediate grade students. *The Reading Teacher, 34,* 261–268.

Drum, P. A. (1984). Children's understanding of passages. In J. Flood (Ed.), *Promoting reading comprehension* (pp. 61–78). Newark, DE: International Reading Association.

Durkin, D. (1978–1979). What classroom observations reveal about reading comprehension instruction. *Reading Research Quarterly, 14,* 481–533.

Durkin, D. (1983). *Teaching them to read* (4th ed.). Boston: Allyn & Bacon.

Favat, F. A. (1977). *Child and tale: The origins of interest.* Urbana, IL: National Council of Teachers of English.

Ferris, J. A., & Snyder, G. (1986). Writing as an influence on reading. *Journal of Reading, 29,* 751–756.

Fitzgerald, J. (1983). Helping readers gain self-control. *The Reading Teacher, 37,* 249–253.

Fitzgerald, J. & Spiegel, D. L. (1983). Enhancing children's reading comprehension through instruction in narrative structure. *Journal of Reading Behavior, 15,* 1–18.

Fitzgerald, J., & Teasley, A. B. (1986). Effects of instruction in narrative structure on children's writing. *Journal of Educational Psychology, 78,* 424–442.

Flood, J., Lapp, D., & Farnan, N. (1986). A reading-writing procedure that teaches expository paragraph structure. *The Reading Teacher, 39,* 556–562.

Gibson, E., & Levin, H. (1975). *The psychology of reading.* Cambridge, MA: M.I.T. Press.

Goodman, K. S. (1986). Basal readers: A call for action. *Language Arts, 63,* 358–363.

Goodman, Y. M., & Burke, C. L. (1972). *Reading miscue inventory manual: Procedure for diagnosis and evaluation.* New York: Macmillan.

Gough, P. B. (1984). Word recognition. In P. D. Pearson (Ed.), *Handbook of reading research* (pp. 225–253). New York: Longman.

Graves, D., & Hansen, J. (1984). The author's chair. In J. M. Jensen (Ed.), *Composing and comprehending* (pp. 69–76). Urbana, IL: ERIC/RCS.

Gray, L. L. (1970). *Better and faster reading.* New York: Cambridge Book.

Hailey, J. (1978). *Teaching writing K–8.* Berkeley: University of California Press.

Hidi, S., & Anderson, V. (1986). Producing written summaries: Task demands, cognitive operations, and implications for instruction. *Review of Educational Research, 56,* 473–493.

Hudgins, B., & Spies, J. (1977). Improving word comprehension of remedial readers. *Journal of Educational Research, 70,* 299–303.

Hunter, P., & Beaty, J. (Eds.). (1981). *The Norton introduction to literature* (3rd ed.). New York: W. W. Norton.

Jett-Simpson, M. (1981). Writing stories using model structures: The circle story. *Language Arts, 58,* 293–300.

Kline, S. (1987). Dear diary. I couldn't teach without you! *Instructor, 96*(5), 80–81.

La Pointe, A. (1986). The state of instruction in reading and writing in U.S. elementary schools. *Phi Delta Kappan, 68,* 135–138.

Lawlor, J. (1983). Sentence combining: A sequence for instruction. *Elementary School Journal, 84,* 53–61.

Loban, W. (1976). *Language development: Kindergarten through grade twelve.* Urbana, IL: National Council of Teachers of English.

Mandler, J. M., & Johnson, M. S. (1977). Remembrance of things passed: Story structure and recall. *Cognitive Psychology, 9,* 111–151.

Manzo, A. V. (1969). The ReQuest procedure. *Journal of Reading, 13,* 123–126.

McGee, L. M., & Tompkins, G. E. (1983). Wordless picture books are for older readers, too. *Journal of Reading, 36,* 120–123.

McNeil, J. D., & Donant, L. (1982). Summarization strategy for improving reading comprehension. In J. A. Niles & L. A. Harris (Eds.), *New inquiries in reading research and instruction.* Rochester, NY: National Reading Conference.

Meyer, B. J. (1975). *The organization of prose and its effects on memory.* Amsterdam: North-Holland.

Meyer, B. J., Brandt, D., & Bluth, G. (1980). Use of top-level structure in text: Key for reading comprehension of ninth-grade students. *Reading Research Quarterly, 16,* 72–103.

Meyer, B. J., & Freedle, R. O. (1984). Effects of discourse type on recall. *American Educational Research Journal, 21,* 121–143.

National Assessment of Educational Progress. (1981). *Reading, thinking, and writing: Results of the 1979–80 national assessment of reading and literature.* Denver, CO: National Education Commission.

Neville, D. D., & Searls, E. F. (1985). The effect of sentence-combining and kernel-identification training on the syntactic component of reading comprehension. *Research in the Teaching of English, 19,* 37–61.

Noyce, R. M., & Christie, J. F. (1983). Effects of an integrated approach to grammar instruction on third graders' reading and writing. *Elementary School Journal, 84,* 63–69.

Noyce, R. M., & Christie, J. F. (1985). Characteristics of subordinate clauses in children's free writing. *Journal of Research and Development in Education, 18*(4), 68–71.

Nutter, N., & Safran, J. (1984). Improving writing with sentence-combining exercises. *Academic Therapy, 19,* 449–453.

Obenchain, A. (1971). *Effectiveness of the precise essay question in programming the sequential development of written composition skills and the simultaneous development of critical reading skills.* Unpublished master's thesis, George Washington University.

Odegaard, J. M., & May, F. (1972). Creative grammar and the writing of third graders. *Elementary School Journal, 73,* 156–161.

Palincsar, A. M., & Brown, A. (1984). Reciprocal teaching of comprehension. *Cognition and Instruction, 1,* 117–175.

Pearson, P. D., & Johnson, D. D. (1978). *Teaching reading comprehension.* New York: Holt, Rinehart & Winston.

Piccolo, J. A. (1986). Writing a no-fault narrative: Every teacher's dream. *The Reading Teacher, 40,* 136–142.

Raphael, T. (1982). Question-answering strategies for children. *The Reading Teacher, 36,* 186–190.

Raphael, T. (1986). Teaching question-answer relationships revisited. *The Reading Teacher, 39,* 516–522.

Raphael, T. E., & Pearson, P. D. (1982). *The effect of metacognitive awareness training on children's answering behavior.* Technical Report No. 238. Urbana, IL: Center for the Study of Reading.

Reutzel, D. R. (1986). The reading basal: A sentence combining composing book. *The Reading Teacher, 40,* 194–199.

Rubin, A. (1980). Making stories, making sense. *Language Arts, 57,* 285–298.

Sebesta, S. L., Calder, J. W., & Cleland, L. N. (1982). A story grammar for the classroom. *The Reading Teacher, 36,* 180–184.

Shugarman, S. L., & Hurst, J. B. (1986). Purposeful paraphrasing: Promoting a nontrivial pursuit for meaning. *Journal of Reading, 29,* 396–339.

Smith, M., & Bean, T. W. (1983). Four strategies that develop children's story comprehension and writing. *The Reading Teacher, 37,* 295–301.

Spiegel, D. L., & Fitzgerald, J. (1986). Improving reading comprehension through instruction about story parts. *The Reading Teacher, 39,* 676–682.

Squire, J. R. (1983). Composing and comprehending: Two sides of the same basic process. *Language Arts, 60,* 581–589.

Stein, N. L., & Glenn, C. G. (1979). An analysis of story comprehension in elementary school children. In R. O. Freedle (Ed.), *New directions in discourse processing.* Norwood, NJ: Ablex.

Sternberg, R. J. (1984). How can we teach intelligence? *Educational Leadership, 42,* 38–48.

Stotsky, S. (1975). Sentence-combining as a curricular activity: Its effect on written language development and reading comprehension. *Research in the Teaching of English, 9,* 30–71.

Stotsky, S. (1982). The role of writing in developmental reading. *Journal of Reading, 25,* 330–340.

Stotsky, S. (1983). Dictation: Building listening, writing, and reading skills together. *The Leaflet* (Journal of the New England Association of Teachers of English), *82*(2), 6–12.

Straw, S., & Schreiner, R. (1982). The effect of sentence manipulation on subsequent measures of reading and listening comprehension. *Reading Research Quarterly, 17,* 339–352.

Strong, W. (1976). Close-up sentence combining: Back to basics and beyond. *English Journal, 65*(2), 56–64.

Strong, W. (1981). *Sentence combining and paragraph building.* New York: Random House.

Sullivan, J. N., & Thompson, M. O. (1985). Two methods of using reading in a writing class. *Virginia English Journal, 35*(1), 88–93.

Tierney, R. J., & Pearson, P. D. (1983). Toward a composing model of reading. *Language Arts, 60,* 568–580.

Whaley, J. F. (1981). Story grammar and reading instruction. *The Reading Teacher, 34,* 762–771.

7

Writing and Reading in the Content Areas

The relation between thought and word is a living process; thought is born through words.
— Vygotsky, Thought and Language

If we think with language, we also learn with language, and this means that writing can enhance learning in every class.
— Russell, Writing across the curriculum in 1913: James Fleming Hosic on "cooperation"

In Chapters 5 and 6 we explained how writing can help students activate and organize their own knowledge prior to reading, promoting interest and comprehension. We emphasized the effectiveness of writing as a prereading activity and described the beneficial effects of engaging in certain kinds of writing before and during the reading of narrative passages. Writing can serve similar functions with respect to expository texts, the type of reading material children typically encounter in the content areas of social studies, science, and math.

Because of their structure, vocabulary, and concept loads, expository texts tend to be more difficult than narrative stories to read and comprehend. This chapter begins with a discussion of ways in which writing can facilitate comprehension of these challenging texts by acquainting students with their structure and organization and by encouraging the active processing of text information. In the second section, the focus changes from writing as a facilitator of reading to writing as a tool for learning new information. Our attention centers on the theoretical evidence supporting writing as an instructional device in the various content areas of the curriculum and on related strategies which can be used to help students learn the subject matter in those fields. This section is based upon the premise that writing, as well as reading, should be taught in every subject area, because both skills are basic to thinking, learning, and communicating knowledge in all fields. The final section presents reading/writing strategies for use in science, mathematics, and social studies.

READING AND WRITING EXPOSITORY TEXTS

■ ■   Expository writing differs in purpose from narrative and descriptive writing. The intent of a narrative is to entertain by telling a story, and the purpose of a description is to present the details about a topic in a somewhat static context. Exposition, on the other hand, seeks to instruct, explain, and persuade. While the three types of writing can be blended in any piece of writing, the difference with expository writing is that the informational transaction with the reader is central, even though narrative may play a supporting role in elaborating the writer's ideas. Narrative discourse (the language of literature) and expository discourse (the language of textbooks) are the kinds of text which elementary and middle school children most commonly read and write.

As we pointed out in Chapter 5, narration and exposition differ in structure. The story grammar of narratives has chronological links, proceeding from a beginning through episodes and outcomes to an ending. It relates a story involving characters, setting, plot, and theme. Most children have a basic knowledge of narrative story structure before entering elementary school. Expository writing, on the other hand, has logical links, presenting information through paragraphs with main topics and subtopics. Just as there are various story genres, there are different types of paragraphs and structural patterns. The organizational patterns most frequently used in children's textbooks are: listing, time order, cause/effect, comparison/contrast, and problem/solution (Horowitz, 1985a). Research has shown that children's knowledge of these expository text structures is extremely limited (Englert & Hiebert, 1984), posing possible barriers to comprehension of this type of discourse.

While children's lack of knowledge of expository structure is partly due to the complexity of the structures themselves, instructional practices may also be a contributing factor. Reading instruction in the elementary grades focuses primarily on narrative discourse (Calfee & Curley, 1984). According to Stotsky (1983), as many as 95 percent of the selections in most basal readers are narratives. Piccolo (1987) notes that the few expository writings found in basal readers tend to be narrative in nature, reporting information by using fictional techniques. In addition, they emphasize, for the most part, one text structure—listing. Basal reader expository writing often lacks the main headings and subheadings which characterize the structure of content-area expository texts (Hennings, 1982).

Primary-grade writing activities are also predominantly narrative. Children's abilities in expressive writing develop naturally with the frequent story experiences they have, while other types of writing, such as expository and descriptive, are less common and require direct, focused instruction. Because children have so many experiences with narrative material both at home and in school, they are able to develop their story schemata at an early age. However, because they see so few good models of expository writing in their reading materials and seldom engage in the production of expository text, they are not as familiar with the organizational patterns of this important type of discourse.

TEACHING EXPOSITORY TEXT STRUCTURE

■ ■   The ability to identify the structural patterns used by writers of expository texts leads to better understanding and recall of text information. Skilled readers are like expert cab drivers, according to Horowitz (1985a):

> Cab drivers must know the layout of a city, have an internal, global represen-
> tation of the patterning of roads, including main highways (the macro-level
> structures), and side roads (micro-level structures). They must also know how
> to work with the cue system on the road — highway marks, road signs, and
> lights. . . . Much like the expert cab driver, readers who are successful in
> schools somehow acquire a specialized knowledge about the patterning of
> their texts. This may include knowledge of overall text design, of chapter
> formats, of substructures within chapters, of paragraph structures, and so on.
> (p. 449)

Schema theory research has confirmed this at various grade levels. Englert and Hiebert (1984) reported that third- and sixth-graders who were familiar with the different expository text structures had better reading comprehension than those who were not. Barton (1983) found that high-ability, fourth-grade readers applied global strategies dealing with macro-level text structures more often than their average-ability counterparts when reading expository material.

Researchers have found that intermediate-grade students can be taught to recognize and use textbook patterns through writing activities. Junior high school students in Bartlett's study (1978), who were required to recognize expository text structures in reading material and then use them in written retellings, retained more information than students who were not taught the structures. Taylor and Beach (1984) determined that middle school students who were taught to write summaries using the organizational structures of social studies textbooks remembered more new content than untrained students.

Direct instruction focused on both macro- (global) and micro- (word and sentence) level textbook structures should begin in the intermediate grades. Researchers have emphasized the need for developing reading and writing strategies for this purpose, based on the premise that comprehending and producing textbook patterns require similar skills (Horowitz, 1985b). The sections that follow describe several integrated strategies that can be used to acquaint children with expository text patterns. These strategies are most appropriate for grades three through eight, although primary-grade teachers will find several activities which can be adapted for use with younger children.

■ Graphic Organizers

Piccolo (1987) suggests that teachers follow these recommendations when teaching children to identify textbook structures:

1. Use writing as an instructional technique.
2. Use good model passages to demonstrate various structures, preferably teacher-written material in which target structures are easily identified.
3. Use a graphic organizer with each structure to help students write and understand it.

A graphic organizer is a spatial outline representing the organization of a text and is presented with the text as a structural aid for the reader (Readence, Bean, & Baldwin, 1981). These organizers function in much the same manner as the story diagrams discussed in Chapter 5, making the relationships between text elements more concrete and easier for students to conceptualize.

A first step in using graphic organizers to teach text structure is to introduce children to organizers for two passages which are identical in structure but different in content. Figures 7.1 and 7.2, from McGee and Richgels (1985), illustrate this approach. Comparing the graphic organizers for the two passages helps the children begin to understand the difference between content and structure.

The next step is to use organizers to teach children to identify the common paragraph structures used in content-area textbooks: listing, time order, cause/effect, comparison/contrast, and problem/solution. Each structure can be effectively taught through a multi-lesson sequence developed by Piccolo (1987):

1. Define the structure and present sample paragraphs with an appropriate graphic organizer, pointing out their "critical attributes."
2. Compose a model paragraph together, using the organizer as a guide. Then have students write their own paragraphs which follow the pattern.
3. Share good and poor examples of the student paragraphs, and have the group revise the poor examples so they follow the target pattern.
4. Have students extract elements from model passages and fit them into blank organizers.

FIGURE 7.1   Sample Causation Passage and Graphic Organizer #1   Source:
From Lea M. McGee and Donald J. Richgels. Teaching Expository Text Structure to
Elementary Students. *The Reading Teacher, 38,* pp. 739–748. Reprinted with permission
of Lea M. McGee and the International Reading Association.

Camels in the Desert

Camels are still ridden by the people of the desert today. They are well suited for carrying people and heavy burdens for long distances in hot, dry places because they can
got for a long time without water. As a result of their thick hooves, camels can easily
walk on the hot sand. Finally, camels can live off the desert because they are able to
the smallest plant to eat hidden in the desert soil.

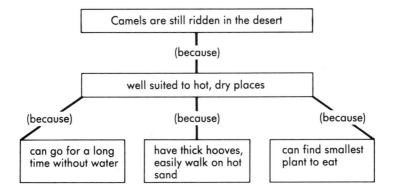

5. Ask students to examine content-area textbooks to find examples of
   paragraphs that follow the pattern.

In the Strategy Example, we have developed a lesson sequence similar
to Piccolo's to introduce third-grade children to the enumerative or listing
pattern, the most common organizational scheme found in content-area
textbooks.

––––––––––––––– **STRATEGY EXAMPLE 7.1** –––––––––––––––

Teaching the Listing Pattern

Lesson 1
   A. The teacher introduces the idea that there are various kinds of
paragraph structures, just as there are different kinds of stories, explaining
that each type of structure answers a specific question (Figure 7.3).

FIGURE 7.2 Sample Causation Passage and Graphic Organizer #2   Source:
From Lea M. McGee and Donald J. Richgels. Teaching Expository Text Structure to
Elementary Students. *The Reading Teacher, 38*, pp. 739–748. Reprinted with permission
of Lea M. McGee and the International Reading Association.

New Life for Lake Erie

Lake Erie is now once more a favorite vacation spot for residents of Ohio and other
nearby areas. The lake can be used for boating, fishing, and swimming because it is no
longer polluted. Pollution in the lake was controlled by making industries process their
wastes instead of dumping them in the lake. The lake became cleaner because sewage
was no longer dumped in it. Finally, farmers were warned not to use certain fertilizers
which were washing into the lake and causing too much algae to grow.

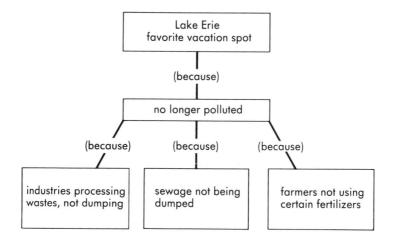

B. On an overhead transparency, the teacher shows the class a
graphic organizer for an enumerative paragraph (Figure 7.4), pointing out
that it shows the pattern of the passage they are about to receive.

C. The students are given a copy of the paragraph corresponding to
the organizer:

THE HONEYBEE'S GIFTS

In spite of the fact that humans fear the honeybee's sting, we appreciate
this insect for the gifts it provides. Most importantly, the honeybee
furnishes over 200 million pounds of honey every year. In addition, its
hives give us beeswax for making candles, furniture polish, and shav-
ing cream. The honeybee also helps farmers raise fruits and vegetables
by cross-pollinating orchards and gardens.

D. The students and teacher read the "Honeybee" passage together
and identify signal words that indicate the listing organizational pattern

FIGURE 7.3 Questions Students Can Use to Help Identify Text Structures or to Write Original Paragraphs Source: From JoAnne Piccolo, Expository Text Structure: Teaching and Learning Strategies. *The Reading Teacher, 40,* pp. 838–847. Reprinted with permission of JoAnne Piccolo and the International Reading Association.

Descriptive
Do you want to tell the reader what something is?

Sequence
Do you want to tell someone how to do something or make something?

Enumerative
Do you want to give a specific list of things that are related to the topic and tell about each?

Cause/effect
Do you want to give reasons why something happens or exists?

Problem/solution
Do you want to state some sort of problem related to your subject and offer some solutions?

Comparison/contrast
Do you want to show the similarities or differences between a certain topic and the topic you are writing about?

FIGURE 7.4 Graphic Organizer for the Listing Pattern

Topic Sentence:

Item 1:

Item 2:

Item 3:

(*most importantly, in addition, also*). Then, as a class, they complete a graphic organizer for the passage on an overhead transparency:

Honeybees provide gifts to humans

1. honey
2. beeswax
3. cross-pollination

Lesson 2
After a prewriting activity in which they select a topic and brainstorm ideas related to it, students complete an individualized graphic organizer based on their idea lists. They then use their organizers to write an original listing paragraph.

Lesson 3
In group discussion, the teacher shows selected examples of student-written paragraphs on the overhead projector. The class identifies good features and suggests possible revisions. Students are then asked to revise their paragraphs in peer groups.

Lesson 4
The teacher gives each student a copy of another paragraph to read and shows a blank organizer for the paragraph on the overhead, directing the students to fill in the organizer slots after reading the paragraph. Through this activity, students learn to read a paragraph and extract listed information by taking notes, guided by a graphic organizer.

After learning several paragraph patterns, students are given guided practice in locating structures in content-area textbooks and reference books. They are also required to incorporate the various structures into their report writing. Teachers can provide additional reinforcement of text structure knowledge through prereading questioning and discussion. Piccolo (1987) reports that the strategies described above are effective in teaching children to identify expository text patterns and to take notes while reading expository texts. In her opinion, "When teachers and students process these new expository text based skills, old problems about ways to improve comprehension in the content areas disappear" (p. 847).

■ Writing Expository Paragraphs

Flood, Lapp, and Farnan (1986) recommend a four-step writing procedure for helping intermediate-grade children understand the structure of expository text. A series of fill-in-the-blanks graphic organizers (Figure 7.5) guides

FIGURE 7.5   Steps in Learning to Write an Expository Passage   Source: From James Flood, Diane Lapp, and Nancy Farnan. A Reading-Writing Procedure that Teaches Expository Paragraph Structure. *The Reading Teacher, 39,* pp. 559–562. Reprinted with permission of James Flood and the International Reading Association.

Step 1. Teacher helps student select topic and list background knowledge

Topic: _____

Facts I already   1. _____
knew about the   2. _____
topic   3. _____
                         4. _____
                         5. _____

Step 2. Student turns to other sources of information

Facts I have learned	Source		Fact
about the topic	1. (reference material, e.g., encyclopedia) _____		1. _____
	2. (reference material) _____		2. _____
	3. (teacher) _____		3. _____
	4. (other informed adult or child) _____		4. _____
	5. (miscellaneous) _____		5. _____

Step 3. Student plots the paragraph

Theme or main idea _____

Supporting details   1. _____
                     2. _____
                     3. _____
                     4. _____
                     5. _____

Step 4. Student writes the expository paragraph

My final paragraph

_____
_____
_____
_____
_____

Note: To help children focus on the task, the teacher will want to start by putting the blank form for each step on a separate piece of paper and handing them out to be used one step at a time.

them through the process of writing an expository paragraph built on a main idea with supporting details about a topic of interest. According to Flood and associates, practice in writing paragraphs of this kind equips children to separate main from supporting details in their reading materials.

"Because of the clear and effective structure, this type of writing represents a first logical step for teaching children how well-organized text fits together" (p. 559).

The first step in this strategy is a prewriting interview with the teacher to explore a topic of interest to each child. After this discussion, children fill out the Step 1 organizer, "Facts I already knew about the topic" (see Figure 7.5). Then children proceed to collect information on their topic, selecting the most important ideas from each source to record in the Step 2 organizer, "Facts I have learned about the topic." Step 3 requires the children to formulate a main idea from the information gathered in the previous steps and plan the structure of a paragraph based upon that main idea, with supporting details. The main idea and details are then written into the third organizer. Finally, in Step 4, they write an expository paragraph, beginning with the statement of the main idea. The writing process is completed through a peer-partner feedback session during which partners read each others' paragraphs, write the main idea below the paragraph, and underline any supporting statements that are unrelated to the main topic. An excellent follow-up activity is to have students examine other pieces of writing containing explicitly stated main ideas and fill in the main idea and details on an organizer such as the one used in Step 3. Then students could search through their textbooks to find other examples of paragraphs following the "main idea/supporting detail" pattern.

According to the designers of this strategy, it is effective because it:

> capitalizes on the relationship between reading and writing to guide students toward an understanding of the nature of expository text. Students are not merely given an application task and asked to complete it for a grade. They are guided by direct instruction through the process of composing and evaluating reading in what for many students is a mode of discourse difficult to comprehend.
>
> (Flood et al., 1986, p. 560)

■ Pattern Guides

Another way graphic organizers can teach expository text structures is when used as pattern guides which students fill in while reading. Pattern guides, a variation of the traditional study guide, are handouts prepared by the teacher which require students to make written responses while reading. What differentiates pattern guides from regular study guides is that they require students to pay attention to text organization as well as text content.

Slater (1985) reported that ninth-graders who were given pattern guides in the form of outline grids to fill in while reading showed increased comprehension and recall of expository passages. According to Slater,

"With only one class period of instruction, students who received a structural organizer and completed an outline grid recalled 77% more idea units than those who merely read the texts. If teachers devoted more time to such instruction, it is likely that even larger gains could be achieved" (p. 718).

Slater's strategy was to introduce students to structural organizers by showing examples of expository text paragraph patterns and to explain the importance of using pattern guides as reading aids. Then he gave the students an outline grid which followed the organization of the passage they would be reading. They were directed to fill in the blank spaces of the guide as they read. After completing the passage, students were asked to recall the organization of the passage and write a summary of it.

We have adapted Slater's approach for use with intermediate-grade children by combining it with the graphic organizers of McGee and Richgels (1985). The result is a blank graphic organizer which students fill in as they read a textbook passage. The following example illustrates how this strategy can be used to teach the cause/effect pattern:

1. *Introduction.* The teacher introduces a graphic organizer for the cause/effect pattern and explains that it is important for a reader to know how an author has organized informational material because it gives clues to help in understanding and remembering. Sample paragraphs are then presented which follow the graphic organizer. For example, the Lake Erie passage in Figure 7.2 and its graphic organizer could be used. In this passage, the writer tells about an effect – Lake Erie is once again a popular vacation area – and then explains several things that caused this to happen – no more waste dumping, eliminating certain farm fertilizers.

2. *Practice.* After discussion of the Lake Erie passage and organizer, students are given a pattern guide, in the form of a blank graphic organizer, to use while reading the paragraph, "Bamboo and the Panda." The completed organizer is illustrated in Figure 7.6.

BAMBOO AND THE PANDA

Bamboo is the wild panda's best friend. The tender shoots of the plant provide food and the bamboo thickets insure safety. Because visibility in bamboo thickets is poor, the thicket offers privacy from visitors. The dry bamboo plants make a crackling sound when they are stepped on, alerting the panda to approaching predators. The panda's squatty, barrel-shaped body is also a protective device because only pandas can pass under the downed trees in the bamboo thickets.

3. *Summary Writing.* After completing the pattern guide for the "Bamboo and the Panda" passage, students write individual summaries of the passage by recalling the causation pattern.

Another use for pattern guides involves restructuring text. Some researchers maintain that students comprehend and recall expository text

FIGURE 7.6 Sample Completed Pattern Guide for "Bamboo and the Panda"

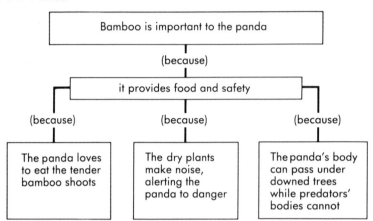

better if they restructure the passages they read, particularly when the organizational structure used by the author is listing (Alvermann, 1982; McGee & Richgels, 1985). The listing pattern is one of the most frequently used in both elementary and secondary text, but is among the least helpful to the reader because no relationships are specified among the listed details other than that they are all related to the main idea. The cause/effect, problem/solution, and comparison/contrast patterns all specify relationships among the elements of a paragraph.

McGee and Richgels (1985) maintain that students who have had experience with graphic organizers may be equipped to rewrite listing passages by imposing another more useful pattern and adding cue words. They suggest, "Since the writers of materials for young students seem to avoid using causation, problem/solution, and comparison passages, you and your students may discover some texts that would work better if rewritten using one of those three structures" (p. 747).

A study by Alvermann (1982) supports this recommendation. Alvermann planned and tested a strategy for teaching tenth-grade students to reorganize listing passages by designing pattern guides based on the comparison/contrast structure. She theorized that the imposing of this alternative structure would make the details of the material more memorable by emphasizing contrasts and offering more cues. Her findings showed that restructuring the listing material resulted in better recall of both main ideas and details, with the greatest gains being made in recollection of main ideas.

For information on other variations of the pattern guide approach plus suggestions for preparing the guides themselves, see Olson and Langnion (1982).

WRITING AS A LEARNING TOOL

■ ■   The dominance of reading in elementary school curriculums is generally recognized. Fulwiler (1987) laments, "Whereas reading is assigned in virtually every academic area as the best way to impart information, introduce ideas, and teach concepts, no such imperative exists regarding writing" (p. 2). Evidence from an investigation of the writing required of American high school students by content-field teachers indicated that most writing assignments were given to measure rather than to promote learning and that only 3 percent of the writing tasks involved the production of anything longer than a sentence (Applebee, 1981). Arguing from Applebee's findings and similar evidence by the American Association for the Advancement of the Humanities, Fulwiler recommends that schools balance the curriculum by increasing the role of writing.

The concept of "writing to learn" has emerged from a growing body of research pioneered by Britton (1978) and Emig (1971). Building upon this seminal work, researchers have produced the well-known model for teaching writing as a process with interactive and recursive stages—i.e., prewriting, composing, revising, editing, and publishing (see Chapter 3). The writing-to-learn thrust has emerged from the intersection of this growing body of research on the composing process with the recommendations from teachers and scholars promoting the use of writing as a learning tool across the curriculum.

Emig (1977), citing the work of Bruner, Vygotsky, and Luria, describes writing as a unique mode of learning that corresponds to some of the most effective learning strategies. For example, writing is integrative. It involves the functioning of the whole brain, requiring both the logical processing of material and the use of emotions, imagery, intuition, and spatial thinking. Writing is also "self-rhythmed," and tends to proceed at a pace that complements learning. Emig explains that "one writes best as one learns best, at one's own pace. Or to connect the two processes, writing can sponsor learning because it can match its pace" (p. 126).

Yinger and Clark (cited in Glatthorn, 1987), extrapolating from the same sources Emig used, propose several arguments for "writing to learn." They point out that, in writing, students employ the three major modes of learning proposed by Bruner: (a) enactive—learning by doing; (b) iconic—learning by depicting images; and (c) symbolic—learning by restating in words. Writing also enhances the learning process through the immediate and long-term feedback it provides for the student, as well as through the diagnostic information it yields for the teacher. In addition, due to the reconstructive and personal nature of the process, writing enables learners to access knowledge they already hold. Glatthorn (1987) adds, "When one writes, the lexical, syntactical, and rhetorical constraints of language demand explicit and systematic symbol manipulation, which in turn facilitates learning" (p. 318).

Although the concept of "writing to learn" emphasizes the learning of new subject matter, it assumes writing skills will improve with practice. In addition, writing in the content areas provides motivation for reluctant writers by furnishing topics to write about. When students have opportunities to play with ideas and concepts by writing regularly, they become more skillful writers and better learners.

Content-area writing develops a variety of reading and thinking skills. For example, writing assignments may generate the higher-level thinking skills needed for critical reading through the application of knowledge to new situations. Hennings (1982) stresses the importance of inferencing and generalizing through writing, urging teachers to require the use of the writer's tools for learning in all subjects. She emphasizes that writing in the content areas entails more than just writing assignments. It requires information gathering, prewriting, drafting, and rewriting, as well as the use of other communication skills: reading, listening, and speaking. Although empirical evidence to support the practice of writing to learn subject matter is still relatively scarce, anecdotal reports from teachers who have used writing successfully to aid learning in their classrooms are providing incentives for developing strategies for writing across the curriculum (Glatthorn, 1987; Newell, 1984).

■ Glatthorn's Planning Strategy

Glatthorn (1987) recommends a framework for teachers to follow in planning writing-to-learn activities for a content area:

> 1. Identify the *continuing* uses for writing in the subject area—ways in which writing is used in an ongoing manner without special assignments. (For example, taking notes, writing essay answers, writing exercises, keeping a journal, and writing in class to reinforce learning.)
> 2. Identify appropriate *special* writing tasks for the discipline—tasks requiring special instruction. (For example, research reports, creative papers, personal responses to reading in the field, papers explaining processes that are important to the subject, persuasive papers discussing issues in the field, and written exercises teaching thinking skills emphasized in the subject area.)
> 3. Identify the important qualities that should be displayed in students' writing in the discipline. (For example, in science, reporting should be objective and accurate; in social studies, historical data are essential to support conclusions; in English, personal thoughts are vital to the interpretation of literature; and in math, precise verbal translations are needed.)
>
> (pp. 319–320)

Glatthorn comments further that elementary teachers find the task of determining ongoing and special uses of writing in the various areas easier than secondary teachers because they work with the total curriculum.

Once these ongoing and special writing activities have been identified, they should be implemented on a regular basis. Tchudi and Huerta (1983) recommend that teachers observe the following principles when conducting writing-to-learn assignments:

1. Keep the content at the center of the writing process, addressing yourself to *what* the writing says, allowing *how it is said* to be treated incidentally.

2. Make certain students know their material before writing; content understanding shines through in student writing.

3. Design writing activities that help students structure and synthesize their knowledge, not merely regurgitate it.

4. Teach the process of writing:

a. Spend much time with prewriting, helping students acquire a solid grasp of the material.

b. Provide assistance and support as students write, helping them to solve problems as they arise, rather than waiting until they turn in the paper.

5. Let students revise one another's papers. Provide support through revision checklists and guidelines.

6. Don't confuse revising with copy editing:

a. Teach revision first, having students clarify the content and substance of their work.

b. Turn to copy editing of spelling, mechanics, and usage only in the final phases of writing.

7. Display or otherwise publicize student writing through shows, demonstrations, book publishing (duplicated or one-of-a-kind), and oral readings. Don't be the only reader of your students' work.

8. *Keep content at the center of the writing process.*

(p. 45)*

■ Summary Writing

In an earlier chapter we emphasized the value of summarization skills for improving recall and monitoring comprehension. Because the summarization process can also facilitate learning by helping readers "clarify the meaning and significance of discourse" (Brown, Campione, & Day, 1981), we are discussing it again within the context of strategies for learning from textbooks.

Researchers studying the behaviors of proficient readers during the reading of expository text have found that such readers can find the important ideas, relate information across sentences, question themselves to

*Condensed from S. N. Tchudi and M. C. Huerta. *Teaching Writing in the Content Areas: Middle School/Junior High.* Copyright © 1983. Reprinted with permission of the National Education Association.

check understanding, and hypothesize about what will come next (Barton, 1983; Gruen, 1981). These are strategies that deal with the macro-structure or underlying meaning of the text as a whole. The average and less able readers in these studies have demonstrated a preference for using micro-structure, or word-level, strategies in their reading.

Reading instruction in elementary classrooms has tended to focus on micro-structure techniques, emphasizing isolated decoding skills and word meanings rather than the skills needed to understand units of text larger than the sentence. This lack of instruction in macro-structure strategies is particularly evident as children reach the third and fourth grades and begin to read concept-packed content-area materials (Durkin, 1978). One of the macro-structure strategies we propose to remedy this situation is summary writing.

The ability to summarize the important information in a text is vital to learning because repetition of material strengthens memory of it (Gagné, 1985). Researchers have found that summary writing following the reading of social studies material improved sixth-graders' comprehension and recall of text information as well as the quality of their expository compositions (Doctorow, Wittrock, & Marks, 1978; Taylor & Berkowitz, 1980). Students were required not only to read and understand a text but also to select and reject information for their summaries on the basis of its importance.

Summary writing is a unique composing activity in that it involves processing ideas from previously generated discourse, requiring the reader/writer to make choices about what to include or eliminate from the original text (Hidi & Anderson, 1986). The summarization process, therefore, demands the use of two higher cognitive skills—selecting and reducing. Flood (1986, p. 790) contends that these skills help students "see the big picture" and "determine whether the pieces of information they selected and remembered were the critical pieces for learning."

□ Four-Step Summary Writing

A set of rules for summary writing developed by Kintsch and van Dijk (1978) has been widely accepted, modified, and adapted for teaching students of various ages. Our writer-based interpretation, which can be adapted for all grade levels, including primary, consists of four steps (eliminating the polishing stage involved in the production of a reader-based summary):

1. *Select a topic sentence.* If you do not see a sentence by the author that summarizes the paragraph, write your own.
2. *Delete unnecessary information.* Text information may be repeated in a passage, or it may be trivial. Delete both redundant and unimportant ideas.
3. *Collapse lists of items.* Substitute a collective term for a number of things that fall into the same category, e.g., instead of *bracelets, neck-*

laces, pendants, pins, and *watches,* you might use jewelry. Also, substitute one encompassing action for a list of subcomponents of the action.
4. *Collapse paragraphs.* Some paragraphs expand on others and can be combined with them. Others are unnecessary and can be deleted.

Explicit instruction in the use of these rules is necessary. Students should be shown through teacher modeling with sample passages how to apply the rules and instructed to check to see that they have found a topic sentence, deleted redundancies, and so forth. The Strategy Example illustrates how teachers can demonstrate the Four-Step Summary Writing strategy.

――――――――― **STRATEGY EXAMPLE 7.2** ―――――――――

A Teacher Demonstration of the Four-Step Summary Writing Procedure

The summary writing demonstration, appropriate for the intermediate grades, begins with an explanation by the teacher that a summary is a shortened version of a passage which says the same thing as the original in fewer words. No new information is added by the writer of the summary even though it is written in the writer's own words.

The following passage is projected on the overhead for the class to read:

> There are still great expanses of the world's deserts which are not crossed by such modern travel routes as roads, railroads, pipe lines, or regular air lanes. Some of these areas are so desolate that they are seldom if ever crossed by human beings. No man has any reason to enter them. Other areas echo occasionally to the noise of a bouncing jeep, which can travel over roadless country that is not too rough or hilly. Still others are crossed today, as they have been for centuries, only by pack trains of animals. The best desert travelers are camels, llamas, or other beasts of burden such as the sturdy burros of Mexico and our own Southwest.
>
> Camels, llamas and burros may someday be crowded off the main travel routes of the world's deserts. But probably there will always be places where desert travel is done with the help of animals or not done at all.
>
> (excerpt from *All About the Desert,* by Sam and Beryl Epstein, pp. 68−69)

Assignment: Write a three-sentence summary of this paragraph, following the Four-Step Summary Writing process.

Step 1: Write a Topic Sentence

The teacher asks the class to suggest several topic sentences, and discussion follows to determine how to state the author's most important idea in a sentence. The students are reminded to use their own ideas. An acceptable sentence might be:

> Although some of the main routes of the desert may become too busy to allow beasts of burden on them, pack animals will always be needed in certain areas.

Step 2: Delete Unimportant or Redundant Materials

As the class rereads the passage, the teacher points out that sentences 2 and 3 say almost the same thing and therefore can be combined. Sentences 4, 5, and 6 contain nonessential information which can be deleted, making it possible to collapse the three sentences into one.

Step 3: Collapse Lists of Items and Actions

The teacher explains that a series of items in the first sentence can be categorized under one name, i.e., roads, railroads, pipelines, and air lanes can be called "modern transportation." Students are asked to find another such list (camels, llamas, and burros) and find a suitable category label (e.g., "beasts of burden").

Step 4: Collapse Paragraphs

Discussion of the content of paragraph 2 is led by the teacher, culminating in the combining of paragraphs 1 and 2, since they both deal with the same topic.

The teacher's revised version on the overhead would look something like this:

> *Some areas*
> There are still great expanses of the world's deserts ~~which~~ are not crossed by ~~such~~ modern travel routes as roads, railroads, pipe lines, or
> *They*
> regular air lanes. ~~Some of these areas~~ are so desolate that ~~they are seldom if~~
> *no one has a*
> ~~ever crossed by human beings.~~ No man has any ∧ reason to enter them.
> *are*
> ~~Other areas echo occasionally to the noise of a bouncing jeep, which can~~
> *crossed* ~~travel over roadless country that is not too rough or hilly.~~ Still others are
> *by jeep* ~~crossed today, as they have been for centuries,~~ only by pack trains of
> *or pack* ~~animals. The best desert travelers are camels, llamas, or other beasts of~~
> *animals.* ~~burden such as the sturdy burros of Mexico and our own Southwest.~~
> *Beasts of burden*
> Camels, llamas and burros may someday be crowded off the main travel routes of the world's deserts. But probably there will always be places where desert travel is done with the help of animals ~~or not done at all~~.

The final stage of the demonstration process is the writing of a suitable three-sentence summary by the teacher and class together:

Some areas of the world's deserts are not crossed by modern transportation because they are too desolate for people to enter. Other areas are crossed by jeeps and animal pack trains. Although some of the main routes of the desert may eventually become too busy to allow beasts of burden on them, pack animals will always be needed in certain areas.

☐ ***The Hierarchical Summary***

Taylor (1982) discovered that middle-grade students who were taught a Hierarchical Summary procedure that focused on the organization of ideas in content textbooks could recall more information from their reading and could write better quality expository compositions. Taylor's students were taught to write summaries of informational selections by following this procedure:

Previewing

Students skim through a three- to five-page expository selection containing headings and subheadings, generating an outline with Roman numerals for each heading and capital letters for each subheading as they read. They leave space for numbered details under each capital letter:

```
I.
    A.
          1.
          2.
          3.
    B.
          1.
          2.
          3.
```

Reading and Outlining

Following their skeleton outlines, students write a summary for each major heading as they read the passage, putting main idea statements for each subheading after the capital letters and listing details after the numbers. Then they generate a topic sentence for the entire subsection and write it next to the Roman numerals.

```
I.   Topic sentence for main heading #1
    A.   Main idea statement for subheading #1
          1.   Detail
          2.   Detail
          3.   Detail
```

    B. Main idea statement for subheading #2
      1. Detail
      2. Detail
      3. Detail

Students repeat this procedure for each major heading. In the left margin, they write key phrases which combine the subsections, drawing lines to connect them.

Studying and Retelling Orally
After studying their summaries, students tell a partner everything they remember about what they have read while the partner follows the summary and reminds them of information they overlooked.

In Figure 7.7 we have applied Taylor's strategy to a selection from *Our America* (Allyn & Bacon, 1977), a seventh-grade social studies text.

FIGURE 7.7 Hierarchical Summary for "British Acts and Colonial Anger"—A Selection with One Main Heading and Two Subheadings Source: Adapted from Barbara M. Taylor (1982). A summarizing strategy to improve middle grade students' reading and writing skills. *The Reading Teacher, 36,* pp. 202–205.

    I. British policy toward the American colonies angered the colonists.

      A. The British passed laws that were unpopular with the colonists

        1. The Grenville Program

        2. The Stamp Act

Actions**   3. Strange taxes (beards, windows, soap)

        4. The Townshend Acts

        5. The Intolerable Acts

      B. The colonists rebelled against the British laws, which led to war between England and the colonies.

        1. The Stamp Act Congress

        2. The Boston Massacre

Reactions**   3. Crispus Attucks—becomes freedom fighter

        4. The Boston Tea Party

        5. The First Continental Congress

*Topic sentence written by the students after filling the main ideas (A and B) and details for the two subheadings.

**Key phrases connecting subsections.

Taylor suggests that students have three guided experiences with the teacher in order to learn to write summaries of this kind and that, after writing about six Hierarchical Summaries, most students should be independent summary writers. She points out that her strategy is an attractive alternative to the traditional practice of having students answer questions after reading. Not only does Hierarchical Summarizing promote recall; it has the additional "advantage of being a study strategy that students can use without outside help" (1982, p. 205).

■ Inquiry-Centered Reading and Writing

Individual and group inquiry activities in the elementary and middle grades build a solid foundation of research skills for children to carry with them through high school and college. Vacca and Vacca (1986) emphasize the need for careful planning by teachers in order to ensure that young researchers are given adequate training and direction for their investigations:

> The inquiry process isn't a "do your own thing" proposition, for budding researchers need structure. Many an inquiry project has been wrecked on the shoals of nondirection. The trick is to strike a balance between teacher guidance and student self-reliance. An inquiry activity must have just enough structure to give students (1) a problem focus, (2) physical and intellectual freedom, (3) an environment where they can obtain data, and (4) feedback situations to share the results of their writing
>
> (p. 221).

Conducted properly, inquiry activities are an ideal context for integrating reading, writing, and content-area learning.

In this section we discuss procedures for teaching the skills involved in individual and group inquiry activities. We give special attention to motivation, difficulty level, and scholastic utility in the strategies we recommend for use with elementary and middle school learners because we believe all three have strong impact on the success and worth of early inquiry experiences. We suggest simplified alternatives to the traditional research papers that are appropriate for younger learners. Our variations on the formal research report have three features in common:

1. Students have the opportunity to *choose the topic* they are investigating.
2. They are given *specific tools for data gathering,* i.e., they are shown how to find information, where to look, and how to use an information-collection chart for comparing and summarizing findings.
3. They *use their research findings for a particular purpose,* i.e., to entertain, inform, or persuade an audience. Their written projects include other forms of discourse in addition to traditional reports.

☐ ***Choosing Topics***

Children need the help of their teachers and peers to locate and define research topics. Nance (1982) finds that asking upper-grade students to write an arguable question about something that interests them has been a successful approach to the topic search in her classroom. She starts the question-generating process by giving students sample questions, to demonstrate that: (a) topics can come from any area; (b) questions that are arguable cannot be answered yes or no; and (c) you have to know something about a topic to write a question, even though you cannot answer it. Nance recommends class brainstorming sessions, browsing through books and magazines, and discussion groups for helping students find topics.

Macrorie (1980) reminds teachers that students usually dread research paper assignments when they must investigate a topic selected by the teacher rather than a question they would like to answer for themselves. He recommends changing the concept of "re-search" to "I-Search," turning the task around from a detached chore to an exciting exploration that means something to the learner. The major difference between I-Search and research is the personal involvement that comes with inquiring about a topic the investigator cares about and chooses, rather than one the teacher selects. (It must be acknowledged, though, that the two are not mutually exclusive.) The I-Search paper which reports the students' findings also has a first-person focus, allowing them to tell the story of their search in a three-section narrative, including: (a) "What I Already Knew"; (b) "The Story of My Search"; and (c) "What I Learned" (see the "I-Search" section below).

☐ ***Tools for Data Gathering***

Although it does provide new information, the traditional practice of copying material from a reference book discourages the development of good writing and thinking skills and promotes the practice of plagiarism. In suggesting better ways for students to use writing to learn about the world, Jacobs (1984) proposes the use of lead-in activities to arouse curiosity and to stimulate children to seek answers to their own questions rather than "a prepackaged sort of truth" (p. 336). She advocates replacing broad research topics with specific questions, maintaining, "Topics are too easily hooked to chunks of information in sourcebooks. Questions, because they set a direction for information to follow, are less easily attached to the ready-made phrasing children find" (p. 359).

One way to wean children away from source book copying in the elementary grades is to require them to impose their own order on the data they collect through their research. Suzanne Brady uses a simple technique to introduce her fourth- and fifth-graders to the reorganizing process when they are in the early stages of learning data-collection skills (Jacobs, 1984). She instructs her students to fold a large piece of newsprint into several rectangular sections and to write a question in each rectangle, allowing space for the answers they will be finding in their investigations. In Brady's opinion, this data-collection system forces the breaking-up of information into units smaller than a topic, while allowing the students to provide the structure and encouraging them to answer the questions directly. Brady believes that large paper is less confusing for young children to work with in organizing information than note cards.

More complex types of data charts can play a vital role for children during the information-collecting stage of their research projects by helping them make connections between their prior knowledge and new information. The tasks of organizing material into manageable units and relating the units of information to each other can be formidable without the assistance of an organizing structure. A variety of data-gathering charts designed by teachers and researchers can be used by children for these purposes. We describe two strategies, the Interview Grid and the Data Retrieval Chart, both of which are appropriate for information-gathering activities in elementary and middle grades.

Interview Grid   QuIP (Questions into Paragraphs) is a three-step strategy developed by McLaughlin (1987) to guide children in open-ended inquiries. The first step of the process is the preparation and completion of an Interview Grid by individual students. The grids are used initially to organize information collected in oral interviews. Students select a topic of interest and ask questions of peers, family, and others, and write their responses in the proper boxes of the grid. Once students are familiarized with the grid format, they can use grids to organize information collected from reference books and other printed sources.

The preparation of a grid begins with the writing of three interview questions about a chosen topic in each of the question boxes of the grid. The answers found through interviews or through reading reference books are then recorded, completing the Interview Grid. Figure 7.8 illustrates the use of the grid with fourth-grade printed resource material dealing with the topic of forts in the United States.

In the second step of the QuIP process, the completed grid is transposed into an outline, with the name of the topic as heading and the questions as subheadings. The interviewees' or books' answers provide supporting information under each subheading. Figure 7.9 shows an outline emanating from the Interview Grid on forts.

The third step involves writing a report based on the outline, composing a paragraph for each subheading of the outline. An introductory topic sentence can then be generated to tie the paragraphs together.

McLaughlin has observed that one of the advantages of the Interview Grid is its ability to make students aware of similarities and differences among their findings from different sources. This encourages them to use the comparison/contrast organization in their compositions, giving them experience with one of the most difficult and complex types of expository text structures.

FIGURE 7.8 Completed Interview Grid Source: From Elaine M. McLaughlin. QuIP: A Writing Strategy to Improve Comprehension of Expository Structure. *The Reading Teacher, 40,* pp. 650–654. Reprinted with permission of Elaine M. McLaughlin and the International Reading Association.

Topic: Forts in the U.S.A.
Student's name: Keith (4th grade)

	Source: *The American Republic*	Source: *New Standard Encyclopedia*
Question 1: A. What were some famous forts in America?	1. There was Fort McHenry where Francis Scott Key wrote the "Star Spangled Banner," and 2. Fort Sumter that started the Civil War.	3. Fort Donelson: Grant's civil war victory here led to his promotion to general. 4. Fort Bridger: waystation on Oregon Trail.
Question 2: B. Why were forts built?	1. Protection from Indians on the frontier.	2. To protect seaports from other countries.
Question 3: C. What kinds of forts were there?	1. Star forts have regular designs with many sharp angles.	2. A bastion has works called bastions which go out from the main fort.

FIGURE 7.9 Outline Developed from an Interview Grid Source: From Elaine M. McLaughlin. QuIP: A Writing Strategy to Improve Comprehension of Expository Structure. *The Reading Teacher, 40,* pp. 650–654. Reprinted with permission of Elaine M. McLaughlin and the International Reading Association.

U.S. military in the 1800s

I. Forts in the USA
   A. Famous forts in America
      1. Fort McHenry
      2. Fort Sumter
      3. Fort Donelson
      4. Fort Bridger

   B. Reasons for forts
      1. Protection from Indians
      2. Seaport defense

   C. Kinds of forts
      1. Star fort
      2. Bastion

Data Retrieval Charts   Hennings (1982) has devised a strategy for helping young learners to compile and interpret information from multiple sources that makes these tasks seem less arduous by dividing the responsibilities. The Data Retrieval Chart, which structures a group of students through the process of reading and recording information on a topic, culminates in a collectively written research report. The chart takes the form of a grid, with the vertical columns containing questions or topics relating to the main topic under investigation, and the horizontal rows containing the names of different research sources. Hennings suggests dividing a class into investigative groups and directing them to assign each member of their group the responsibility of collecting data from one of the sources on the chart. After the children compile their data using one master retrieval chart for their group, they use the information to write one paragraph about each subtopic and a final paragraph which requires the drawing of conclusions from their research.

In Hennings's example (Figure 7.10), upper-elementary-grade children studying Colonial America gathered information on schooling in the Middle Colonies, the Southern Colonies, and the New England Colonies. The students worked in three-person teams, with each team choosing to study a different subtopic (e.g., schooling, agriculture). Each team member was given different source material and required to collect information relevant to the subtopic for all three colonial areas and then to fill out the appropriate row of the group Data Retrieval Chart. Using data from this group chart, students were then required to write a paragraph for each subtopic (e.g., one describing schooling in each of the three areas) and finally, to compose a paragraph telling where they would prefer to have lived and why, based on the information gathered in their research (e.g., the educational practices of the various colonies).

The Data Retrieval Chart strategy adapts well for individual use, as demonstrated in the version we have designed for use in an I-Search experience (see below).

☐ ***Using Research Findings***

The Interview Grid (QuIP) and Data Retrieval Chart illustrate the types of collection devices that provide structure for children's investigative activities. By displaying information in an organized manner, they facilitate the selection of relevant material for reports, essays, and other writing purposes. We recommend that teachers offer students options in the forms of discourse they use for sharing the newly acquired knowledge appearing on their data charts.

After reading Applebee's (1981) finding that mechanical forms of writing, such as slotting information on worksheets and copying from textbooks, were the most prevalent types of writing in American classrooms, Levine (1985) explored the most effective kinds of writing for concept development. She hypothesized that content-area teachers, who begin with expressive writing and ease children into other forms of dis-

FIGURE 7.10 Data Retrieval Chart on Colonial America Source: From D. G. Hennings. *Teaching communication and reading skills in the content areas.* Copyright © 1982 by Phi Delta Kappa, Inc.

Name of Researcher: _____ Subtopic Investigated: _____

I. Directions: Record in the appropriate column material on the subtopic from the reference named. Each member of your three-person team will collect data from one of the references named and complete one column of the chart.

References	Middle Colonies	Southern Colonies	New England Colonies
textbook: *Your America*			
textbook: *World Book*			

II. Directions: When each member of your team has gathered data from one reference named, compile your data on one master chart. Then using the data from that chart, complete the following writing assignments:

A. Draft a paragraph that describes schooling in the New England colonies.

B. Draft a paragraph that describes schooling in the Middle colonies.

C. Draft a paragraph that describes schooling in the Southern colonies.

D. In your group, decide where you would have preferred to live during colonial days. Draft a paragraph expressing your preference based on the schooling practices there. Make sure your paragraph tells why.

course as they gain familiarity with concepts, would find that their students learn more from their information searches. She discovered that her seventh- and eighth-grade science students became much more specific and concrete when they were writing to explain ideas to audiences other than the teacher (i.e., peers and real or imaginary adults) than when they were writing traditional reports. Levine also found that allowing students to investigate a topic of interest to them and report their findings in a manner of their choice had impressive results. Among the writing activities that helped her students develop mastery of science concepts were writing to the President about the effects of nuclear war and writing an account of a hands-on lab experience to read to their peers the next day.

The three strategies that follow—Spin-Off Writing, I-Search, and Saturation Reporting—are examples of high-interest alternatives to the traditional research report. These strategies enable students to use their findings in enjoyable, satisfying ways.

Spin-Off Writing   Nance (1982) adds variety to the inquiry activities in her classroom by following three steps: (a) having students pose an arguable question about some topic that interests them; (b) teaching them how to write an abstract containing the important facts they found while exploring the question; and (c) allowing the students to use their research findings by writing for a variety of purposes and audiences.

The topic search in her classroom begins with a listing of sample topics by the teacher, to demonstrate the kinds of questions that are arguable and to emphasize that it is necessary to know something about a topic before formulating a question. Brainstorming and book-browsing follow, and then students are placed in triad groups to help each other finalize their research questions before proceeding with the reading of reference sources.

After information collection is completed, students prepare a draft containing the important facts from their inquiries. After the teacher models the writing of an abstract from one student's fact paper, they then write individual abstracts of their own fact papers. The abstract, which is part of a self-revision process, equips the students with a map of their drafts to assist them in organizing the information they have gathered. Students are instructed to follow three steps in writing these abstracts: (a) write the research question; (b) write the topic sentence from each paragraph of the draft; and (c) write a summary sentence or two, developing each topic.

Students in Nance's classroom have used their abstracts as the basis for a variety of types of writing, including poems, short stories, letters, formal speeches, editorials, and pamphlets. Spin-Off Writing based on their research activities has added an interesting new dimension to the writing process in her classroom. As a result, she has heard her students remark, " 'Hey, you know, that research paper wasn't so bad after all' " (p. 288).

Whenever possible, Tchudi and Tchudi (1983) build real or imaginary audiences, including friends and parents, into the sharing stage of their students' research activities. The Strategy Example lists some of the discourse forms which the Tchudis use with their students, all of which are appropriate for Spin-Off Writing activities.

——————————— **STRATEGY EXAMPLE 7.3** ———————————

Some Discourse Forms for Content-Area Writing

Journals and diaries
   (real or imaginary)
Biographical sketches
Anecdotes and stories:
   from experience
   as told by others
Thumbnail sketches:
   of famous people
   of places
   of historical events
Guess who/what descriptions
Letters:
   personal reactions
   observations
   persuasive:
      to the editor
      to public officials
Requests
Applications
Memos
Resumés and summaries
Poems
Plays
Stories:
   fantasy
   adventure
   science fiction
   historical
Dialogues and conversations
Children's books
Telegrams
Editorials
Commentaries
Response and rebuttals
Fact sheets
School newspaper stories
Stories for local papers
Proposals
Case studies:
   school problems
   local issues

Reviews:
   books (including textbooks)
   films
   television programs
Historical "you are there" scenes
Science notes:
   observations
   notebook
   lab reports
Math:
   story problems
   solutions to problems
   record books
   notes and observations
Responses to literature
Interviews:
   actual
   imaginary
Directions:
   how-to
   school or neighborhood guide
Dictionaries and lexicons
Future options, notes on:
   careers, employment
   school and training
   military/public service
Written debates
Taking a stand:
   school issues
   family problems
   state or national issues
   moral questions
Radio scripts
TV scenarios and scripts
Dramatic scripts
Notes for improvised drama
Cartoons and cartoon strips
Slide show scripts
Puzzles and word searches
Prophecy and prediction
Photo captions

national concerns	Collage, montage, mobile,
historical problems	sculpture
scientific issues	Poster displays
Songs and ballads	

I-Search   Searching for information about a topic of special interest and relating the details of that search to others is a natural adventure in learning. Macrorie (1980) uses the term "I-Search" to remind students that there is a personal story behind their research papers, even though the word "I" is rarely used in such texts. He emphasizes that students enjoy the freedom of telling the story of an information search that has meaning for them.

Bay Area Writing Project teachers (Olson, 1986) attest to the effectiveness of the I-Search strategy, or "hunting story," for teaching skills students will need throughout their lives for reading and writing research reports. Freedman (1986) promotes the introduction of the I-Search approach at the third-grade level when children first learn to write reports, explaining that it meets the objectives of traditional reporting—i.e., recognizing responsible sources of information, distinguishing between fact and opinion, knowing accepted forms of writing research, testing facts, and drawing conclusions.

Freedman teaches the I-Search process in three stages: (a) identifying the problem to be studied; (b) searching for information; and (c) writing the report. She advises teachers who are introducing the I-Search technique in the classroom to begin with a prewriting exercise in which students write statements about topics of interest and list things they would like to know. After some ideas have been generated, students select one topic of special interest from their lists to explore. Freedman explains: "This warm-up activity stimulates thinking and assures students of having the key ingredient of the I-Search process: finding a problem which they can get involved in" (1986, p. 115). The second step is to show children how to obtain information through library sources (reference and trade books), interviewing, and resource people. Finally, an I-Search reporting format is taught, giving students a structure to follow in preparing their papers:

1. Statement of the problem: What did I want to know?
2. Procedures followed: How did I find the information?
3. Summary of findings: What did I learn?
4. Conclusion: What will I do with this information?

(Freedman, 1986, p. 115)

Acknowledging the demands of the prescribed curriculum on teachers, Freedman points out that children can find high-interest topics related to any subject matter being studied by the class if they are encouraged to do so in the problem-identification stage.

We recommend the use of an I-Search data chart for guiding children through the process — from problem identification to conclusions — and for preparing them to write the personal narratives describing their searches. Figure 7.11 illustrates an I-Search data chart appropriate for use in the third grade and above. The topics for individual I-Searches in this sample activity are generated from the teacher's oral reading of Byrd Baylor's *When Clay Sings* (Scribner's, 1972). After learning the term "artifact" and the facts reported by Baylor about Indian cultures of the American Southwest — facts gathered from piecing together pottery remnants found in the desert — children are given the opportunity to discuss the information in the book. After this experience, some students may decide to explore artifacts from other cultures to make comparisons among them. For example, the designs on the bowls seen in *When Clay Sings* differ in a number of features from the Pueblo designs found in Gerald McDermott's *Arrow to the Sun* (Viking, 1974). Other students may decide to compare the artifacts of several Native American cultures that are of special interest to them. A list of other informational trade books about Native Americans is located in the "Recommended Children's Books" section at the end of this chapter.

The first step children follow in completing the I-Search data chart is writing their question at the top of the chart. In our example in Figure 7.12, the student has chosen to study the artifacts of the Woodland Indians. The question to be answered is: What can I discover about the Woodland Indians from their artifacts? Next, in the "What I Knew" section, the student lists facts learned about Indian artifacts from *When Clay Sings* (documenting the source) and other facts from prior knowledge. In this section of the chart, the investigator may also state "What I Want to Know." This material will constitute the first paragraph of the I-Search paper. The story of the research is told in the next section of the chart, including the procedures followed ("Where I Looked") and the findings ("What I Found"), providing the facts for the second section of the paper. Finally, the student's conclusions are stated as summary sentences in the bottom section of the chart ("What I Concluded"), serving as the basis for the last paragraph of the paper. A reference list containing the sources used, in alphabetical order by the author's last name, concludes the I-Search paper.

The I-Search paper is ready to be written upon completion of this chart. Newly discovered facts and their sources have been listed and properly organized so that the writer's task is simply to combine the three sections into an I-Search report. Through this experience, children are introduced to fundamentals of research and standard bibliographic form (underlining book titles, listing authors alphabetically by last name, and

FIGURE 7.11   Blank I-Search Data Chart
QUESTION:

I-SEARCH PAPER What I Knew	*FACTS*	
The Story of My Search	*WHERE I LOOKED*	*WHAT I FOUND*
What I Concluded	*SUMMARY SENTENCES*	

including publisher and date in the entry). These are skills on which they can build in the future.

Saturation Reporting   Using fictional techniques for nonfiction writing, as newspaper reporters do in feature stories, has been referred to as the "new journalism" (Wolfe & Johnson, 1973). When children are engaged in this kind of writing, they act like reporters who are on the scene writing about first-hand observations. They "saturate" themselves with the facts about their subject and select the details to report. Bernstein (1986) promotes the use of this Saturation Reporting technique at all grade levels, explaining, "You ask your students to make all the sophisticated choices professional writers make: which points of view to use; which details and

FIGURE 7.12 I-Search Data Chart Example

QUESTION: *What can I learn about Native Americans of the past from their artifacts?*

I–SEARCH PAPER	FACTS
What I Knew	*Bowls found in the Southwest desert were decorated with animals, fish, and designs. They show that these people hunted rabbits, mountain lions, bears, deer, antelope, and wildcats. Designs with the moon, sun, and stars showed their interest in the solar system. They wore masks when they danced. They had pet dogs. Source: Baylor, Byrd. When Clay Sings, Scribners, 1972*

The Story of My Search	WHERE I LOOKED	WHAT I FOUND
	Glubok, Shirley. The Art of the Woodland Indians, Macmillan, 1976.	*Beaded wampum belts, snowshoes, toboggans, quillwork, deerskin clothing, medicine pipes, birdstones, fire bags, gourd jars, flutes, drumsticks, turtle shell rattles, masks*
	Glubok, Shirley The Art of the Northwest Coast Indians, Macmillan 1975	*Totem poles carved from cedar trees, long dugout canoes, large supernatural figures and feast dishes, wolf head helmets, masks, ivory charms, whale tusks, hollowed-out frog-shaped bowls, black shale figures.*

What I Concluded	SUMMARY SENTENCES
	1. Ceremonial masks and pottery bowls were found among the artifacts of all Native American cultures studied. 2. Each culture had its own special artifacts depending upon its location (desert, seacoast, or woodlands). 3. By studying and comparing artifacts from the various Native American cultures, we can learn about their lives and traditions.

dialogue to include; which research, if any, to pursue; and finally, how to structure the nonfiction experience" (p. 93).

Bernstein demonstrates the production of a saturation report for her high school students by sharing her own experiences in writing about a weight-loss clinic. After brainstorming her observations during thirty days of daily trips to a clinic, she developed a collage of scenes, which she later described separately and put in final order from A to G (see Figure 7.13).

The next step involves introducing the students to a listing of the features of Saturation Reporting (see Strategy Example). The students then choose their topics after brainstorming people, places, and events they might like to write about and selecting the most promising. In this early planning stage, Olson (1986b) asks her students to write a one-page ab-

FIGURE 7.13   Brainstorming of Observations for Saturation Reporting   Source: Reprinted, by permission, from "Using Fictional Techniques for Nonfiction Writing," by Ruby Bernstein, in *Practical Ideas for Teaching Writing as a Process* (pp. 105–107), edited by Carol Booth Olson, copyright 1986, 1987, California State Department of Education, P.O. Box 271, Sacramento, CA 95802-0271.

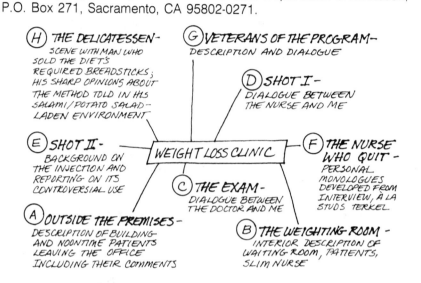

stract, explaining what their topic is, why they chose it, and how they will gather information. She encourages them to observe their person, place, or event for about a week, recording everything they can about it and noting their own personal impressions. After the information-gathering stage, Olson asks her students to design a scene-by-scene cluster of their reports, following Bernstein's model (see Figure 7.13). Then the students are required to write their opening scenes and share them in "read-around" groups. Olson (1986a) explains that this sharing enables students to return to their own reports "with a fresh perspective on their own writing, some new ideas gained from seeing other students' works, and the motivation of writing for their peers" (p. 99).

––––––––––––– **STRATEGY EXAMPLE 7.4** –––––––––––––

Saturation Report Features

1. *Writing about some place, some group, or some individual that you know well or can get to know well firsthand.*   You "saturate" yourself with your subject.
2. *Writing a nonfiction article using fictional techniques.*   There will be scenes, characters, and characterizations, dialogue, and subtle, rather than overt, statement.

3. *The appeal of information and facts.* You are writing nonfiction, and the reader will want to "know" about your subject; in short, be sensitive to this thirst for facts on the part of your reader.

4. *Author identification.* Your point of view can be quite flexible. You can be an active participant in the action; you can remove yourself; or you can come in and then move out.

5. *Microcosm.* You are focusing on some particular subject, but in so doing you are saying something more. As you capture an isolated segment of today's world, you say something about the total world.

6. *Implication.* Much of what you attempt to "say" in your article (because of the use of fictional techniques) will be said through implication—through dialogue and through your manipulation of details.

7. *Reporting.* You will observe your subject with a keen eye. You will note interesting "overheard" conversations. You might want to interview someone.

8. *Form.* You might write your article in pieces—conversations, descriptions, interviews, facts—and then piece it together, finding the best form for your subject (time sequence and so forth). A "patchwork"—working sections together with no transition—can be quite acceptable.

9. *Choice of subject.* You can pick some subject from the present or recreate some subject from your past.

Source: Reprinted, by permission, from "Using Fictional Techniques for Nonfiction Writing," by Ruby Bernstein, in *Practical Ideas for Teaching Writing as a Process* (pp. 105–107), edited by Carol Booth Olson; copyright 1986, 1987 by the California State Department of Education, P.O. Box 271, Sacramento, CA 95802-0271.

Linda Bowe (1986) teaches Saturation Reporting to her second-graders in connection with science and social studies, using an add-on technique. The children write daily about different aspects of a phenomenon they are observing and studying about in their classroom, developing an ongoing story which integrates facts with their own ideas. For example, she describes her students as "very capable of writing about the experience" while they are observing silkworms passing through their life cycle in the classroom. Bowe helps her students focus on a special topic each day in their Saturation Reporting by requiring that they choose one of two approaches. They may decide to study one aspect of the life cycle closely and write about it each day or describe a different stage of the cycle each time they write.

The add-on Saturation Reporting activity increases enthusiasm for science study, according to Bowe, by allowing children to combine creative writing with science reporting. They are also eager to communicate what they have learned through their interesting and informative stories.

CONTENT-AREA SPECIFIC STRATEGIES

■ ■   The skills required to read science must be acquired through reading science. The skills required in writing science can be learned only by writing science. . . . Equally important is experience in writing in every content area. A child who writes science or social studies or industrial arts acquires the basic vocabulary of the subject. . . . Over several years, practice in writing in subject areas will contribute strongly to the performance in reading and thinking in the disciplines.

(Squire, 1983, p. 583)

Children who process subject matter by writing learn to think in that discipline. Therefore, if children's comprehension of material in science, math, social studies, and other content areas is to improve, writing should be taught in every subject area across the curriculum. In *Becoming a Nation of Readers* (Anderson, Hiebert, Scott, & Wilkinson, 1985), the Commission on Reading reminds teachers that reading and thinking skills are also more effectively taught within the context of content-area-specific experiences than in separate reading lessons. According to the commission, the integration of reading instruction and subject matter instruction seldom occurs, although the idea is an old one in American education. In current practice, expository reading skills are usually taught in reading classes through such approaches as the SQ3R formula in SRA reading labs and study skills units in basal reading programs.

Basal reader stories are unable to provide practice with the skills needed to read science, math, and social studies textbooks because the basic structures differ (see Chapter 5). In the sections that follow, we describe several reading/writing strategies appropriate for each of the three content areas: science, mathematics, and social studies. We also recommend other sources of teaching strategies for integrating reading and writing with each subject area.

■ Science

Learning science concepts requires children to process information in unique ways. In order to read science materials successfully, they must learn to perceive important relationships, make inferences, and evaluate. In order to write appropriately in science class, they must learn to formulate questions, record, classify, compare, explain, distinguish fact from opinion, and separate important from subordinate data. The following are several strategies that can help children develop these important reading/writing skills and learn science concepts at the same time.

☐ *Joining Bits of Information*

This science writing strategy, developed by Giroux (1979), involves students in the writing of the main thesis of a science passage after reading it. They are instructed to write an "organizing sentence" that reports the most important relationships in the passage in their own words by joining "bits of information" listed below the reading material (Figure 7.14).

Koeller (1982) advises that, before asking students to write topic sentences by themselves, teachers should illustrate the procedures for completing the writing task by discussing examples and then allowing small groups of students to write organizing sentences for the examples. When the technique is introduced, teachers list the bits of information themselves. Later, students are required to select information bits, discriminating

FIGURE 7.14 Joining Bits of Information Example Source: Reproduced with permission from S. Koeller. Expository Writing: A Vital Skill in Science. *Science and Children,* September 1987. Copyright © 1987 by the National Science Teachers Association, 1742 Connecticut Avenue, NW, Washington, DC 20009.

Question: How big is an insect?

Quotation:

The world of insects includes some of the most beautiful and fantastic animals on earth. No other branch of the animal kingdom has such great variety in size, color, and form.

Most insects are less than 6 millimeters (mm) long. The smallest ones include fairy flies and some beetles. They are about 0.25 mm long and could easily crawl through the eye of the smallest needle. Giant insects include the Goliath beetle, which grows more than 10 centimeters (cm) long, and the Atlas moth, which has a wingspread of about 25 cm. An Atlas moth is about 1,000 times as large as a fairy fly. Among mammals, the blue whale—the largest of all animals—is only about 500 times as large as a shrew.

(Source: *World Book Encyclopedia*)

Task: Join the following bits of information from the above quotation into an organizing sentence that represents *your* idea of the writer's main message:

variety
0.25 mm
25 cm

Possible organizing sentence: Insects are found in a variety of sizes, from as small as 0.25 mm to as large as 25 cm.

among important and less important details. Koeller comments, "As students learn to select, record and join key bits of information into sentences, they are learning to explain the *relationships* between individual pieces of information" (p. 14).

☐ *Writing to Record Data*

Koeller (1982) stresses the value of exposing children to models for recording data from science reading. "Just as students are shown a format for writing a simple letter, they must view and understand numerous formats for recording science information" (p. 14). Science assignments, which involve students in enumerating and/or organizing data from observations, surveys, and interviews and which require them to translate that material into expository paragraphs, facilitate the development of basic research skills. These kinds of experiences provide children with experience in recording, classifying, and analyzing information as scientists do, while also teaching them science concepts and vocabulary.

In the beginning, children should be taught a simple writing format for recording science learning. An example suggested by Koeller is found in Figure 7.15. Before children tabulate their observations individually using this type of chart, they should have a teacher-directed group experience which takes them through the procedures for using the chart step-by-step. Koeller adds: "Possibilities for organizing written data are endless, but the best formats convey information with fluency, clarity, and drama. Reference reading will yield additional items and categories for these formats. Encourage children to be on the lookout for alternative ways to classify data" (p. 14).

It is important for students to know that the recording and classifying of data are not ends in themselves for scientists. By explaining their findings and drawing conclusions from them, researchers make their discoveries useful to others. It becomes evident to students, as they attempt to convey

FIGURE 7.15 Tabular Form for Recording Science Observations Source: Reproduced with permission from S. Koeller. Expository Writing: A Vital Skill in Science. *Science and Children,* September 1987. Copyright © 1987 by the National Science Teachers Association, 1742 Connecticut Avenue, NW, Washington, DC 20009.

Count of Birds in the North Hedgerow			
Time	Robins	Sparrows	Bluejays
10:00 AM			
10:10 AM			
10:20 AM			
10:30 AM			

what they have learned, that science writing has its own organizational patterns and that it requires a clear and concise writing style.

☐ ***Already-Know Time***

Reading specialist Dianne Hampton (1984) reports that children learn more from their science textbooks and from each other when they participate in Already-Know Time before reading science assignments. Writing for ten minutes about what they already know about the solar system, for example, activates prior knowledge and increases student interest in the topic. Hampton explains that this type of prereading writing assignment "teaches them that they know more than they think they do and that they themselves are dispensers of information" (p. 5). This gives students a sense of being in control of their learning and also prepares them for reading their textbooks.

Students participating in Hampton's Already-Know Time begin by individually brainstorming and writing what they know about a topic, making up questions and predictions as they go along. Then they find and read resources that provide answers to their questions and write these answers as informational statements. After studying their questions and answers, they select their most interesting "now-know" material (knowledge statements) to share with others in small groups.

Hampton uses Already-Know Time with success, claiming that "information and ideas become firmly cemented to what students already know" (p. 5), no matter what the subject area. This, in turn, improves their understanding and recall of material in their science reading assignments. As explained in Chapter 5, activating prior knowledge about text topics before reading promotes both interest in the topic and comprehension of the text.

☐ ***Sources for Other Strategies***

Armes, R. A., & Sullengar, K. (1986). Learning science through writing. *Science and Children, 23*(8), 15–19.

Barrow, L. H., Kristo, J. V., & Andrew, B. (1984). Building bridges between science and reading. *The Reading Teacher, 38,* 188–192.

Clem, C., & Feathers, K. M. (1986). I LIK SPIDRS: What one child teaches us about content learning. *Language Arts, 63,* 143–147.

Esler, W., & Merritt, K., Jr. (1976). Teaching reading through science experience studies. *School Science and Mathematics, 76,* 203–206.

Fisher, R. J., & Fisher, R. L. (1985). Reading, writing, and science. *Science and Children, 23*(2), 23–24.

Gatlin, P. (1986). Science search—The write way. In Olson, C. B. (Ed.), *Ideas for teaching writing as a process* (pp. 41–42). Sacramento: California State Department of Education.

Horninger, J. (1986). How students can write to learn science. *Learning, 14*(8), 37–38.

Langer, J. A., & Applebee, A. N. (1985). Learning to write: Learning to think. *Educational Horizons, 64*(1), 36–38.

Lawrence, P., Skoog, G., & Simmons, B. (1984). At their level: LEA in the science classroom. *Science and Children, 21*(4), 103–105.

Levine, D. S. (1985). The biggest thing I learned but it really doesn't have to do with science. *Language Arts, 62,* 43–47.

Lowe, J. (1984). Writing across the curriculum: Focus on science. In G. Archibald, L. Spina, J. Krater, & J. Flinn (1984) (Eds.), *New Routes to Writing K-8* (pp. 71–73). St. Louis: University of Missouri, Gateway Writing Project.

Matthews, K. (1984). Language everywhere: Community journals. *Livewire, 1*(1), 2–3.

Rezba, R. J. (1979). By emphasizing writing in science. *Today's Education, 68,* 28–29.

Shuman, B. (1984). School-wide writing instruction. *English Journal, 74*(6), 54–57.

Switzer, T., & Voss, B. (1982). Integrating the teaching of science and social studies. *School Science and Mathematics, 82,* 452–462.

Toothaker, R. E. (1980). Language arts: Getting kids to write about science. *Instructor, 89*(4), 123–125.

Wotring, A. M., & Tierney, R. (1982). *Using writing to learn science.* Berkeley: University of California, Bay Area Writing Project.

■ Mathematics

National Assessment results in mathematics show that the computational skills of students are improving. However, a large proportion of these students lack the ability to solve word problems requiring the use of those skills (Burns, 1983).

Poor reading skills are frequently blamed for these problem-solving deficiencies. However, Burns and Richardson (1981) refute this position, citing evidence from a 1979 study by Knifong and Holtan. The study, conducted with sixth-graders, investigated how the students' reading comprehension abilities related to their ability to solve word problems. The investigators asked individual students, who consistently made word problem errors that were not computational mistakes, to read a problem aloud (95 percent could do so), and to explain the situation the problem described (98 percent answered correctly). Then they asked, "What is the problem asking you to find?" (92 percent replied correctly) and "How would you work this problem?" (only 36 percent responded correctly). Knifong and Holtan concluded that, in spite of the students' accurate comprehension of the problem, they were still unable to select the proper operation to solve the problem. Lack of arithmetic understanding, not lack of reading ability, appeared to be responsible for their failure to solve word problems.

Others contend that writing is a major factor in solving word problems. Graves (1978) maintains that children are unable to fully comprehend word problems in math until they have written examples of their own. Writing in math class pays other dividends as well by raising the level of cognitive activity and increasing students' understanding of mathematical concepts. Among the benefits of writing that make it an appropriate skill to integrate with math instruction are the focusing of thought, making thought available for inspection, and the translating of mental images (Haley-James, 1982). Language experiences with word problems also help children see the purposes of computational skills.

□ *Story Problems*

Believing, as Graves does, that students must write word problems before they can be expected to understand them, Jerry Kennedy, an upper-elementary teacher from the Gateway Writing Project in St. Louis, asks his students to write their own story problems about things that interest them. His premise is that they will be more likely to remember and apply math concepts if the story problem material relates to their experiences. His students collect their story problems in special folders that become part of the regular math program along with the textbook. Kennedy explains that his fifth-graders start by writing one-step problems using their own names and the names of their friends and pets. Before long, they are applying their writing skills to come up with story problems like this one:

> On my way to school this morning, I noticed two thick strings wiggling on the sidewalk. I stooped down and saw that they were big, fat worms. I decided to give them both a name and write about them for my math folder. So, Willie the worm and Wilma the worm were playing a really slow game of tag on the sidewalk and decided to have a race. Willie started out at 9:15 A.M. and made it to the corner by 10:12 A.M. How long did it take Willie? Wilma started out at 9:24 A.M. and made it to the corner by 10:48 A.M. How long did it take Wilma to finish the race? Which worm won and by how many minutes?
>
> (from p. 72 of an unpublished paper, n.d. sponsored by the Gateway Writing Project)

Writing fully developed story problems is a time-consuming process, according to Kennedy, who cautions teachers not to require students to write a series of problems at once.

Frank (1979) also recommends involving students in individual ways when mixing math and writing. In addition to suggesting the writing of imaginative word problems using classmates' names, she offers a potpourri of activities in her writing idea book, *If You're Trying to Teach Kids How to Write, You've Gotta Have this Book,* including such assignments as:

> Write up a CONTRACT between yourself and someone who is buying your bike on time payments.
> Write a MENU for a restaurant where a family of four could eat dinner for under $12.00.
> Make a NO NUMBER booklet telling what the world would be like without numbers.
> Write DIRECTIONS telling how to make a cube or any other geometric figure.

Write ADVERTISING FOLDERS for resorts, camps, cruises, hotels. Figure out what your rates will be for individuals, families and groups.

(excerpts from p. 170)

The suggestions listed by Frank are particularly suitable for individualized math situations and learning centers which allow students to choose activities.

☐ *Letter Writing and Learning Logs*

Bill Kennedy (1985) uses writing to relieve "math anxiety" in his middle school classroom. He claims that children relax and keep trying when they have opportunities to write about their past experiences and present concerns with mathematics.

Kennedy requests that his students write him a letter periodically about whatever the class is studying in math. He requires that the letter include: (a) examples of what they understand in math; (b) examples of what they do not understand; and (c) questions about any aspect of what the class is studying in math. He finds that students are not reluctant to admit they do not understand something in the privacy of a letter to the teacher. Kennedy prepares for the next class by taking notes from the letters, sometimes planning a review of material for the entire class and other times planning to meet with individuals or small groups to discuss their "I don't get the part about" statements.

Kennedy comments that his letter writing strategy is efficient and valuable, enabling him to learn more about his students' needs than he can from more time-consuming observing and testing.

In class the next day, I can sometimes clear up their questions with a brief explanation. Other times, the letters show me that I've gone too fast or taken too many leaps, so the next day I back up and retrace my steps.

(1985, p. 59)

Kennedy's students also write to themselves in Learning Logs. In their own words, they keep a regular record of learning "as it happens." Kennedy points out that instead of *taking* notes, his students are *making* notes. Taking is copying someone else's information; making notes is writing interpretive comments and personal reminders such as "Ask about this" or "Why?" One of his eighth-grade students used an analogy and a reminder to herself when writing about square root in her log: "Square root is like a question that asks what number times itself will be the number under the square root sign (which is called a radical). One thing to remember is that if a number has an odd number of zeros, it is not a perfect square" (1985, p. 61).

According to Kennedy, this kind of personal and exploratory "writing in math" identifies problems students are having and helps them raise questions while clarifying their thinking. He advises teachers to create an atmosphere of trust in the classroom before initiating Learning Logs so that students will be assured of the confidentiality of what they write and realize judgments are not being made about their personal worth or their math grade through that writing.

□ **Evans's Strategies**

Inspired by a report from the Bay Area Writing Project describing how high school students used writing to learn biology content, Evans (1984) conducted a research study to discover if writing could help her fifth-grade students learn math. She taught and tested two units, one on writing with multiplication computation and the other on writing with geometry, an area with a heavy vocabulary load. She used three strategies in her study—How-To Descriptions, Definition Writing, and Troubleshooting—and learned that each of them helped less capable students improve their mathematical skills.

How-To Descriptions   Students wrote to an uninformed third party, explaining how to perform a specific mathematical calculation—for example, multiplying with a zero in the multiplier or drawing a sixty-degree angle. Evans found that writing these explanations improved students' understanding of the principles underlying the mathematical operations. The task of explaining the procedure to an "uninformed" party, rather than to the teacher, required students to write clear, detailed descriptions. Evans noticed that some students also included graphics to aid the reader. In order to write a complete process description, students had to thoroughly understand the mathematical concepts involved.

After reading about Evans's success with the How-To Description strategy, Marilyn Poor experimented with a variation in her fifth-grade classroom, with similar results. She combined Evans's strategy with Kennedy's (1985) Letter Writing procedure, described in the preceding section. Poor asked her students to write a letter to a person in history, explaining three points: (a) what they understood about the mathematical operation; (b) what they found confusing; and (c) what questions they had about the operation. Figure 7.16 gives an example of a student's letter to Davy Crockett about subtracting numbers containing fractions.

Definition Writing   Noticing that her students seemed to have difficulty understanding and even memorizing the precise definitions of mathematical concepts in the textbooks, Evans decided to have them describe the concepts in their own language by writing definitions. The greatest benefit she reported as a result of definition writing activities was the opportunity for her to see immediately which of her students understood the concepts she was teaching and which did not. She also noted that her students discovered their own definitions were easier to remember than the textbook definitions. Figure 7.17 illustrates a fourth-grader's definition for the term "parallelogram."

FIGURE 7.16   Letter to Davy Crockett about Subtracting Fractions

Dear Davy Crockett,

The example is going to be $18\frac{7}{8}$ – $10\frac{3}{4}$. Check to see if the denominator are the same. They aren't, but 8 is a mutipil of 4. That meens all you have to change is $\frac{3}{4}$. After you change it, it should be $\frac{6}{8}$. But you still can't subtract, because you can't subtract $\frac{6}{8}$ from $\frac{7}{8}$. You have to borrow 1 from 18. It would be now $17\frac{11}{8}$. Now you can subtract. $17\frac{11}{8} - 10\frac{6}{8} = 7\frac{5}{8}$. This is what I understand

I think I understand everything.

Since I understand everything I haven't any questions.

Sencerly,
Joshua

Fourth- and fifth-grade teachers in the Jayhawk Writing Project at the University of Kansas used Evans's definition writing technique in their classrooms as a directed journal activity. Their students wrote definitions, responding to teacher questions, throughout the year in a special section of their journal entitled "Math Concepts." The Jayhawk Writing Project teachers were enthusiastic about the definition writing strategy, claiming that the "Math Concepts" journal section was an excellent review source for their students.

Troubleshooting   Evans's Troubleshooting strategy required her fifth-graders to examine each problem marked incorrect on their quiz and home-work papers to determine what mistakes they had made. Then they wrote an

FIGURE 7.17   Fourth-Grade Student's Own Definition of a Math Term

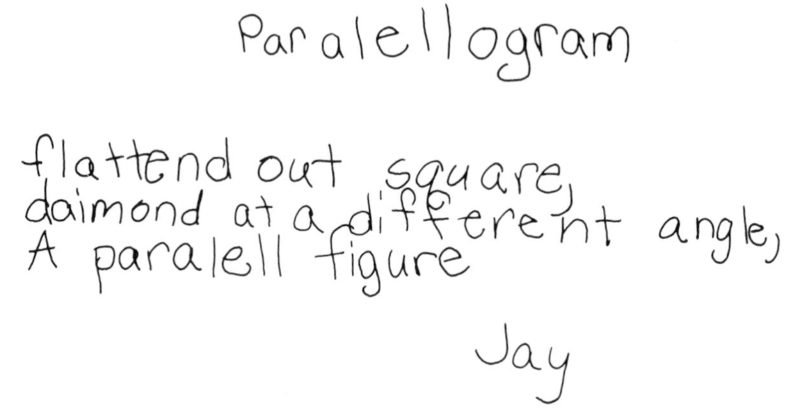

Paralellogram

flattend out square,
daimond at a different angle,
A paralell figure

Jay

explanation of the reason for each error before returning the paper to her. For example, students wrote: "I missed this problem because I put forty-two down on seven times seven instead of forty-nine" and "I made my mistake by multiplying instead of adding" (1984, p. 833).

After assessing the results of her students' Troubleshooting writing, Evans exclaimed:

> This was most enlightening! Troubleshooting forced students to go beyond the red "X" and find out what they did wrong. For most students, this was a brand new experience. As the teacher, I know I didn't have to worry about those who could analyze their mistakes. But when Pati wrote:
>
> I did not get 1, 4, and 5 correct and I don't know why.
>
> I knew I had to do some immediate reteaching. Best of all, Pati knew she needed help and was open to further help.
>
> (1984, p. 834)

Evans concluded from her experimentation with writing and math that writing, like reading, is an effective aid for learning.

☐ *Sources for Other Strategies*

Fennell, F., & Ammon, R. (1985). Writing techniques for problem solvers. *Arithmetic Teacher, 33*(1), 24–25.

Fisher, C. J. (1986). Enhance learning through writing. *Middle School Journal, 17*(3), 4, 7, 31.

Geeslin, W. (1977). Using writing about mathematics as a teaching technique. *Mathematics Teacher, 70,* 112–115.

Moore, D. W., Moore, S. A., Cunningham, P. M., & Cunningham, J. W. (1986). *Developing readers and writers in the content areas: K–12.* New York: Longman.

Pradl, G. M., & Mayher, J. S. (1985). Reinvigorating learning through writing. *Educational Leadership, 42*(5), 4–6.

Schnell, V. J. (1982). Learning partners: Reading and mathematics. *The Reading Teacher, 35,* 544–548.

Vukovich, D. (1985). Ideas in practice: Integrating math and writing through the math journal. *Journal of Developmental Education, 9,* 19–20.

■ Social Studies

Learning in social studies relies heavily upon the ability of students to read for information, grasp the facts, and think beyond them. By integrating writing with the social studies reading process, students can be served in two ways: (a) writing is an aid for clarifying the meaning of textbook material, promoting understanding of concepts and generalizations; and (b) writing is a catalyst for higher-level thinking. The three strategies we describe here illustrate ways in which teachers can use writing for both purposes in social studies class. Textbook Activity Guides and Glossing are effective techniques for improving students' comprehension of social studies textbooks; the During Reading Activities help teachers guide students to higher levels of thinking about social studies concepts through writing while reading.

□ *Textbook Activity Guides*

In order to be efficient readers of social studies textbooks, students need to develop flexible approaches for learning information and self-evaluation strategies for insuring comprehension. Textbook Activity Guides (TAG) can help students in grades three and higher read textbook material successfully by providing strategy cues to indicate appropriate skills to apply in specific situations. According to Davey (1986), "textbook activity guides engage students in using content-area materials actively and successfully. These written guides specify what is to be learned and how it should be learned" (p. 489). A TAG example appears in Figure 7.18.

The codes—DP, PP, WR, Map, Skim—listed at the top of the sample TAG indicate common strategies students have been taught to implement with a partner. DP (discuss with partner), for example, refers to a cooperative learning strategy in which pairs of students talk together, exchanging ideas about the information without writing responses. PP suggests to partners that they make predictions together without writing responses, and WR requires them to write an individual response to information. Map signals the students to prepare a semantic map of the material, and Skim requires them to read the passage quickly and discuss it with their partners. Self-monitoring cues (+, ✓, ?) indicate how well they understand the information after self-evaluation. Students learn through use of the various strategies to approach learning with flexibility.

The TAG focuses the students' attention on selective material related to the teacher's instructional objectives and is designed to be completed in

FIGURE 7.18 Sample TAG: Geography Affected Indian Ways
Source: From Beth Davey. Using Textbook Activity Guides to Help
Students Learn from Textbooks. *Journal of Reading, 29,* pp. 489–494.
Reprinted with permission of Beth Davey and the International Reading
Association.

Names: _____ Date initiated: _____

_____

Strategy codes:
  DP = Read and discuss with your partner
  PP = Predict with your partner
  WR = Each partner writes response on separate paper
  Map = Complete the semantic map
  Skim = Read quickly for the purpose stated; discuss with your partner

Self-monitoring codes:
  __+__ I understand this information
  __✔__ I'm not sure if I fully understand this information
  __?__ I do not understand this information. I need to restudy.

---

1. PP pp. 21–25 title and headings
    What do you think you will learn about from this section? List at least eight things.
2. DP p. 21 heading and first three paragraphs
___ Explain the second sentence in this section, beginning "The type of shelter . . ."
    What are some examples from the passage? What are some examples from today?
3. WR p.21 right column, first and second paragraphs
___ a. Why did the Haidas and the Iroquois need different kinds of boats?
___ b. Using other resource books in the classroom, draw an Iroquois canoe and a
    Haida boat. Add them to your booklet on Indians.
4. Skim p. 21, last two paragraphs, p. 22, first paragraph
___ Purpose: Find out about the shelter and food of the Plains Indians.
5. DP p. 22 second to sixth paragraphs
    How did the climate of the Southwest affect:
___ the materials the Pueblo Indians used for their shelters?
___ the way they built their shelters?
___ the way they grew their food?
6. Skim p. 22 second to last paragraph of section
___ Purpose: Find out about the features of homes of the Mayan Indians.
7. WR p. 22 last paragraph of section
    Give an example from the section to prove each of the following:
___ Geography influenced Indian homes.
___ Geography influenced Indian clothing.
___ Geography influenced Indian food.
8. DP, Map pp. 24, 25
___ Compare and contrast two types of Indian homes.

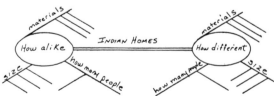

9.   WR Add at least three new words to your vocabulary file.
10. Get an answer key 1-A to check your work. Record your summary score.
     Evaluation: _____ Summary score
                  _____ Written check up
                  _____ Teacher conference

Adapted from a TAG created by Sandra Bensky

one class period. Davey follows five steps in constructing this type of study guide:

1. Clearly state the learning objectives.
2. Designate all sections and features of the text that are related to the objectives.
3. Select and sequence the text material to be used in the TAG, keeping in mind the need for manageability.
4. Develop an appropriate reading task for each objective, e.g., discussion, diagram.
5. Design a code system to communicate the tasks to the students. Place a line marker by each task for students to use in checking their understanding $(+, \nearrow, ?)$.

Davey offers several recommendations to teachers using TAGs in content-area classrooms: (a) explain and model the use of TAGs before assigning them; (b) use them for short periods (about twenty minutes) in the beginning, covering a small amount of material; (c) team students with similar skills at the start, monitoring the pairs closely; (d) try a TAG with some able students at first; and (e) do not overuse TAGs to the point of boredom.

Davey has helped a number of teachers to incorporate TAGs into their content-area reading assignments, with great success. He reports:

> Using the guidelines, content area teachers at the middle and secondary school levels have implemented TAGs successfully over the past 3 years. All 48 teachers in a TAG project reported increased student involvement with textbooks and more opportunities for flexible small group work or individualized instruction in their content classes. Forty-five reported enhanced overall learning of material.
>
> (1986, p. 493)

□ *Glossing*

The teacher-made graphic organizers described in the "Teaching Expository Text Structure" section of this chapter can assist students in identifying important social studies concepts in textbooks. However, students seldom have the opportunity to determine their own purposes for reading and to select the appropriate skills for accomplishing those purposes while using teacher-produced comprehension guides (Richgels & Mateja, 1984). The

Glossing technique, a strategy developed by Otto (1981), integrates content and process by promoting the learning and application of self-monitoring skills while reading, adding another dimension to the use of structural organizers.

According to Otto, Glossing is "an attempt to share a mature (expert) reader's insights into the reading process with developing (novice) readers" (p. 5). Marginal notes made by the teacher in specific areas of expository text focus students' attention on process as well as content by prompting them to use prior knowledge, text structure, and purpose setting to facilitate comprehension. As students use these skills, the role of the teacher as integrator of process and content diminishes, and students become more successful readers of content-area materials.

Richgels and Mateja (1984) describe the successful use of Glossing in secondary classrooms through a four-step process leading from teacher modeling to the stage where students make their own mental notations and apply Glossing independently. We consider the first step in this process, teacher demonstration, to be appropriate and effective for use in the elementary and middle grades. Figure 7.19 presents an example of demonstration Glossing designed for fourth-graders. Although teachers who use Glossing with older students generally write their notations either on ditto masters or the text itself, we recommend that teachers of younger children "walk through" the material verbally with them, using a glossed transparency on the overhead to show children the questions they ask and the skills they use while reading.

☐ *During Reading Activities*

Devine (1986) emphasizes the importance of During Reading Activities which allow students to express themselves in writing as they are learning concepts and facts in a discipline. By making their own responses, they not only increase their knowledge of content through better comprehension but also develop thinking processes which enable them to relate and invent in relation to that content. Devine presents teachers with an "idea box" of During Reading Activities which have been used successfully by middle-grade teachers. We have selected three we consider especially appropriate for social studies classes:

> 1. *New-to-Me Lists.* One teacher has developed a technique for helping his students concentrate their attention on new information in the material they are reading. He explains to them that they will be reading some facts they already know and points out that the new ideas are the ones which need their attention. He asks them to keep track of the new ideas as they read on a separate journal page for each reading assignment. After reading, the students discuss the information they have recorded, which gives them the opportunity to reinforce it in their minds and assess its importance.
>
> 2. *Half-Page Outline.* Another middle school teacher uses a half-page outline technique for sensitizing students to the structure of the textbooks they

FIGURE 7.19 Glossing Example Source: Lawrence Pauline. *Our America.* Copyright © 1977 by Allyn and Bacon. Reprinted with permission.

The Panama Canal

The Spanish-American War showed the need for a canal to connect the Atlantic and Pacific Oceans. Battleships from the east coast had to sail more than 22,000 kilometers (14,000 miles) around South America to reach the west coast of the United States. A canal in Panama would shorten the distance by about 11,000 kilometers (7,000 miles). The idea of a canal became very important to the United States because it now owned lands in the Pacific Ocean.

President Theodore Roosevelt offered Columbia $10,000 in cash and $250 thousand a year for the land on which to build a canal. Columbia refused the American offer. They wanted more money. Teddy Roosevelt said that the United States might use force to take Panama.

The leaders in Panama were afraid the United States might build a canal somewhere else. Panama could accept the American offer if it were an independent nation. Only a revolution could free Panama from Columbia. Many people in Panama were willing to revolt, if the United States gave them protection. President Roosevelt said he would be happy if Panama was an independent country. The people took this to mean that he would protect them.

A revolution broke out in Panama in 1903. American warships were sent to the area. They kept Columbian troops from stopping the revolution. A few days later, Panama became an independent country. Panama accepted American money. In return, the United States got the right to build a canal. Work on the canal began in 1904. Thirty-five thousand people worked on it for ten years. They removed mountains, built dams, and made lakes. The cost of the canal was almost one-half billion dollars. When it was finished in 1914, a ship could go from the Atlantic to the Pacific Ocean in about eight hours. The United States had again involved itself in foreign affairs.

The title and first paragraph suggest that we will be learning the story of the Panama Canal. This passage tells why a canal connecting the Atlantic and Pacific Oceans was important to the United States.

Would we use force to get the canal land if Columbia would not take money? Read on to find out.

The causes of the Panama revolution are given here. The last two sentences describe America's role. The effects of the revolution should come next.

As I read this passage I'm making 2 lists: 1. The results of the revolution and 2. The steps in building the Panama Canal. I'm wondering... was it worth the cost? Another involvement in foreign affairs... How does it compare to previous ones?

are reading. He prepares an outline of the material to be read, folds the page in half vertically, and duplicates the half pages, giving one copy to each student. He instructs the students to complete the outline while they read. After they have read the assignment, he gives them the missing half of the outline so they can check to see how their outlines compare with his. He claims that the students better understand the structure of the textbook after several half-page experiences.

3. *History Digests.*   An eighth-grade history teacher uses a digest magazine approach to improve her students' comprehension of their history textbook. She requires them to write a list of the main idea sentences, paragraph by paragraph, as they are reading. When they have finished a section, they compose a digest of it by putting the main idea sentences together into a paragraph. A book chapter with ten subsections then becomes a ten-paragraph digest made up of main idea sentences. The students in her class gave their ever-expanding digest the title, "Everything You Wanted to Know about American History at (Practically) a Glance."

(pp. 170–171)*

□ *Sources for Other Strategies*

Beach, J. A. (1983). Teaching students to write informational reports. *Elementary School Journal, 84,* 213–220.

Bell, M., & Cohn, S. (1985). The use of abstract modeling to teach note-taking skills. *Middle School Journal, 16*(3), 12–14.

Beyer, B. K. (1982). Using writing to learn social studies. *The Social Studies, 73,* 100–105.

Diamond, I. (Ed.). (1980). *Interdisciplinary writing: A guide to writing across the curriculum.* Madison: Wisconsin Writing Project.

Dittmer, A. (1986). Guidelines for writing assignments in the content areas. *English Journal, 75*(8), 59–63.

Ehrenberg, S. (1981). Concept learning: How to make it happen in the classroom. *Educational Leadership, 39*(1), 36–43.

Hoffman, S. (1983). Using student journals to teach study skills. *Journal of Reading, 26,* 344–347.

Lunstrum, J., & Irwin, J. (1981). Integrating basic skills into social studies content. *Social Education, 45,* 169–171.

McKenzie, G. R. (1979). Data charts: A crutch for helping pupils organize reports. *Language Arts, 56,* 784–788.

Melton, V. (1985). Reading, thinking, writing, learning. *Middle School Journal, 16*(3), 10–12.

Pooler, A. E., & Perry, C. M. (1985). Building higher level thinking and writing skills in social studies. *The Social Studies, 76,* 125–128.

Queenan, M. (1986). Finding the grain in the marble. *Language Arts, 63,* 666–673.

Simpson, M. L. (1986). PORPE: A writing strategy for studying and learning in the content areas. *Journal of Reading, 29,* 407–414.

Welton, D. A. (1982). Expository writing, pseudowriting, and social studies. *Social Education, 46,* 444–448.

SUMMARY

■ ■   This chapter has focused on strategies for teaching reading and writing in the various content areas of the curriculum. In the first section, we explained how writing can improve students' comprehension of expository reading by familiarizing them with text structure and organization. We also described how writing can encourage the active processing of information from reading. After contrasting the structure of narrative and expository text, we recommended the direct teaching of expository structures using graphic organizers. The strategies described in this section demonstrated how graphic organizers can be used in three different ways to improve students' comprehension of the material in their content-area textbooks: (a) to teach students to identify expository text structures; (b) to equip students to write their own expository paragraphs; and (c) to guide them in attending to text organization as well as content while reading in the subject areas.

In the next section of this chapter we looked at writing as a mode of learning and reemphasized that reading and writing should be taught throughout the curriculum because they are vital skills for learning and communicating in every field. In the first part of this section, we defined the concept of "writing to learn" and presented the arguments of educators supporting it, noting that content-area teachers are reporting success with using writing to enhance learning. We included a summarized version of Glatthorn's framework for planning write-to-learn activities and recommended two kinds of summary writing — Four-Step and Hierarchical — as valuable strategies for facilitating learning. We turned our attention to inquiry-centered reading and writing in the latter part of this section. The strategies recommended for teaching research skills were alternatives to the traditional research paper, allowing students to choose their topics, giving them special tools for data gathering, and requiring them to use their findings to entertain, inform, or persuade an audience. Two types of data collection devices were described — the Interview Grid and the Data Retrieval Chart — as well as several options for sharing findings: Spin-Off Writing, I-Search, and Saturation Reporting.

In the final section of this chapter, we stressed the need for students to practice writing in each specific content area in order to improve their ability to read and think in that particular discipline. Similarly, we pointed to their need to practice reading through content-area specific experiences rather than basal reader stories alone. Strategies for teaching reading and writing in the fields of science, mathematics, and social studies were recommended and sources of teaching ideas integrating reading and writing with each subject were listed.

──────── **RECOMMENDED CHILDREN'S BOOKS** ────────

Informational Books about Native Americans

Batherman, Muriel. *Before Columbus*. Houghton Mifflin, 1981.
Clark, Ann Nolan. *Circle of Seasons*. Farrar, 1970.
Erdoes, Richard. *The Native Americans: Navajos*. Sterling, 1979.
Folsom, Franklin. *Red Power on the Rio Grande*. Follet, 1973.
Glubok, Shirley. *The Art of the North American Indians*. Harper & Row, 1964.
_____. *The Art of the Southwest Indians*. Macmillan, 1971.
_____. *The Art of the Northwest Coast Indians*. Macmillan, 1975.
_____. *The Art of the Plains Indians*. Macmillan, 1975.
_____. *The Art of the Woodland Indians*. Macmillan, 1976.
Hofsinde, Robert. *Indians at Home*. Morrow, 1964.
_____. *Indian Warriors and Their Weapons*. Morrow, 1965.
Holling, Holling C. *The Book of Indians*. Platt & Monk, 1962.
Hoyt, Olga. *American Indians Today*. Abelard-Shuman, 1972.
Keegan, Marcia. *The Taos Indians and Their Sacred Blue Lake*. Messner, 1972.
LaFarge, Oliver. *The American Indian*. Golden, 1960.
Loh, Jules. *Lords of the Earth: A History of the Navajo Indian*. Macmillan, 1971.
McNeer, May. *The American Indian Story*. Farrar, 1963.
Pine, Tillie S., and Levine, Joseph. *The Indians Knew*. McGraw-Hill, 1957.
Poatgieter, Alice H. *Indian Legacy: Native American Influences on World Life and Culture*. Messner, 1981.
Siegel, Beatrice. *Indians of the Woodland Before and After the Pilgrims*. Walker, 1972.

REFERENCES

Alvermann, D. E. (1982). Restructuring text facilitates written recall of main ideas. *Journal of Reading, 26,* 754–758.

Anderson, R. C., Hiebert, E. H., Scott, J. A., & Wilkinson, I. (1985). *Becoming a nation of readers: The report of the Commission on Reading*. Newark, DE: International Reading Association.

Applebee, A. N. (1981). *Writing in the secondary school: English and the content areas*. Urbana, IL: National Council of Teachers of English.

Bartlett, B. J. (1978). *Top-level structure as an organizational strategy for recall of classroom text*. Unpublished doctoral dissertation, Arizona State University.

Barton, B. (1983). *Problem solving in text comprehension: A study of elementary readers' strategy use in reconstructing the macro-structure*. Unpublished doctoral dissertation, University of Kansas.

Bernstein, R. (1986). Using fictional techniques for nonfiction writing. In C. B. Olson (Ed.), *Practical ideas for teaching writing as a process* (pp. 93–95). Sacramento: California State Department of Education.

Bowe, L. (1986). The add-on saturation report. In C. B. Olson (Ed.), *Practical ideas for teaching writing as a process* (pp. 99–100). Sacramento: California State Department of Education.

Britton, J. N. (1978). The composing process and

the functions of writing. In C. R. Cooper and L. Odell, (Eds.), *Research on composing: Points of departure* (pp. 13–28). Urbana, IL: National Council of Teachers of English.

Brown, A. L., Campione, J., & Day, J. D. (1981). Learning to learn: On training students to learn from texts. *Educational Researcher, 10,* 14–24.

Burns, M. (1983). *Problem solving: The math challenge of the 80's.* Belmont, CA: Pitman.

Burns, M., & Richardson, K. (1981). Making sense out of word problems. *Learning, 9*(6), 26–28.

Calfee, R. C., & Curley, R. (1984). Structure of prose in the content areas. In J. Flood (Ed.), *Understanding reading comprehension* (pp. 161–180). Newark, DE: International Reading Association.

Davey, B. (1986). Using textbook activity guides to help students learn from textbooks. *Journal of Reading, 29,* 489–494.

Devine, T. G. (1986). *Teaching reading comprehension: From theory to practice.* Boston: Allyn & Bacon.

Doctorow, M., Wittrock, M. C., & Marks, C. (1978). Generative processes in reading comprehension. *Journal of Educational Psychology, 70,* 109–118.

Durkin, D. (1978). What classroom observations reveal about reading comprehension instruction. *Reading Research Quarterly, 14,* 481–533.

Emig, J. (1971). *The composing processes of twelfth graders.* Urbana, IL: National Council of Teachers of English.

Emig, J. (1977). Writing as a mode of learning. *College Composition and Communication, 28,* 122–128.

Englert, C., & Hiebert, E. (1984). Children's developing awareness of text structures in expository materials. *Journal of Educational Psychology, 76,* 65–74.

Evans, C. S. (1984). Writing to learn math. *Language Arts, 61,* 828–835.

Flood, J. (1986). The text, the student, and the teacher: Learning from exposition in middle schools. *The Reading Teacher, 39,* 784–791.

Flood, J., Lapp, D., & Farnan, N. (1986). A reading-writing procedure that teaches ex-

pository paragraph structure. *The Reading Teacher, 39,* 556–562.

Frank, M. (1979). *If you're trying to teach kids how to write, you've gotta have this book.* Nashville, TN: Incentive.

Freedman, A. (1986). Adapting the I-Search paper for the elementary classroom. In C. B. Olson (Ed.), *Practical ideas for teaching writing as a process* (pp. 114–116). Sacramento: California State Department of Education.

Fulwiler, T. (1987). *Teaching with writing.* Montclair, NJ: Boynton/Cook.

Gagné, R. (1985). *The conditions of learning* (4th ed.). New York: Holt, Rinehart & Winston.

Giroux, H. A. (1979). Teaching content and thinking through writing. *Social Education, 43,* 190–193.

Glatthorn, A. A. (1987). *Curriculum leadership.* Glenview, IL: Scott, Foresman.

Graves, D. (1978). *Balance the basics: Let them write.* New York: The Ford Foundation.

Gruen, E. R. (1981). *A comparison of fluent and non-fluent readers' use of strategies in text comprehension as measured by reconstruction of the macrostructure.* Unpublished doctoral dissertation, Teachers College, Columbia University.

Haley-James, S. (1982). Helping students learn through writing. *Language Arts, 59,* 726–731.

Hampton, D. W. (1984). Already-know time. *Live Wire, 1*(1), 5.

Hennings, D. G. (1982). *Teaching communication and reading skills in the content areas.* Bloomington, IN: Phi Delta Kappa.

Hidi, S., & Anderson, V. (1986). Producing written summaries: Task demands, cognitive operations, and implications for instruction. *Review of Educational Research, 56,* 473–493.

Horowitz, R. (1985a). Text patterns: Part I. *The Reading Teacher, 28,* 448–454.

Horowitz, R. (1985b). Text patterns: Part II. *Journal of Reading, 28,* 534–541.

Jacobs, S. (1984). Investigative writing: Practice and principles. *Language Arts, 61,* 356–363.

Kennedy, B. (1985). Writing letters to learn math. *Learning, 13*(7), 59–61.

Kintsch, W., & van Dijk, T. (1978). Toward a model of text comprehension and production. *Psychological Review, 85,* 363–394.

Koeller, S. (1982). Expository writing: A vital skill in science. *Science and Children, 20*(2), 12-15.

Levine, D. (1985). The biggest thing I learned but it really doesn't have anything to do with science. *Language Arts, 62,* 43-47.

Macrorie, K. (1980). *Searching writing.* Rochelle Park, NJ: Hayden.

McGee, L. M., & Richgels, D. J. (1985). Teaching expository text structure to elementary students. *The Reading Teacher, 38,* 739-748.

McLaughlin, E. M. (1987). QuIP: A writing strategy to improve comprehension of expository structure. *The Reading Teacher, 40,* 650-654. 650-654.

Nance, E. H. (1982). The research paper: New variations on an old theme. *Curriculum Review, 21,* 285-288.

Newell, G. E. (1984). Learning from writing in two content areas: A case study/protocol analysis. *Research in the Teaching of English, 18,* 265-287.

Olson, C. B. (1986a). Preparing students to write the saturation report. In C. B. Olson (Ed.), *Practical ideas for teaching writing as a process* (pp. 96-99). Sacramento: California State Department of Education.

Olson, C. B. (1986b). A sample prompt, scoring guide, and model paper for the I-Search. In C. B. Olson (Ed.), *Practical ideas for teaching writing as a process* (pp. 117-121). Sacramento: California State Department of Education.

Olson, M. W., & Langnion, B. (1982). Pattern guides: A workable alternative for content teachers. *Journal of Reading, 25,* 736-741.

Otto, W. (1981). *A technique for improving the understanding of expository text: Gloss* (Theoretical paper no. 96). Madison: Wisconsin Center for Educational Research, University of Wisconsin.

Piccolo, J. A. (1987). Expository text structure: Teaching and learning strategies. *The Reading Teacher, 40,* 838-847.

Readence, J. E., Bean, T. W., & Baldwin, R. S.

(1981). *Content area reading: An integrated approach.* Dubuque, IA: Kendall/Hunt.

Richgels, D. J., & Mateja, J. A. (1984). Gloss II: Integrating content and process for independence. *Journal of Reading, 27,* 424-431.

Russell, D. R. (1986). Writing across the curriculum in 1913: James Fleming Hosic on "Cooperation." *English Journal, 75*(1), 34-37.

Slater, W. (1985). Teaching expository text structure with structural organizers. *Journal of Reading, 28,* 712-719.

Squire, J. R. (1983). Composing and comprehending: Two sides of the same basic process. *Language Arts, 60,* 581-589.

Stotsky, S. (1983). Research on reading/writing relationships: A synthesis and suggested directions. *Language Arts, 60,* 627-642.

Taylor, B. M. (1982). A summarizing strategy to improve middle grade students' reading and writing skills. *The Reading Teacher, 36,* 202-205.

Taylor, B. M., & Beach, R. W. (1984). The effects of text structure instruction on middle-grade students' comprehension and production of expository text. *Reading Research Quarterly, 19,* 134-146.

Taylor, B. M., & Berkowitz, S. (1980). Facilitating children's comprehension of content material. In *29th yearbook of the National Reading Conference* (pp. 66-68). Washington, DC: National Reading Conference.

Tchudi, S. N., & Huerta, M. C. (1983). *Teaching writing in the content areas: Middle school/ junior high.* Washington, DC: National Education Association.

Tchudi, S. N., & Tchudi, S. J. (1983). *Teaching writing in the content areas: Elementary school.* Washington, DC: National Education Association.

Vacca, R. T., & Vacca, J. L. (1986). *Content area reading* (2nd ed.). Boston: Little, Brown.

Vygotsky, L. (1962). *Thought and language.* Cambridge, MA: M.I.T. Press.

Wolfe, T., & Johnson, E. W. (1973). *The new journalism.* New York: Harper & Row.

8

Reading, Writing, and Oral Language

We are now in a new era of language arts research and theory. The processes of learning to read and write, to speak and listen, are recognized as holistic processes in which the child is actively seeking out and constructing meanings. Schools with elaborate sub-skill sequences are looking for more promising approaches. This is the time to build new, more effective integrated language arts curricula based on well-grounded principles.

—Busching & Lundsteen, Curriculum models for integrating the language arts

Language studies strongly support the correlation of achievement in oral language with achievement in reading and writing (Loban, 1976; Hall & Raming, 1978). One of the major implications of this finding is that the interrelationship of speaking, listening, reading, and writing should be an important consideration in curriculum planning. Teachers can promote learning in all four areas by teaching the language arts in holistic and natural ways.

Busching and Lundsteen (1983) describe three types of language arts integration. The most basic kind takes place when learners actually use various language subskills to read, listen, speak, or write, rather than practice subskills in separate exercises. We stressed the importance of learning language in this way—by using it in natural contexts—in our discussions of oral language acquisition and emergent literacy in Chapter 2. A second, broader approach to integration is based on the assumption that students can develop language skills while learning subject matter, which is the focus of Chapter 7.

Wagner (1985) defines language arts integration in a third way, as:

learning each of the language arts in terms of the others. Reading is learned through appropriate oral and written activities; writing is learned by attending to reading as a writer would—composing orally, reading drafts to peers, and engaging in related activities; and oral language is learned in the context of rich opportunities for receiving and producing written language.

(p. 557)

The strategies for using reading to promote writing in Chapters 3 and 4 and those for using writing to enhance reading in Chapters 5 and 6 are examples of this third type of integration.

Throughout this book we have treated reading and writing as composing processes which have certain skills in common, advocating that they be taught together in order to increase skill development in both areas. In earlier chapters we have also mentioned the importance of oral language experiences such as roleplaying and discussion for both prereading and prewriting. In this chapter we extend the oral language emphasis by: (a) examining the theoretical basis for integrating oral and written language activities; (b) describing curriculum models that integrate all of the language arts; and (c) suggesting instructional strategies for integrating reading, writing, and oral language.

RESEARCH AND THEORY

Classroom-based studies indicate that oral language skills are essential to the development of reading and writing skills. The positive effects of oral interaction upon children's writing has been demonstrated convincingly in the case studies of Graves (1983) and Calkins (1983). Evidence that experiences with oral language and writing improve children's reading abilities is also presented in these studies. Clay (1986) is among the language researchers who argue for integrated instruction on the basis that learning in one area enriches the potential for learning in other areas, explaining that children learn much about talking/listening through writing/reading and vice versa.

In a recent ERIC/RCS report, Wagner (1985) noted that there are numerous studies which link the development of reading and writing skills with oral language, citing the work of King and Rentel (1981) and others. After completing a meta-analysis of writing studies, Hillocks (1984) concluded that oral interaction is important to the writer at all stages of the writing process. In a correlational study of the reading and writing performance of sixth-graders, Evanechko, Ollila, and Armstrong (1974) reported that fluency of writing and competency with the use of varied structures in writing were the most influential factors in reading success; they recommended that teachers begin with the development of fluency and syntactic skill in oral language as a first step toward the development of reading skills.

An examination of current literature on oracy (listening and speaking) and its relationship to literacy (reading and writing) led Sticht and James (1984) to conclude that research evidence argues "for the soundness of an approach to reading development which includes extensive activities to develop oral language knowledge and skills" (p. 315). According to Goodman and Goodman (1979), "Written language development draws on competence in oral language, since both written and oral language share underlying structures and since, for most learners, oral language competence reaches a high level earlier. As children become literate, the two systems become interactive, and children use each to support the other when they need to" (p. 150).

PATTERNS FOR INTEGRATING THE LANGUAGE ARTS

■ ■   One approach that has been widely used for teaching reading and writing from an oral language base is the Language Experience Approach, described in Chapter 2. The Language Experience Approach allows children to talk about their own experiences and to have these experiences recorded in written form to read themselves or to share with other readers. Lehr (1981) explains that in Language Experience Approach classrooms, the language arts are integrated when children "talk about topics of interest, discuss those topics with others, listen to the language of many authors, dictate their own stories or poems to teachers or other adults, tell stories, explore writing as a recreational activity, write their own books, and relate reading to speaking and writing through hearing their own stories read aloud" (p. 960).

Whole Language classrooms (Newman, 1985) incorporate essential elements of the Language experience approach by building instruction on children's own language. Whole Language teaching is based on the belief that children learn language best as they use it for personal and social purposes. Rather than drilling on isolated bits and pieces of language, Whole Language teachers allow children to learn oral and written language skills in real and functional contexts. According to Watson (1987), "Whole language teachers think learners are terribly interesting and that by watching them intelligently they can find the center of gravity for everything that goes on in their classroom" (p. 4). This "kid-watching" enables teachers to build the curriculum around children's natural language and interests.

The teaching of oral and written language skills through meaningful language experiences is the central theme in a joint statement issued by five professional organizations (Association for Supervision and Curriculum Development, International Reading Association, National Association for the Education of Young Children, National Association of Elementary

Principals, and National Council of Teachers of English). One of the major concerns of the group, the Early Childhood and Literacy Development Committee (1986), was that "too much attention is focused upon isolated skill development or abstract parts of the reading process, rather than upon the integration of oral language, writing, and listening with reading" (p. 11). Among the recommendations emerging from this group were:

1. Build instruction on what the child already knows about oral language, reading and writing. Focus on meaningful experiences rather than merely on isolated skill development,
2. Respect the language the child brings to school, and use it as a base for language and literacy activities.
3. Ensure feelings of success for all children, helping them see themselves as people who can enjoy exploring oral and written language.
4. Provide reading experiences as an integrated part of the broader communication process, which includes speaking, listening, and writing, as well as other communication systems such as art, math, and music.
5. Present a model for students to emulate. In the classroom, teachers should use language appropriately, listen and respond to children's talk, and engage in their own reading and writing.
6. Make parents aware of the reasons for a total language program at school, and provide them with ideas for activities to carry out at home.
7. Encourage children to be active participants in the learning process rather than passive recipients of knowledge, by using activities that allow for experimentation with talking, listening, writing, and reading.

(pp. 11–13)*

Several curriculum models have been developed to promote large-scale integration of the language arts. The New Brunswick Comprehensive Reading/Language Arts Program (NBCRP), for example, was developed over a decade ago by one school district and adopted as the district-wide curriculum. Five critical experiences make up the core of the NBCRP model:

1. *Sustained Silent Reading.*   Students read self-selected materials at their own pace for an uninterrupted period every day.

2. *Oral and Written Composing.*   In the early grades, children dictate stories, which the teacher writes down. The children then copy the sentences for writing practice. Older students respond to the literature they read by writing in their ungraded journals. They are given direct instruction in structured writing and opportunities to take their writing through the peer-editing process.

3. *Reading Aloud to Children.*   Teachers read literature to the students at all grade levels in order to provide a rich language environment.

*From *Literary Development and Pre-First Grade* (1986), a statement prepared by the International Reading Association. Reprinted with permission.

4. *Responding to Literature.*   Students are asked to respond to the litera-ture they hear and to read in personal, literal, critical, and inferential ways.

5. *Investigating and Mastering Basic Skills.*   Students are placed at ap-propriate instructional levels in skill development materials and taught read-ing through problem-solving approaches to sound, structure, and meaning.

(adapted from Christensen, Haugen, & Kean, 1982, pp. 5–7)

Concern over the fragmented teaching of language skills apart from meaningful contexts led elementary administrator Jerome Green (1983) to propose a school-wide plan for integrating language arts instruction. His plan included:

1. Experiences involving children with the four language modes in each lesson by including a specific objective for each.
2. Teaching units requiring the use of listening, speaking, reading, and writing.
3. Motivating students through participatory activities (e.g., field trips) and visiting resource people.
4. Using dramatic performances, publications, language arts fairs, and li-brary/media center activities which involve children in integrated language experiences.

Another type of integration model, the Wisconsin Writing Project (WWP), uses writing as the unifying thread. The basic structure of the WWP program evolves from the steps in the writing process: prewriting, writing, and rewriting (Christensen et al., 1982). At each of the three stages, students engage in a variety of language experiences which involve oral activities as well as reading and writing. The designers of the model explain that communication, not writing alone, is the context of the writing process. Students use a variety of language skills as they prepare to write, read, discuss their own writing and that of their peers, and edit each other's works.

STRATEGIES

■ ■ Unfortunately, it is unlikely at this point that many teachers have had the benefit of involvement in a district-wide integrated approach such as the New Brunswick Comprehensive Reading/Language Arts Program, nor have many participated in school-wide plans of the type Green instigated. The challenge facing most teachers is the development of strategies for integrating language experiences within their own classrooms, as the Wis-consin Writing Project teachers have done.

In the sections that follow, we describe suitable strategies for unifying oral and written language instruction through informal drama, interview-ing, and oral reading activities.

■ Informal Drama

Participants in informal drama activities have the two-fold task of inventing and acting out a drama. Some formats require the use of reading and writing skills in the preparatory stages. For example, Heathcote's (1980) approach, which uses drama as a learning medium rather than an end in itself, emphasizes the dramatizing of events from study units. In order to build their drama, students must study reference materials to increase their understanding of the topic. Similarly, story drama is based on the reading of literature and often requires some written plans in the structuring stages. Informal drama differs from Readers Theatre, a strategy discussed later in this chapter, in that the actors' lines are spontaneously generated rather than read from a script. Drama in the informal context is used as a means rather than an end, with the primary goal being the development of the learner rather than audience appeal (although attention is usually given to both process and product). The fact that it has well-defined dramatic form, with beginning, story, climax, and conclusion, distinguishes it somewhat from the dramatic play of younger children described in Chapter 2.

Informal drama is an ideal setting for stimulating language growth—both oral and written—whether in the form of role playing, creative drama based on a story or the imagination, or the simulation of a real event. Wagner (1983) explains, "Since what makes language good in a drama is not different in kind from what makes language good in a written composition, both forms of expression are enhanced by their integration." She adds, "both demand that the language user stay in role, elaborate appropriately, use language relevantly, provide coherence, choose words precisely, and craft discourse for a desired rhetorical effect" (p. 162).

Bolton (1984) suggests that drama be made a "pivot" around which the curriculum revolves in order to help students make connections for assimilating new information. He recommends that teachers use drama as the core of project activities and as a central subject with which all other subjects can be integrated. He contends that drama has the potential to make abstract ideas understandable by allowing students to act them out in concrete, explicit ways. Drama provides contexts which require meaningful uses of language skills, and it increases the functions that reading and writing can serve for children. Fluency of oral expression is also nurtured as children communicate their thoughts extemporaneously. McCaslin (1987) also promotes the concept of drama at the center of the language curriculum, stating that leading educators believe that "drama can motivate writing and improve oral skills; they believe that it stimulates reading. Some insist that it can be used to teach any subject effectively" (p. 181).

There is a growing body of evidence to show that informal drama experiences can also improve reading proficiency. After reviewing studies related to drama and reading, Ross and Roe (1977) concluded that creative drama promotes children's use of critical and creative reading skills by encouraging them to apply their own knowledge, make interpretations, and draw inferences. Dramatizations have also been shown to increase vocabularies and to provide motivation for further reading.

The use of informal drama in language programs is consistent with Busching and Lundsteen's (1983) three basic principles of language learning:

1. Drama promotes *broad communication effectiveness*. It provides opportunities for children to use all forms of oral and written language in real, meaningful situations.
2. Drama provides opportunities for children to *learn about language in a variety of contexts* — social, cognitive, and expressive.
3. Drama *maximizes interrelationships between the language arts* by facilitating movement from one language mode to another.

The role drama and story drama strategies we describe in this section are connected, language-in-use strategies that integrate reading, writing, and oral language.

☐ *Role Drama*

Role drama, one of the drama formats recommended by Bolton (1984), occurs when the teacher contrives a situation in which students explore problems and develop new insights by taking roles in a dramatization. The dramatizations themselves are planned cooperatively by the teacher and students. The following are two examples that illustrate how role drama can be used as a medium to encourage reading and writing.

Improvised Drama Unit   Wagner (1985, p. 559) maintains that "a good way to integrate the language arts is to focus on something else — the study of flight, or cats, or the water cycle, or energy-giving foods, or Boston in 1773." An excellent example of this principle is Wagner's (1983) account of an improvised drama unit in which third- and fourth-graders moved from role drama to writing to reading while learning concepts in science (water usage) and social studies (Brazil). She and a colleague, Ruth Trethar, set up a situation in which their students pretended to be members of an Indian tribe living in a valley where Brazilian engineers were planning to build a dam. The students improvised a drama about their tribal life, writing about their experiences as members of the tribe. When the children began to feel like a tribe, the teachers introduced the problem facing them: their homeland would soon be flooded because workers were blocking the river to build a dam. The children then improvised a drama dealing with the conflict between the Indians and the dam builders, giving rise to questions about Brazilian tribal life and the reasons for constructing dams. They became eager to read and gather information to answer these questions. One group of children played the roles of anthropologists, moving among the tribe members, questioning them and writing accounts of what they saw and heard. Figure 8.1 is the first paragraph of a five-page report written by one of the young anthropologists about the Moqui tribe.

When the drama activities were ended, the teachers helped the class develop a list of questions for which they wanted to search out answers. Their list included:

> What do the Moqui eat?
> Do they have clay pots?
> Do they plant things?
> Do they fish with spears or nets?
> How do they make baskets?
> What do their homes look like?
> How do you start to build a dam?
> What keeps a dam from being washed away?
> Why do people build dams?
>
> (Wagner, 1983, p. 161)

Wagner suggested that a culminating activity might involve reenacting the life of the tribe in a more accurate fashion than was done in the initial dramatizations. The students could use the information obtained through their reading to make their improvisations more authentic and true-to-life. They might want to develop a formal play to present to another class to show what they have learned about the Brazilian Indians.

Narrative Theater. Edmiston, Encisco, and King (1987) describe a unique form of drama in which discussion, reading, and writing take place within the role drama itself—Narrative Theater. Drama contexts which involve the use of language skills are "framed" for the students by the teacher. The format requires participants to "think from inside situations" and link these situations with their own experience, which Heathcote (1980) claims children must do if they are to become good comprehenders. Narrative Theater differs from Readers Theatre in that discussion is emphasized and the text is not necessarily read aloud in a theatrical manner. Unlike story drama, in which a drama is performed after the reading of a story, the reading and discussion of Narrative Theater are part of the drama itself.

A museum drama experience in which children centered around Jean Fritz's biography, *Where Do You Think You Are Going, Christopher Columbus?* (Putnam, 1980), illustrates how Narrative Theater was carried out in one classroom (Edmiston et al., 1987). The nine- and ten-year-old children in this classroom played the roles of members of the "Columbus 1992 Society," which agreed to accept the responsibility of preparing a museum exhibit on Christopher Columbus for the five-hundredth anniversary of his voyage. Their project took shape within a six-week drama which involved them in reading and writing from several different frames of reference related to their museum responsibilities. In order to facilitate easy access to the information in Fritz's biography of Columbus, their teachers arranged copies of the book pages on the floor of the classroom, enabling

FIGURE 8.1   A Young "Anthropologist's" Report on the Moqui Tribe   Source: From B. G. Wagner. The Expanding Circle of Informal Classroom Drama. In *Integrating the Language Arts in the Elementary School,* edited by B. A. Busching and J. I. Schwartz. Copyright © 1983 by the National Council of Teachers of English. Reprinted with permission.

The Moqui Tribe

Once there was a tribe that lived on the tip of the Amazon River, and the tribe had to fish and hunt for their food. so one day they were fishing for their food and one of the tribe members called for the witch Doctor. and the witch Doctor came runing over to the tribe member and said "What do you want?" the witch Doctor said. and then the member of the tribe said "This is a bad Luck fish is it not?" he said. hm said the witch Doctor and then he said it is a very Bad Luck fish you have to hold By the tail Like you are now. Do not move while I go get the Chief of the tribe I will Be Back soon." So the witch Doctor came Back with the Chief and they came to a council meeting in the village. the witch Doctor was holding The fish now. the witch Doctor spoke up and said "we have to Burn this fish!" ...

the students to read, reread, and discuss parts of the book related to their purposes.

The 1992 Society "frame" gave them a purpose for reading the entire book because it was necessary for them to learn about the various decisions

Columbus had to make on his voyage in order to develop an organizational plan for their exhibit. Another perspective involved becoming crew members themselves, talking about and acting out the problems of the sailors, in order to decide how to depict the situation on the Santa Maria in the exhibit. After dramatizing events on shipboard, they wrote pieces from the viewpoints of crew members and of Columbus himself. They used words from the text as well as improvised language as they acted the roles of Columbus and his crew. For example, one "crew member" wrote this description of the "scarfing" process after researching fifteenth-century shipbuilding:

SCARFING

It's complicated work men, she'll have to be watertight. If she's not that'll not only spoil the cargo, but take us flat to the bottom of the sea. The plan that Christopher drew isn't too specific. I wouldn't be surprised if we sunk, he's mad. He can not scarf the keel properly let alone the rest of the ship. Scarfing must be done skilfully. The stem of the keel is plenty stright but the shapes are all wrong. The first shape in the stem must be a rectangle with a slanted edge. The slant fits into a trapexoid that fits into a triangle. It has 5 edges. The last piece is very long it has five sides all these blocks form a curve. Smooth cuts and straight angles form the keel.
That boat'll sink I tell ya.

(Edmiston et al., 1987, p. 225)

In discussing the implications of this Narrative Theater experience, Edmiston and associates explained that the creation of museums is a well-established endeavor in American society. The museum motif created a context in which the students could compose and comprehend texts related to real purposes. Their main objective was to create the museum exhibit. The reading, writing, and discussion in which the students engaged "functioned as tools helping them to fulfill their primary goal" (p. 226).

☐ *Story Drama*

The dramatization of stories can have a powerful effect on children's reading and writing. Booth has been applauded for his work with drama in education, particularly for having used story drama techniques successfully with young children who were poor comprehenders (Kukla, 1987). Booth found that when these children improvised a drama after reading a story their comprehension improved. He speculated that the dramatizations caused the children to explore the deeper meanings of the story and to clarify concepts. It is also likely that knowing they would later get to dramatize the story motivated them to put more effort and attention into their reading.

Booth's story drama sessions begin with the reading of a story and discussion of the important ideas and issues in order to develop a focus for dramatic activities. Then small groups work in roles to improvise mini-dramas about the situations identified in the class discussions, after which they meet together as a class to let the larger drama unfold, as each child takes part in the action.

Kukla (1987) describes one of Booth's drama episodes with Lloyd Alexander's *The King's Fountain* (E. P. Dutton, 1971). The story is about a king who deprived a village of water in order to build himself an elaborate fountain in the palace courtyard. After the children in his class had read and discussed the story, Booth had them work together in small groups on tasks related to the central theme, using drama techniques such as role playing, tableaux, dialogue, and storytelling. He worked with the groups, both as a player in role and as a coach, as the students assumed the roles of villagers attempting to solve their problems. When they had prepared themselves through interaction within the group to play a role in the larger drama, they came together as a village and let the complete drama happen. Even the most shy children found voices, for they understood that what they had to say would make a difference in the outcome of the drama. All the players had a reason for listening carefully in order to respond effectively. The drama clarified the meaning of the story for them and enabled them to think beyond the facts to become critical readers and imaginative writers.

Cunningham (1981) also considers story drama to be a valuable comprehension activity, pointing out that in order to understand a story the "main idea and supporting details must be clear in your mind. Events must be remembered in the proper sequence. Inferences must be made about characters' motivations and intentions" (p. 468). Her approach involves children in the simple reenactment of a familiar story, after a discussion centered around the characters and plot. After the first dramatization of the story, the class evaluates the performance, discussing good features and needed improvements. Then new roles are assigned for a second enactment of the story, after which comparisons are made between the two presentations. Cunningham emphasizes the importance of familiarity with the story upon which the dramas are based and recommends the rereading of basal reader stories, the retelling of stories read by the teacher, and the listening to or reading along with tapes of stories, as preparation for acting them out. She maintains that the dramatization of familiar stories is a "natural vehicle for improving speaking skills and listening/reading comprehension and fostering that love of stories which separates 'readers' from those who can but don't" (p. 468).

Teachers in the 1982 Wisconsin Writing Project (WWP) designed a story drama lesson for use with elementary and middle school students (see Strategy Example). The lesson, based on *The Shrinking of Treehorn,* by Florence Perry Heide (Holiday, 1981), promotes reading and writing through story drama by leading students to write about the characters in personal ways and by motivating them to read more stories.

STRATEGY EXAMPLE 8.1

Using Creative Dramatics with *The Shrinking of Treehorn*, by Florence Perry Heide

Introduction

1. Who is the person you would go to if you needed a good listener?
2. What does the person you chose do to be such a good listener?
3. How does being listened to make you feel?
4. How does not being listened to make you feel?
5. Listen and find out what happens to Treehorn.

Listening to the Story

1. Read the story to the class.
2. Pick some favorite parts and reread them.
3. Have a child read a favorite scene to the class.
4. Read the story enough times so that the class is familiar with it.

Pantomime and Discuss

1. Have small groups pick a character from the story and discuss how that character would look, feel, walk, gesture.
2. Choose someone from each group to pantomime the chosen character and let the other groups guess who it is.
3. After each character has been presented, discuss with the class:
   a. what was revealing about each character portrayal? (good gestures, expression, action)
   b. what could have been added or changed?

Improvise and Discuss

1. Repeat the activities above, but now let each character speak spontaneously.

Pantomime and Write

1. Have individuals pick a character from the story to pantomime.
2. As each child pantomimes, have the class write down words they can think of to describe the character.
3. Using words from their lists, have them choose one of the charac-

ters and write a three-sentence paragraph about him or her. (Length can be adapted to grade level.)

Dramatize the Story

1. Discuss, decide, and list on the chalkboard the way the story could be divided into scenes.
2. Decide whether props are necessary. (Keep them to a minimum.)
3. Review character traits.
4. Assign students to all characters except the main one (Treehorn). Teacher takes that character to serve as model.
5. Appoint someone to call out the scene numbers at the beginning of each scene and "curtain" at the end of each scene.
6. Dramatize the story.

Evaluate

1. Have the class discuss:
   a. What was revealing about the characters?
   b. What parts of the action were interesting, funny, sad?
   c. What could be added, subtracted, changed?

Follow Up

1. The playing of the story can be done several times so that each child gets a chance to try out a character. Keep this on a voluntary basis until the students feel comfortable. The teacher does not have to participate after the class becomes accustomed to the procedure.

Source: Christensen et al. (1982), pp. 20–22. Used with permission.

The WWP teachers stressed the importance of follow-up discussions after every story drama experience children have, for the purposes of reinforcing ideas and suggesting changes. This type of discussion also promotes critical listening skills.

■ Interviewing

Teachers of children as young as first-graders have reported beneficial results from interviewing experiences. By asking questions of a chosen person and sharing the answers with others, children are engaging in the communication process in a unified way, with one step leading naturally to the next. Haley-James and Hobson (1980) claim, "When children take on the role of interviewer . . . a drive to communicate is released within them. In addition to asking intelligent questions, they become willing writers and readers of their own writing" (p. 499).

One way to ease children into the interviewer's role is to give them opportunities to ask prestructured questions of a peer, writing down notes as they listen to the answers and composing a simple journal entry from the conversation. If they read their entries to each other, they will have come full circle in the communication process. The problem of interview topics can be solved by asking students to bring an object that is important to them to class and having them work in pairs to learn the story behind each other's object. In this way, each student will be both expert and interviewer.

Parent interviews are a logical next step for practicing the skills needed to structure and carry out a good interview. An interviewing assignment asking parents about their own childhoods is an enjoyable task for children to perform. Questions about friends, pets, favorite activities, hobbies, favorite books, nicknames, funny incidents, embarrassing experiences, and jobs are appropriate for inclusion in interviews of this type. Children are likely to be eager to write up the results of this questioning to share with their classmates, and to be motivated to listen to what their peers have to say.

Haley-James and Hobson describe how one first-grade teacher expanded her students' involvement in interviewing by inviting guests into the classroom to be interviewed by the entire class. In one instance, the children asked nonstop questions of a visiting police officer for an hour and twenty-five minutes. After he left, they each wrote stories about him, read them to each other, and later composed a group story giving the information they agreed was most important. The teacher observed increased interest in speaking, listening, reading, and writing during these interviewing experiences, as well as improvement in the children's language skills. Student-team interviews can be used with the guest-interviewee approach as an interesting variation. In this format, teams of three or four students interview the guest for five to ten minutes, taking notes and comparing information as a class before writing up the interview.

Among the other outcomes noticed by the teachers working with Haley-James and Hobson were more fluent writing due to increased interest in the person and topic, more sophisticated language use, a sense of pride in what they wrote, and a desire to have others read their writing.

Haley-James and Hobson, stressing the importance of structure for children who are engaging in interviewing activities, offer suggestions similar to the following for teachers initiating the interview process:

1. Have practice interviews in which students interview the teacher about an interest and a related object.
2. Let students know that you will give them only the information they request, i.e., a yes-no question will get a yes-no answer.

3. Identify and list the most productive questions in a follow-up discussion of the teacher-interest interviews. Repeat the process until the quality of the questioning improves.
4. Ask students to bring objects related to their interests to class and schedule time for them to interview each other. Follow up the interviews with an evaluation of the questioning and set up further interviews.
5. Provide opportunities for students to read the records of these interviews to each other and to the teacher.

☐ *Family Map*

Collecting information about the past histories of their families and communities requires students to gather data firsthand through the interviewing process and to verify the data by reading historical materials. When the "Foxfire" approach to cultural journalism (Wigginton, 1972) is used in a classroom, students are involved in a total class project, and the stories they compose from their written or tape-recorded interviews of family members or older citizens in the community are published in a magazine format.

Ideas for individual cultural journalism projects which culminate in less ambitious products than a class magazine are offered by David Weitzman (1975). The use of interviewing skills is basic to many of the projects Weitzman describes, and others can be structured by teachers to include the interview as an information-gathering technique. We have adapted Weitzman's Family Map strategy here as a means of motivating students for family interviews and facilitating the sharing of results.

Students begin with a blank outline map of the United States on which they trace their parents' moves from their birthplaces, through childhood and adulthood, to their present home, using information collected in an interview with each parent. They mark the locations where both parents lived with dots and connect the dots with lines to show their movements, writing a brief description of each dot (Figure 8.2).

After completing maps for their immediate families and sharing them with family and peers, students may elect to follow Weitzman's suggestions for continuing the process with two other maps, one showing where relatives are now living in the United States and another showing the movements of ancestors (grandparents, great grandparents, and even great, great grandparents) from their countries of origin to the United States. The map formats accomplish the purposes of formal reports based on the interviews, yet they give the students and their audience the enjoyment of a graphic presentation.

☐ *Write Around Town*

Interviewing people in various sectors of the business community is a stimulating activity appropriate for older students. Tchudi and Tchudi (1984) introduce the Write Around Town concept to middle-school students by describing the possibilities of a visit to the butcher, baker, or candlestick

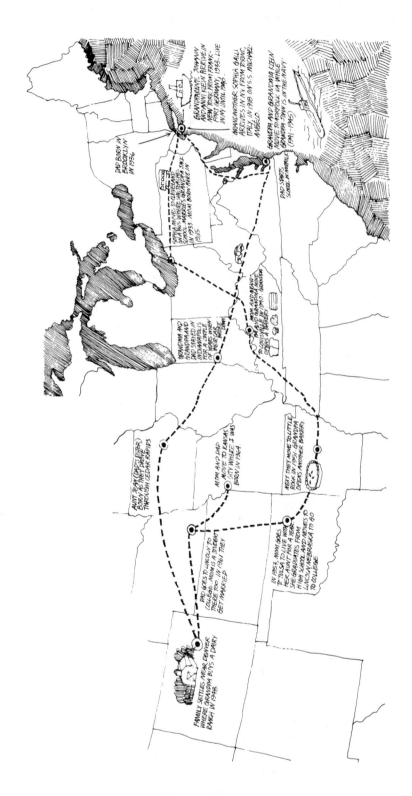

FIGURE 8.2 A Family Map Source: From David Weitzman. *My Backyard History Book.* Copyright © 1975 by the Yolla Bolly Press. Reprinted by permission.

maker. They explain, for example, that questioning a butcher could lead to a story about the training needed for that job, a description of the different cuts of meat, or an essay on the wrapping and labeling of packaged meats. A bakery visit could provide material for a paper on the hours bakers work, how yeast causes dough to rise, the various types of doughnuts, and what is done with the part that is taken from the doughnut holes. In a woodworking shop, a visitor might observe the process of twining candlesticks on a lathe, or in a jewelry store, one might discover the composition and origins of some expensive candlesticks.

The strategy used by Tchudi and Tchudi (1984) to interest students in Write Around Town is to list places from A to Z where they can go for interviews:

> Airport, beekeeper, collectors' shop, detective agency, electric power com-
> pany, florist, gas station, hardware store, ice cream parlor, jukebox distribu-
> tor, key maker, laboratories: medical, dental or scientific; museums: art,
> historical or scientific; newspaper, office supply store, pancake house, quick
> printer, radio station, salvage store, taxidermist, upholstery shop, vacuum
> cleaner store, waste removal service, x-ray laboratory, yacht club, zipper
> repair store (tailor or fix-it shop).
>
> (adapted from pp. 119–122)

In addition to suggesting places from A to Z for Writing Around Town, Tchudi and Tchudi provide a few interesting questions for students to ask at each place as a start for structuring an interview. Their guidelines for data collection include making an appointment, making a list of questions to ask, being on time, taking brief notes, taping the interview, and writing longer notes directly after the interview. A final report is then written and shared with classmates. This strategy is another way to provide students with writing experiences within the context of a project that has personal significance and meaning.

■ Oral Reading

The life purposes that oral reading serves makes it apparent that it is the *communication* aspect that is important, and yet oral reading is most often used in school to test a reader's ability to pronounce words. Oral reading is all too often considered synonymous with round-robin reading in which students take turns reading in a circle as others follow along in their texts, a practice regularly condemned by reading experts as the cause of negative reading and listening behaviors. Round-robin reading is usually an exercise in word pronunciation since the oral reader is usually corrected when words are miscalled. Artley (1972) explained that "word perception, though neces-sary, is only peripheral or incidental to the main and only reason for reading aloud—which is to interpret to interested listeners the ideas, information, feeling, mood or action that is in printed or written form. *It is an act of interpretation"* (p. 47).

There is a scarcity of research focusing on sound instructional practices for promoting oral reading fluency and skill. Allington (1984) alerts educators to the need for more research on the specific tasks of oral reading and the variables involved in the oral reading situation. Recommendations for teaching oral reading skills have come primarily from teachers who have experienced success with certain oral reading strategies.

Heinrich (1976) urges teachers to include oral reading skills among the goals of their language arts programs. She maintains that oral reading competency is vital in the development of good silent readers. Other benefits she lists are improvement in speech skills, development of self-confidence, and increased ability to communicate orally. Artley (1972) agrees that silent reading skills and oral reading skills go hand-in-hand. Silent reading is a necessary part of the oral interpretation process because it enables the reader to reconstruct the writer's ideas and sense the implied mood. This step is necessary before the reader can interpret what the writer has to say for the interested listener.

According to Artley, there are situations throughout the school day that give students "honest-to-goodness" reasons for reading textual material to their peers, such as interpreting portions of personal reading, sharing news items, and reading directions for performing experiments or playing games. There are also opportunities for integrating writing with the oral reading process by allowing students to read their own writing to others. Once again, the importance of the teacher as a model should be noted. Children should hear the teacher's well-rehearsed renditions of good literature in order to "catch" oral interpretation skills by imitation. The teacher's own writing should be shared regularly by the same process.

Most proponents of oral reading instruction agree that teaching strategies should be grounded in these practices:

1. An oral reader deserves an interested audience. This usually means reading something the listeners have not heard before and do not have a copy of before them. If they can read the text themselves, why listen?
2. Oral readers should have a genuine purpose for their reading. For example, it might be to share a passage they have read and enjoyed or something they have written themselves.
3. Oral readers should be given ample time to practice whatever they will read to an audience.

The oral reading strategies we describe—Quick Reads and Readers Theater—conform to the practices we have recommended by giving students opportunities to read their own writing, after practice, to audiences for whom it is a first-time listening experience.

☐ *Quick Reads*

Oral reading can flourish in classrooms where writing is taught as a process, because audiences for oral reading are readily available and students have a real purpose for reading. The peer-group structure in such classrooms allows five or six students to practice oral reading skills at the same time by reading their own written pieces to others in the revising/editing step of the writing process. Finished papers are frequently "published" by being read to the whole class by the author. Journal writing is continuously in progress, and Quick Reads—the oral reading of favorite journal entries by volunteers—are a regular activity.

One of the routine practices of teachers who hold individual press conferences (see Chapter 4) with their students is to ask them to read a self-selected excerpt from the basal reader or trade book they are currently reading, for the purpose of diagnosing skill needs. The student has usually read the passage silently and practiced reading it orally beforehand. Quick Reads from students' own writings can extend this approach by offering students opportunities for additional oral reading practice and discussion of their writing on a one-to-one basis with the teacher.

In addition to teacher-pupil conferences, peer-response groups, and whole-group settings, other contexts can be used to promote Quick Reads:

1. *Pupil Pairs.* Paired oral reading experiences have at least two advantages: (a) a large number of children can practice reading simultaneously; and (b) both children in each pair are actively involved at all times, either as reader or listener. Whisler (1976) recommends that teachers train pupil partners to engage in reciprocal oral reading by modeling the process, using one set of partners to demonstrate how to read, listen, and ask good questions. As soon as pairs of students are competent to carry out the alternate reading and listening/questioning process, they are permitted to read to each other independently. The teacher continues to meet with other pairs until all children are prepared to read and question without teacher direction. Whisler maintains that students learn rapidly through the modeling process to ask higher-level questions than those requiring a simple yes or no answer.

Journal entries and dialogue writing are two recommended sources of reading material. Journal entries guarantee that the material is at children's independent level, making the pupil-pair arrangement appropriate for children as young as first-graders. Pairs of students can also write dialogue to use as Quick Read material. Teachers can assign each partner a role and ask both to play their roles by conversing with each other in writing for about ten minutes, without any oral communication. Pictures or cartoons showing two characters conversing are good sources of roles for students to play. Reading the resulting dialogue to the class gives students a valuable experience in oral interpretation by having to assume a voice other than their own. The activity not only requires them to write from another's point of view, but also furnishes material for later learning of script-writing skills and mechanics of writing, such as the proper use of quotation marks.

2. Parent Partners. Teachers in two third-grade classrooms observed increased proficiency in oral reading after including parents in a plan to improve students' skills in this area (Ross, 1986). After informing parents they would be evaluating pupils' oral reading skills every Friday, the teachers asked them to have their children read assigned pages from the basal reader each night for practice. A note was sent home to parents, telling them which skills their children needed to learn (see Figure 8.3).

Standards for good oral reading were discussed in class, and students were instructed about the procedures to use at home. Selections assigned to children were at their independent reading levels, to permit fluent oral reading free of word recognition problems. The extension of this strategy to include the oral reading of children's self-authored materials can pay additional dividends by promoting interactions between parents and children about the ideas expressed in their Quick Reads, providing extra motivation for writing.

☐ **Readers Theatre**

Readers Theatre is a student-centered format for the oral interpretation of literature which involves students in the total production of a play. They

FIGURE 8.3 Note Sent to Parents about the Parent-Partner Oral Reading Program

Something New For You to Do at Home!

Beginning today, your child is bringing home a reader with a particular page assigned for the purpose of *practicing oral reading*. You may have him/her read any other story or all of the stories if you wish, but on Friday the assigned page must be read for an oral reading grade.

The book which is being brought home is one level below your child's reading group level; therefore, it should be easy to read. Listed below are the areas which will be considered:

1. Reads with proper expression (shows excitement, questioning, etc.).
2. Pauses for commas and dashes.
3. Stops at periods and question marks.
4. Reads in phrases and not by individual words.
5. Does not omit or change words.
6. Does not go back and repeat a word or begin again at the start of a sentence.
7. Pronounces the endings of words, such as in book*s* and go*ing*.

Enjoy reading with your child!

select, read, and discuss the story, write the script, choose the actors and production teams, read the lines, and participate in a follow-up discussion for reinforcement and for ideas to improve the next play. Sloyer (1982) defines Readers Theatre in this way:

> There are no stage sets, no elaborate costumes, no memorized lines. It is not ordinary reading with dull word-by-word reciting. Readers Theatre is an interpretive reading activity for all the children in the classroom. Readers bring characters to life through their voices and gestures. . . . The performers read aloud in a dramatic style while the members of the audience create vivid mental images of things depicted in the literature. . . . As a thinking, reading, writing, and listening experience, Readers Theatre makes a unique contribution to our language arts curriculum.
>
> (p. 3)*

Sloyer presents a series of guidelines to assist teachers in implementing Readers Theater activities. We have adapted her procedures in abbreviated form in the instructions that follow:*

1. *Selection of Material.* Students should choose a short story or single scene to adapt in the beginning and move on to longer pieces of literature as they gain experience with Readers Theatre. Songs, poems, and advertisements also provide appropriate material. It is important to find an imaginative story with tight plot, appealing characters, and quick action. Fairy tales, fables, picture books, and plays make good source material for scripts. Some basal reader stories can also be used as the basis for scripts.

Improvised story drama can also furnish the basic material for script writing. Miccinati and Phelps (1980) observed dramatizations of three different scenes from "Rapunzel" which were improvised in various ways by groups of fifth-graders. The children then wrote a script for Readers Theatre, incorporating ideas from the improvisations. The new version of the fairy tale was well received by an enthusiastic classroom audience.

2. *Getting Started.* After a story has been selected, the teacher should model the writing of a script by adapting a basal reader story that has been read by the class. The class and teacher then work together on the script for the selected story, with the teacher using large poster paper and acting as scribe. The steps to be followed in the script-writing process include:

  a. List the title, time, and setting, and name the characters. Write in as many characters as possible, including groups of actors and two narrators, to insure maximum participation.

  b. Discuss the important events that will be portrayed and decide what part each character will play in the action. Write the names of the characters (and narrators) in the margins of the script and discuss what their lines will be. As decisions are made, write the various characters' lines by their names, working through the entire story in this way.

3. *Complete the Script.* The students revise the lines together to add interest to the production and then reproduce the script for readers to perform.

4. *Preparing for the Presentation.* Name a production team, including a director and stage manager, assigning them the responsibility for working out the details of positions and actions of the players on stage.

Assign several students to play each role so the script can be performed three or four times with different casts. Allow ample practice time for students to become confident readers of their lines.

5. *Follow-up Discussion.* Readers Theatre outcomes should be discussed and evaluated by the entire class in order to give students the information they need to upgrade the quality of the next performance and improve their own oral interpretation skills.

One of the possible pitfalls of Readers Theatre is that it can become so formalized that teachers are seldom able to give time to it. We urge teachers to keep their expectations realistic and not attempt to do overly ambitious scripts and production. In the Strategy Example, eight-year-old Jenny's new version of Aesop's "The Fox and the Stork" illustrates the simplicity of an appropriate script for third-graders to perform with enjoyment and ease.

—————————— STRATEGY EXAMPLE 8.2 ——————————

The Fox and the Stork: The Original Tale and a Derived Readers Theatre Script

THE FOX AND THE STORK
by Aesop

At one time the Fox and the Stork were on visiting terms and seemed very good friends. So the Fox invited the Stork to dinner, and for a joke put nothing before her but some soup in a very shallow dish. This the Fox could very easily lap up, but the Stork could only wet her long bill in it, and left the meal as hungry as when she began.

"I am sorry," said the fox, "the soup is not to your liking."

"Pray do not apologize," said the Stork. "I hope you will return this visit and come and dine with me soon."

So a day was appointed when the Fox should visit the Stork, but when they were seated at the table all there was for their dinner was contained in a very long-necked jar with a narrow mouth, in which the Fox could not insert his snout. So all he could manage was to lick the outside of the jar.

"I will not apologize for the dinner," said the Stork:

"ONE BAD TURN DESERVES ANOTHER."

THE FOX AND THE STORK: VERSION 2
by Jenny

Narrator:	At one time the fox and stork were on visiting terms and seemed very good friends, so the fox invited the stork to play and said,
Fox:	Let's play hide-and-go-seek!
Narrator:	So they did, but just for a joke, the fox made the boundaries a very small place in which the stork could not hide. The stork, however, remembering their last happening, refused. The next day the stork called the fox and said,
Stork:	Come over and play.
Narrator:	And they did.
Fox:	Let's watch T.V.
Narrator:	But the stork knew that the fox was a real couch potato, so he put the T.V. high on the shelf, and the fox could not see it. And the fox said,
Fox:	We won't be seeing each other again!
Narrator:	And they didn't.

Sloyer suggests having a Readers Theatre file in the classroom containing cards children can fill out after they have read a story that would make a good script (see Figure 8.4). The file becomes a storehouse of ideas for future Readers Theatre scripts and motivates students to read passages from possible selections aloud. The interest generated by the file facilitates the formation of production groups for script writing and presentation of favorite stories. Sloyer urges teachers to set aside one period each week for the sharing of these oral interpretations to stimulate Readers Theatre activities.

SUMMARY

■ ■ In this chapter our interest centered on the oral and written language connection. An overview of classroom-based research correlating achievement in reading and writing with competence in oral language supported the practice of integrating language arts instruction so that learning in one area can enrich learning in another. The Language Experience and Whole Lan-

FIGURE 8.4   Readers Theatre File Card   Source: From Shirlee S. Sloyer. *Readers Theatre: Story Dramatization in the Classroom.* Copyright © 1982 by the National Council of Teachers of English. Reprinted with permission.

Pupil Name:

Name of Selection:

Author:

Type: (story, poem, play)

Characters:

Story Line:

guage Approaches were cited as natural integrated contexts which have been proven to be effective for this purpose.

After listing specific guidelines from professional organizations for unifying instruction in listening, speaking, reading, and writing, we described three patterns for integrating the language arts curriculum. One plan was intended for district-wide implementation (the New Brunswick Comprehensive Reading/Language Arts Program); another was developed as a school-wide program (Jerome Green's plan); and the third was designed to be a model for individual classroom teachers (the Wisconsin Writing Project program).

In the next section of the chapter, we suggested teaching strategies for integrating oral and written language instruction through informal drama, interviewing, and oral reading activities. The two types of drama formats we suggested involve students in both the preparation and presentation of informal dramatizations. In role drama, students assume the roles of participants in a situation instigated by the teacher and plan with the teacher to explore solutions to problems through a drama. Wagner's Improvised Drama Unit and the Narrative Theater approach illustrated effective use of role drama in the classroom. Story drama activities planned by teachers in the Wisconsin Writing Project illustrated how improvised dramas based on stories can promote critical and creative reading skills, as well as reading comprehension. We described interviewing as a unified communication process, recommending oral history experiences (Family Map) and the interviewing of people in various businesses (Write Around Town). After examining traditional oral reading instruction, we suggested two strategies that conform to sound practices for teaching oral reading (Quick Reads and Readers Theatre) by allowing children to read something new and preferably self-authored to an interested audience, after practice.

REFERENCES

Allington, R. L. (1984). Oral reading. In P. D. Pearson (Ed.), *Handbook of reading research* (pp. 829–864). New York: Longman.

Artley, A. S. (1972). Oral reading as a communication process. *The Reading Teacher, 26,* 46–51.

Bolton, G. (1984). *Drama as education: An argument for placing drama at the centre of the curriculum.* Essex, England: Longman House.

Busching, B. A., & Lundsteen, S. W. (1983). Curriculum models for integrating the language arts. In B. A. Busching & J. I. Schwartz (Eds.), *Integrating the language arts in the elementary school* (pp. 3–27). Urbana, IL: National Council of Teachers of English.

Calkins, L. M. (1983). *Lessons from a child: On the teaching and learning of writing.* Exeter, NH: Heinemann.

Christensen, L., Haugen, N., & Kean, J. (Eds.). (1982). *A guide to integrating the language arts.* Madison: Wisconsin Writing Project.

Clay, M. (1986). Constructive processes: Talking, reading, writing, art, and craft. *The Reading Teacher, 39,* 764–770.

Cunningham, P. (1981). Story dramatization. *The Reading Teacher, 34,* 466–468.

Early Childhood and Literacy Development Committee (1986). Literacy development and pre-first grade: A joint statement of concerns about present practices in pre-first grade reading instruction and recommendations for improvement. *Young Children, 41*(4), 10–13.

Edmiston, B., Encisco, P., & King, M. L. (1987). Empowering readers and writers through drama: Narrative theater. *Language Arts, 64,* 219–228.

Evanechko, P., Ollila, L., & Armstrong, R. (1974). An investigation of the relationship between children's performance in written language and their reading ability. *Research in the Teaching of English, 8,* 315–326.

Goodman, K., & Goodman, Y. (1979). Learning to read is natural. In L. Resnick & P. Weaver (Eds.), *Theory and practice of early reading* (pp. 132–154). Hillsdale, NJ: Erlbaum.

Graves, D. (1983). *Writing: Teachers and children at work.* Exeter, NH: Heinemann.

Green, J. (1983). An administrator's perspective on integrating the language arts. In B. A. Busching & J. I. Schwartz (Eds.), *Integrating the language arts in the elementary school* (pp. 174–178). Urbana, IL: National Council of Teachers of English.

Haley-James, S. M., & Hobson, C. D. (1980). Interviewing: A means of encouraging the drive to communicate. *Language Arts, 57,* 497–502.

Hall, M., & Ramig, C. J. (1978). *Linguistic foundations for reading.* Columbus, OH: Merrill.

Heathcote, D. (1980). *Drama as context.* Huddersfield, England: National Association of Teachers of English.

Heinrich, J. S. (1976). Elementary oral reading:

Methods and materials. *The Reading Teacher, 30,* 10–15.

Hillocks, G., Jr. (1984). What works in teaching composition: A meta-analysis of experimental treatment studies. *American Journal of Education, 93,* 133–170.

King, M. L., & Rentel, V. (1981). *How children learn to write: A longitudinal study.* Final report to the National Institute of Education. (ERIC Document Reproduction Service No. ED 213 050).

Kukla, K. (1987). David Booth: Drama as a way of knowing. *Language Arts, 64,* 73–78.

Lehr, F. (1981). Integrating reading and writing instruction. *The Reading Teacher, 34,* 958–961.

Loban, W. (1976). *Language development: Kindergarten through grade twelve.* Urbana, IL: National Council of Teachers of English.

McCaslin, N. (1987). *Creative drama in the primary grades.* New York: Longman.

Miccinati, J. L., & Phelps, S. (1980). Classroom drama from children's reading: From the page to the stage. *The Reading Teacher, 34,* 269–272.

Newman, J. M. (1985). *Whole language: Theory in use.* Portsmouth, NH: Heinemann.

Ross, E. P. (1986). Classroom experiments with oral reading. *The Reading Teacher, 40,* 270–275.

Ross, E. P., & Roe, B. D. (1977). Creative drama builds proficiency in reading. *The Reading Teacher, 30,* 383–387.

Sloyer, S. (1982). *Readers theatre: Story dramatization in the classroom.* Urbana, IL: National Council of Teachers of English.

Sticht, T. G., & James, J. H. (1984). Listening and reading. In P. D. Pearson (Ed.), *Handbook of reading research* (pp. 293–315). New York: Longman.

Tchudi, S., & Tchudi, S. (1984). *The young writer's handbook.* New York: Scribner's.

Wagner, B. J. (1983). The expanding circle of informal classroom drama. In B. A. Busching & J. I. Schwartz (Eds.), *Integrating the language arts in the elementary school* (pp. 155–163). Urbana, IL: National Council of Teachers of English.

Wagner, B. J. (1985). Integrating the language arts. *Language Arts, 62,* 557–560.

Watson, D. (1987, April). What is whole language? *Teachers Networking: The Whole Language Newsletter,* p. 4.

Weitzman, D. (1975). *My backyard history book.* Boston: Little, Brown.

Whisler, N. G. (1976). Pupil partners. *Language Arts, 53,* 387–389.

Wigginton, E. (1972). *The Foxfire book.* New York: Doubleday.

AUTHOR INDEX

SUBJECT INDEX

Comprehension, (continued)
  prereading writing assignments, 140,
    144–146
  purposes for reading, 149
  role of schemata, 6, 137, 139, 168
  self-questioning, 150–156
  semantic mapping, 141, 144
  summary writing, 197, 234
  text condensation, 193–200
  text structure, 179–180
  vocabulary knowledge, 168
  word recognition, 168
Computers, 38
Content-area textbooks, 219–221, 226, 234
Content-area writing (*see* Writing to learn)
Copying, 168–170
Creative dramatics (*see* Drama)
Creativity training, 80–83
Creativity (*see* Thinking, creative)
Critical reading
  becoming insiders, 12, 201–203
  content-area writing, 232
  importance of, 200–201
  metacomprehension, 207
  self-authoring, 203–205
Crowhurst's circle strategy, 125–126
Cultural journalism, 287
Curriculum models
  New Brunswick program, 276
  school-wide plan, 277
  Wisconsin Writing Project, 277

Daily edit, 123
Data charts
  data retrieval, 243
  interview grid, 241–242
  I-Search paper, 248–249
  role, 241
  science, 255–256
Data gathering
  data retrieval charts, 243–244
  guidelines, 240
  interview grid, 241–242
Definition writing, 260–262
Dialogue journals, 47–50, 77–79
Dictation
  language experience approach, 34
  prereading, 172
  self-edited, 170–171
  value of, 12, 168
Directed reading activity, 12, 137–139, 165
Directed reading and thinking activity, 12,
    153–154
Display spaces, 26

Divergent thinking (*see* Thinking, creative)
Donaldson's triad strategy, 126–127
Drafting
  composing model of reading, 10
  role in writing process, 62
Drama
  basal readers, 283
  importance of, 278–279
  improvised unit, 279–281
  informal, 278–279
  narrative theater, 280–282
  readers theatre, 280, 292–295
  reading skills, 278
  role, 13, 279–282
  story, 13, 282–285, 293
Dramatic play (*see* Play)
During reading activities, 266–268

Early literacy development
  child engagement, 39
  classroom environment, 24
  demonstrations, 28
  home environment, 22
  processes, 19
  purposeful activities, 40–55
  research, 4, 17
  role of writing, 21
  social interaction, 19
  stages, 19
Early readers, 4, 17, 24
Editing Marks proofreading system, 123
Editing (*see* Revising/editing)
Emergent literacy (*see* Early literacy devel-
    opment)
  Project English units, 71
  traditional instruction, 1, 13
Enlarged texts, 30–33
Experience stories
  follow-up activities, 36–38
  procedures, 34–36
  value of, 33–36
Expository text structure
  basal readers, 220
  characteristics, 220
  children's lack of knowledge, 220
  children's writing, 220–221
  comprehension, 221
  glossing, 265–266
  graphic organizers, 222–231
  paragraph structures, 220
  pattern guides, 228–231
  role in comprehension, 180
  writing paragraphs, 226–228

Syntax, (continued)
  difficult structures, 174
  integrated sentence-modeling cycle, 12,
    111–115
  role in comprehension, 172–173
  sentence combining, 172–179
  sentence reconstruction, 175–179

Teacher/student conferences (*see* Press con-
    ference)
Text structure
  descriptive, 220
  expository (*see* Expository text structure)
  narrative (*see* Story grammar)
  role in comprehension, 179–180
  writing activities, 181–193
Textbook activity guides, 263–265
Thematic fantasy training, 54
Theme centers (*see* Centers, dramatic play)
Theory
  composing model of reading, 8, 203
  interactive, 5
  mirror, 5
  schema, 6, 139–140
  selective attention, 149
Think-alouds, 13, 210–213
Thinking
  creative, 68–70, 80–83, 146–148
  higher-level, 3, 12, 200–201, 263
Topics from classical poetry, 73–74
Troubleshooting, 261–262
Type one interest center, 83–84

Uninterrupted Sustained Silent Reading (*see*
  Sustained silent reading)

Vocabulary knowledge
  copying, 169
  dictation, 170

paraphrasing, 194
role in comprehension, 168

Whole language approach, 275
Whole reading, 2
Wisconsin Writing Project, 277, 283
Word banks, 36–38
Word processors, 38
Word recognition
  copying, 169
  dictation, 170
  role in comprehension, 168
Wordless story books, 194–196, 215–216
Write around town, 287–289
Writing expository paragraphs, 226–228
Writing to learn
  discourse forms, 246–247
  Glatthorn's strategy, 232–233
  importance of, 231–232
  inquiry-centered reading/writing, 239
  instructional principles, 233
  mathematics (*see* Mathematics writing)
  science (*see* Science writing)
  social studies (*see* Social studies writing)
  summary writing, 233–234
Writing to record data, 255–256
Writing
  competence/performance, 99
  expressive, 76, 206–208, 243
  functional, 29, 47
  interactive, 47
  learning content (*see* Writing to learn)
  letter, 50, 102, 202, 259–260
  materials, 25, 27
  process approach, 11, 62, 227, 231, 291
  research reports (*see* Research findings)
  scribble, 43–44
  script, 291–294
  text structure, 181–193
  think-alouds, 213
  traditional instruction, 2